Michael White is a former scien   writer for *GQ*. In a
previous incarnation he was a member of the Thompson
Twins, and then a science lecturer before becoming a full-
time science writer in 1991. He is the author of a dozen books
including the international best-sellers *Stephen Hawking – A
Life in Science* (1992) and *The Science of The X-Files* (1996).
He has also written biographies of Einstein, Darwin, Isaac
Asimov, John Lennon and others. His latest is an alternative
biography of Isaac Newton that concentrates on his work as
an alchemist – *Isaac Newton: The Last Sorcerer* (1997).

Michael White tries to deliver at least one book each year
whilst struggling to find time for his two great loves – his
wife, Lisa, and their baby daughter, India. He may be
contacted at INTERNET: 101465.3301@compuserve.com.

SUPERSCIENCE

Explaining the Paranormal

MICHAEL WHITE

EARTHLIGHT

LONDON · SYDNEY · NEW YORK · TOKYO · SINGAPORE · TORONTO

First published in Great Britain by Earthlight, 1999
An imprint of Simon & Schuster UK Ltd
A Viacom Company

Simon & Schuster UK Ltd
Africa House
64–78 Kingsway
London WC2B 6AH

Simon & Schuster Australia
Sydney

A CIP catalogue record for this book is available
from the British Library.

0–684–85817–7

1 3 5 7 9 10 8 6 4 2

Typeset by Palimpsest Book Production Limited,
Polmont, Stirlingshire
Printed and bound in Great Britain by
Bath Press, Bath

For one of my oldest and dearest friends, Mark

CONTENTS

PREFACE

Back in 1996, I wrote a book called *The Science of the X-Files*. As part of the publicity for the book, I was invited to embark upon a lecture tour of the country, speaking in halls and bookshops as well as appearing on a number of radio and TV programmes.

This was a great educational experience. I had never done a book tour before and was more than a little nervous about it. But as well as learning something about public speaking, I realised two important things during those few weeks meeting my readers. The first was that the paranormal interests an amazingly wide range of people. In the audience on the tour there were children aged five upwards and old folk in their nineties, all keen to know more about how the supernatural could work.

The second thing was less pleasing. This was the clear fact that many people were not only weary of science, but actively hostile towards it.

This last fact was brought home to me when I appeared on a late-night radio phone-in to promote the book. Many of the callers were quite justifiably unhappy about the way scientists fail to communicate their ideas, but others were surprisingly aggressive. One caller claimed I was trying to: 'blind people with science and that I was "out of order!"'

When I got back to my desk, these two lessons – on the one hand the huge interest in trying to find answers to the great mysteries – and on the other, people's genuine fear of, and sometimes anger towards science, inspired me to put pen to paper again and offer my thoughts on a dozen topics where science and the paranormal meet.

Some of these chapters deal with matters at the heart of what people consider the supernatural or the occult – astrology, alien abduction, voodoo; while others explore the periphery – the idea of genetic mutants, clones and superhumans, the possibility that a collision between the Earth and a high speed celestial object could end civilisation, the weird thinking behind cults and gurus. But all these topics, whether traditional paranormal subjects or those that have been brought into the fold in recent decades, offer themselves up for rational explanation.

It goes without saying that it is not my intention to obfuscate free thought and discussion about the paranormal, and I remain one of those who would love to see some 'supernatural' ideas verified; but, equally, I hope I have maintained a degree of scientific detachment in the following discussions. Most of all I want to try to allay people's fears about science and engender the interest in finding *rational* answers, an interest that I know most people have whether they are five or ninety, people who are genuinely fascinated with this endlessly exciting subject.

Michael White, Tuscany, September 1998

1

SWEPT OFF THEIR FEET

'When a man no longer believes in God,
he'll believe in anything.'

G. K. Chesterton

One warm October evening in 1957, a twenty-three-year-old farm labourer named Antonio Villas-Boas, living near the small town of São Francisco de Sales in Brazil was, he claimed, snatched by a group of strange beings and dragged kicking and screaming into their craft hovering nearby. The hapless young man was then laid on a table in a sealed room, smeared with a thick jelly-like substance and had a blood sample taken. But then it seems his luck changed. Minutes later he was visited by a nude female humanoid alien who forced him to have sex with her twice. During this process she apparently yelped like a dog, and bit his chin before being led away by her colleagues. As she left the room, she pointed to her belly and then at the stars, and was gone.

Villas-Boas was examined by a doctor a few months later when the young man had finally plucked up the courage to tell his tale and the full account came out. The doctor found small scars under the man's chin and on other parts of his body and concluded that these marks were similar to radiation burns.

Although it sounds ridiculously far-fetched, this account,

the first widely-publicised abduction case in the world, is actually quite typical and has been repeated with slight variations ever since. In fact, reports of alien abductions are on the increase and one poll has proposed that during the past fifty years in the United States alone, five million people could have been abducted.

It might sound flippant to call this incident 'quite typical' but this is not the case, since claims of abduction fit into a very limited pattern. In fact investigators have established five distinct criteria for abduction reports. These are: reporting seeing lights in the sky, missing time, flying through the air without any apparent means of support, paralysis in the presence of strange beings and later, after the physical ordeal has ended, finding strange marks on the body or small, seemingly alien objects located inside the body.

Another famous case will serve to illustrate many of these classic elements.

One night in late September 1961, an interracial couple, Betty and Barney Hill were driving through the White Mountains of New Hampshire in the north-east of the United States when they spotted bright lights in the sky above the car. They stopped and an object 'pancake in shape, ringed with windows in the front through which we could see bright blue lights' hovered over the road. The next thing they knew, they were travelling along the road again and noticed that two hours were unaccounted for. Travelling at 40–50 m.p.h., the 190-mile journey to their home should have taken five hours, but it had taken them seven.

The couple said nothing, but each started to experience disturbing dreams in which they were captive aboard a strange craft. It was only after strains in their marriage led them to get psychiatric help and they underwent hypnosis that they discovered what has since been claimed to be repressed memories of the experience. According to their accounts, they were taken aboard a craft, medically examined, poked and prodded by bald-headed beings with huge, lidless eyes. A large needle was pushed into Betty's abdomen, a process she later took to be a pregnancy test, and she found herself discussing 'great matters of the Universe' with the captain of the craft. Barney had a similar account which came out during individual hypnosis sessions during 1963.

To this day, Betty Hill (now a widow) sticks by her story, and it has become the most famous account in UFO lore, probably because it was also the first publicised case which had come from the USA.

It is interesting to note the marked similarities between this case and that of Antonio Villas-Boas and to link them with the countless thousands of documented cases over the years. UFO enthusiasts would point to this consistency as some form of verification that the experiences of these people are examples of genuine abductions by aliens from another world (what are called 'close encounters of the fourth kind'). Sceptics would say the uncanny similarities of cases is actually a point against the possibility, and that rather than verifying these extraordinary claims, they demonstrate the extreme gullibility and straightforward lack of imagination of those who report them.

Perhaps one of the most intriguing aspects of the Hills' case is that it was what is called a 'multiple-abduction scenario'. In other words, more than one person was abducted and their stories corroborated. There have been many such cases where either several people were abducted or the abduction was seen by a group of witnesses.

A case almost as famous as the experiences of the Hills was the story reported in 1975 by one Travis Walton who was snatched by a UFO whilst driving home to Snowflake, Arizona, with six colleagues, all of whom had been working in a nearby forest. They too saw lights in the sky; Mr Walton got out of the car to investigate, disappeared and was found five days later delirious and half-naked in the forest close to where the abduction occurred. His account has a familiar ring to it: 'I was lying on a table . . .' he reported. 'I saw several strange creatures standing over me. I became completely hysterical and flipped out. I knocked them away, but I felt so weak I collapsed. They forced me back on the table, placed a mask over my face and I blacked out.'

So, what should be made of these accounts and thousands of similar stories?

For the followers of paranormal phenomena, alien abduction really is 'The Big One'. As we approach the end of the millennium there are no half measures when it comes to alien abduction: either you believe that the experiences of many people are delusions or explicable using ideas from psychology and neurophysiology or else it is all terrifyingly real and part of a massive conspiracy.

The enthusiasts claim that advanced alien beings are visiting our world in large numbers and with the full knowledge of many Western governments. Furthermore, they believe state agencies are working with some groups of aliens and against others. In short, we are engaged in some form of galactic intrigue that, to the non-believer, sounds reminiscent of badly-written and very dated science fiction. The purpose of many of the alien abductions, it is claimed, is to conduct on-going genetic experiments. Some of the aliens are keen to breed alien-human hybrids and to this end they are 'tagging' humans in order to find the most fruitful genetic crossovers. Apparently they have no qualms about what they are doing.

Of course, this theory 'explains' the similarity in accounts. People are invariably snatched at night before being medically examined, and there is often a sexual aspect to their stories. In order for this scheme to work, say the believers, the governments of the industrialised nations, in particular the US and Russia, as well as British and other European states, are all involved with the conspiracy. In other words, at some senior level, government agencies are aware of what is happening and are party to the political network connecting what are thought to be at least three or four different alien races.

This is an entertaining and interesting story – the back-bone of *The X-Files* television series. One of the recurring threads and the original intrigue of the programme is that Mulder and Scully are caught up in a web of information and disinformation and an alien intelligence is intimately linked with human agencies to suppress knowledge of breeding experiments.

Is there any way in which this tale could be true? Is it possible that we are not only being visited by alien beings, but that the Earth is a key interchange for all the experimenters and political schemers of the galaxy?

Firstly, we have to accept that there is almost certainly life on other planets. In fact, the galaxy is likely to be teeming with life of all types, and there are probably alien civilisations more advanced than ours living happily and unhappily all over this galaxy and beyond. Secondly, it is extremely difficult to travel interstellar distances, to cover the vast expanse of space between stars. But that does not mean it is impossible. It is currently impossible for *us* and will remain so for the foreseeable future unless some stunning revolutionary set of ideas is stumbled upon and used properly. However, we live on a tiny speck of dust in an almost infinite universe. This universe began some fifteen billion years ago and life on this planet started about four billion years ago. The series of factors that lead from the first bacteria to you reading these words was staggeringly complex and dependent on an almost infinite number of events all working towards this end. One of those factors is: The point in time at which life began here. Another is: The speed at which we evolved. If either of just these two has a different answer for another world it would make a huge difference to the present level of advancement of a civilisation on that planet.

On Earth, the dominant species is just about capable of reaching nearby planets. On another world where evolution acted faster or was set in motion earlier there could live alien life forms we would view as 'super-beings', aliens who could travel between the stars using one of the loopholes in the theory of relativity or perhaps some process we cannot even begin to imagine.*

So, the idea that we are being visited by aliens is not beyond the realms of reason. In fact it is quite possible that at some time in our history a craft built by an advanced race could have passed this way. It is even possible that we are still being visited from time to time. But, as I will try to show in this chapter, the idea that we are being visited by hoards of aliens and that millions of humans have been snatched for genetic experiments and that there is some vast cover-up is pure science fiction, the result of overactive imaginations. It does not make any logical sense, and rather than being the start of an alien invasion, it is actually, I believe, a result of very human and sadly, rather mundane events.

Alien abduction is a huge phenomenon in the United States. Although America cannot lay claim to the first publicised case (that of Mr Villas-Boas), UFO lore has a rich and fertile past in the United States. The term 'flying saucer' was first coined by a USAF pilot, Kenneth Arnold flying over Washington State near the Canadian border in 1947. And a few days later several thousand miles south, the *Beowulf* of UFO legend occurred – the Roswell Incident, a case I will discuss in detail later in this chapter.

American culture has always encouraged open exchange of ideas and views, freedom of speech lies at the heart of the American dream, the moral structure of the nation; so it is perhaps inevitable that the wilder limits of human imagination find fertile ground there. The other two countries with high numbers of cases are England and Brazil. The fact that England has bought into the phenomenon will also surprise few. Enthusiasts would argue that the US and the UK are obvious sites of alien activity because, along with Russia

* For much more information on this, see Chapter 1 of my book: *The Science of the X-Files*, published by Legend, 1996.

and China, they are the most important military powers in the world.

Until recently, the former Soviet bloc has been as secretive about interest in the paranormal as it has about military matters and the authorities in China are so secretive about anything that may be linked to military matters we can hope to learn little from there just yet. Sceptics would also argue that the UK follows trends started in America and that Brazilians are particularly keen to report imagined or deliberately made-up cases because Villas-Boas has set a precedent.

America has also produced the vast majority of experts in the field of alien abduction and not all of these are fringe figures but include university professors and established intellectuals. Best-known of these is the abduction investigator John Mack, who is a Pulitzer prizewinner and Professor of psychiatry at Harvard University.

Mack believes that the human race is the subject of a huge breeding programme, and that its perpetrators intend to produce a race of alien-human hybrids. 'A huge, strange interspecies or interbeing breeding programme has invaded our physical reality and is affecting the lives of hundreds of thousands, if not millions of people,' he has written.[1]

However, he seems a little confused about the precise nature of these alien experimenters and has said that they: 'Penetrate and enter the physical world, and to that extent they're a little different from spirit entities.'[2]

Instead of being a fully paid-up member of what has been called a Hidden College of UFO researchers (important academics and intellectuals who believe but keep their heads down), Mack is an evangelical, proselytising believer who goes out of his way to publicise his ideas and appears to take the wroth of his superiors and the anxieties of his friends in his stride. He has written widely on the subject of UFOs and lectures around the world. His most important contribution so far is a book called *Abduction: Human Encounters With Aliens* in which he models his elaborate theory about abduction based upon the testimony of over one hundred abductees (or 'experiencers' as they prefer to be called) who have found their way to his couch during his many years of research in the field.

John Mack's academic credentials are impeccable but his past reveals him to be a man who desperately wants to find alternative paths through life rather than following any form of orthodoxy. Now in his late sixties, he has been in and out of every possible form of alternative research and experimentation. He has conducted psychology experiments with psychedelic drugs, became involved with EST – a form of alternative 'therapy' widely discredited in the late 1970s – and travelled to India to find enlightenment in Eastern religion and philosophy.

There is nothing wrong with any of this, but to some sceptics it does imply that Mack is not merely open-minded, but has left the door to his mind flapping wildly in the breeze – a state which many scientists believe to be the wrong approach to a subject like alien abduction. Mack and many other enthusiastic believers around the globe would of course argue the exact opposite – that the problem with scientific investigators is that they approach fields like this with closed minds and are therefore unqualified to deal with something so far outside their normal mode of thinking.

To study those who claim to be experiencers, Mack uses the technique of *hypnotic regression*. For many researchers this is the most invaluable tool in the armoury of the investigator. It involves relaxing the subject and putting them into what some psychologists call a 'non-ordinary state' in which they can remember experiences they have suppressed and which they cannot recall in an 'ordinary state'. It is used by some researchers of the paranormal to open up what they claim to be experiences individuals have had in previous lives.

Hypnotic regression may be a useful tool for the investigator, but it has its pitfalls. It is highly susceptible to deliberate fakery, but most importantly, it can be used to plant ideas in the minds of subjects and, in extreme cases, to create what has recently been dubbed *false memory syndrome*.

False memory syndrome has made headlines recently because of the suggestion that some claims of child abuse investigated by psychologists are actually fictional ideas planted by the investigator and expanded upon by the distraught subject. In some accounts these false memories are incredibly vivid and the result of these investigations has meant shattered families and even police probings. It has been suggested, not without reason, that the use of hypnotic regression could also explain many cases of so-called alien abduction.

Naturally, researchers like John Mack strongly deny this claim. They may not be planting the ideas deliberately, and from all accounts Mack genuinely believes in what he is doing and is deeply committed to the idea that alien abduction is not a human invention. However, the similarity between alien abduction experiences as described by investigators using this technique and to stories created by adults regressed to childhood and later proven to be relating false memories is uncanny.

At one point in his book about alien abduction, Mack writes: 'The undoing of denial is effected by having the abductee stare into the "engulfing, searching eyes" of the alien. This will make them real and remove once and for all the denial that has operated as a psychological defence.' With this, Mack found there is: 'a shift in their relationship to the alien being.'[3]

Recently there appears to have been a reversal in the interest shown in hypnotic regression, and within the orthodox psychiatric community it is now viewed as questionable, and possibly damaging. Although it continues to be used enthusiastically by psychologists like Mack who work on the fringe, it is losing credibility in the mainstream. Psychiatrist-in-Chief at Boston's Beth Israel hospital, Professor Fred Frankel has said of the technique: 'Hypnosis helps you regain memories that you would not have otherwise recalled . . . But some will be true, and some will be false. The expectation of the hypnotist and the expectation of the person who is going to be hypnotised can influence the result.'[4]

A huge dent in the credibility of Mack's experiments with experiencers as well as the entire practice of hypnotic regression has come from the work of a forty-one-year-old Boston-based writer named Donna Bassett. Hearing that Mack was 'strip-mining the emotional lives of distraught people and failing to help them with follow-up therapy',[5] she decided to pose as an abductee to test out Mack's techniques and to question the entire phenomenon.

She read everything she could find on the subject of UFOs and took method-acting lessons to produce convincing testimony in a faked hypnotic state and gradually ingratiated herself with Mack. She told him she had been visited by 'little people' whom she called 'angels from God' and described how she had been experiencing weird events since childhood – balls of fire hovering above her parents' house at night, the healing touch of an alien who visited her after she had burned her hands. Mack spent hours with Bassett and became so convinced of her story he even used her account of an abduction in his book.

Other American investigators are just as enthusiastic. David Jacobs, who is a historian specialising in modern American history at Temple University, is becoming almost as well known as Mack and suggests ideas every bit as radical. In a recent magazine article, he was asked why it was that during over 50 years of investigation there has never been a clear-cut abduction incident in daylight with reliable witnesses and with complete corroboration and without underlying psychological abnormalities linked to any of the participants. He retorted: 'The secret aspect of the phenomenon is remarkably efficient and extraordinarily effective. The way in which the alien programme is instituted mitigates against having a lot of cases from the same day. And so does the way in which we find out about the cases. Most people who have had abduction experiences don't really know what has happened to them. They might know that an odd thing has happened here and there, but linking it to a UFO abduction is not something most of them would probably do. So of all the abductees out there we only hear from about 0.001 percent of them. But every once in a while we'll have a case where somebody who is an abductee will come up to another person and say, "I know you. I've seen you before." And they will trace it back to an abduction event they have shared.'[6]

Jacobs is particularly interested in multiple abductions. There are a surprising number of these; one estimate suggests that about one quarter of all cases involve more than one individual and there have been reported incidents involving up to eight people being abducted simultaneously. But these run into all the same pitfalls as individual cases – questionable techniques applied to extract the story and clear inconsistencies that are surprisingly overlooked by investigators.

A good example is the testimony of an anonymous man who was supposedly abducted along with his entire family. One of the things he remembered about the incident was lining up in a hall with dozens of others who had been abducted around the same time before being led into an investigation or interrogation room by his alien hosts. Whilst standing in line he noticed that a man in front of him had a mole on his left shoulder. To Jacobs, this was a convincing detail that added weight to the man's story. To a dispassionate outsider, it seems ridiculous that anyone would notice such a thing when about to be examined by an alien, let alone in what experiencers happily relate as being in an otherworldly or 'trippy' state.

Another aspect of reports often ignored by believers is what independent-thinking investigators call 'contamination'. Frequently in multiple abduction cases, those involved are all interested in UFOs, they have all read the literature and they invariably behave in a highly competitive manner. Psychologists investigating many of these cases believe that quite often, one of the individuals will suggest to the others that something has happened when it has not and so the idea spreads amongst them. Peer pressure and simple wishful thinking eventually leads them to actually believe a false memory themselves and to let this come out in whichever way is most suitable – usually by having the story teased out under hypnosis.

So, if in fact humans are not being abducted by aliens then what do we make of the swelling flood of reports coming in not just from the United States and Europe but from all over the world? By applying ideas from psychology and neuroscience, as well as a sprinkling of common sense and logic, there may be some answers.

First, the common-sense part – some statistics. I mentioned earlier in this chapter that a survey has shown that as many as five million Americans could have had experiences that indicate they have been abducted by aliens. This survey was actually carried out on 6000 people during 1991. Of these, 119 people fitted the stereotype of a classic abduction scenario. When this figure is extrapolated up to the population of America we arrive at a figure of five million abductions. Strictly speaking, this in itself is not a reliable figure because extrapolating from 6000 to some 350 million (the population of the United States) is not statistically valid. But ignoring this, let us look at a more significant absurdity offered by these figures.

Taking the figure of five million American abductees, an investigator named Robert Durant has reached an interesting conclusion. He assumed that the average abductee has been taken ten times, (some have claimed many more abductions, some have had only one or two experiences). If five million individuals have been abducted an average of ten times during the past fifty years then that constitutes one million abductions per year or 2740 per day in the United States. He went on to assume that each abduction required an average of six aliens; (this was based upon the growing abduction lore and data gathered by enthusiasts) and that this team can carry out twelve abductions per day. This means that each day there are 288 teams of aliens operating which constitutes a total of 1370 alien visitors.

Perhaps more startling than these figures is Durant's conclusion, which inadvertently reveals more about the sort of sloppy thinking of UFOlogists than any statistics could alone. Starting his investigation, he claimed, 'very sceptically', Durant concluded that the figure of 1370 alien visitors per day was actually not too absurd a number. He concluded that even with backup and support the figure of 1370 aliens would only need to be increased to say 5000; a figure, he pointed out, that is about equal to a single aircraft carrier crew. But where he fell down in his argument was with the simple fact that he had considered only American statistics. In a breathtaking display of parochialism he ignored the other ninety-five percent of the world's population. This would mean that to account for the figures presented by the community of UFO enthusiasts themselves, there needs to be in excess of *100,000* aliens on earth engaged upon missions to abduct humans, all undercover, all going about their business without a single convincing verifiable piece of evidence for a period of at least fifty years.

But it gets worse. If there have been five million abductees during the past fifty years in America, there must have been 200 million abductees during that time throughout the world. This is about one in twenty people.

These statistics offer just one argument against the entire notion of alien abduction. A counter argument could be that the vast majority of incidents are accountable by some other means – hallucination, hysterical reaction, hypnotic suggestion, so that perhaps only one percent of reported cases are genuine alien abductions. This then admittedly lowers the alien population on earth to a believable 1000, and the number of abductees worldwide to just two million. But there are other logical arguments used by sceptics against the entire abduction lore.

It is impossible to convincingly explain each and every

case of abduction but, argue the sceptics, this is actually quite unnecessary. The concept of alien abduction as it is reported by thousands of experiencers is not logical – the overall story simply does not work; it is internally inconsistent.

First, imagine human explorers visiting a remote part of the Amazon jungle. During their travels they discover a new, as-yet-unheard-of species of animal or plant. Within six months of the discovery, the BBC would have made a documentary about the creature, complete with David Attenborough wandering through the undergrowth. Within a year, books about the new species would have appeared in shops and there would be CD-ROMs available detailing every aspect of the creature's anatomy, behaviour and habits.

Now, when we are talking about alien visitors, it is easy to forget just how technologically advanced these beings must be to have travelled here in the first place. Any scientist will admit that we cannot hope to travel interstellar distances at practical speeds in the foreseeable future and until we can crack the light-speed problem a journey, even to the nearest star system, would take thousands of years. With this in mind, it is clear then that any alien visitors must possess technology thousands of years in advance of ours. In which case, why would they possibly need to spend at least fifty years snatching a total of perhaps millions of humans in order to learn about our species?

Looked at from this perspective it is clear that the very notion of alien abduction is an example of human vanity at its worse. We are imprinting upon an alien race our own technological limitations and lack of imagination and at the same time implying that we are so special and important as a race that firstly they are drawn here, and secondly we are so endlessly fascinating and complex that they can't stop snatching us to find out how we tick.

Enthusiasts would argue that this misses the point. They claim that alien abductors are not merely studying our anatomy and behaviour as we would a new species of animal from the Amazon jungle, but they are engaging in complex genetic research.

This is again indicative of human egocentricity and a lamentable lack of imagination. Genetic engineering is an exciting new field of research and it has sparked the public's imagination, but to an advanced race able to travel across the galaxy it would be ancient knowledge. If they have advanced in the areas of physics needed to accomplish interstellar travel then they will almost certainly be equally advanced in the field of genetics. *We* might need to abduct creatures, dissect them, stick metal probes into them and conduct simple genetic experiments using sperm and eggs, but is it reasonable to assume that such an advanced people would also need to do this?

Even assuming they would be interested in experimenting with less advanced life forms, aliens who can travel across interstellar or even intergalactic distances would be able to extract materials from other beings without needing to resort to anything so crude as physical abduction and internal examinations.

Abduction lore includes many cases in which women have been abducted, impregnated and then discovered the foetus has disappeared. None of these cases have been proven and it is a very simple matter to explain them as phantom pregnancies, or to show a mitigating psychological disorder in the experiencer. But, even if we assume for the moment that this really happens, that aliens somehow dematerialise a foetus and transport it to their craft in *Star Trek* fashion, would not those same aliens be capable of creating the hybrid pregnancy without recourse to abduction and impregnation?

Some sceptics have also pointed out that the entire idea of abduction is a nonsense because advanced civilisations would be advanced morally as well as technologically so they would think it unethical to interfere with other less advanced civilisations and to abduct innocent, unwilling individuals. This may be true, but it is by no means a certainty. Although we are far more advanced technologically than our ancestors, are we any more developed ethically or morally? We may kill each other in different ways today, but we still kill. Skilled individuals may steal using the Internet rather than pickpocketing, but it is still theft; the rich Western nations may exploit their poorer neighbours in a clandestine manner, but it is still a form of imperialism.

However, the matter of whether or not an advanced alien race is morally more advanced than us and would or would not stoop to abduction is actually irrelevant. Far more significant is our total insignificance as a species and our unremarkable position in the galaxy. The Earth is a tiny planet, lost in an ocean of stars and other worlds. Why would an alien race want to come here? Furthermore, why would they want to bother with us? What could an advanced race possibly gain by interbreeding with humankind? Perhaps there is a plentiful supply of dilithium crystals somewhere on Earth!

Putting even these logical arguments aside, the fact that large numbers of seemingly sane individuals are experiencing something strange cannot be ignored easily. If not alien abduction, what then could they be experiencing? If they are not part of some massive global conspiracy and millions of individuals who appear to be caught up in the web are not in fact smuggled aboard alien vehicles, what are they living through?

As we have seen, stories related by experiencers follow a very clear template, but there are also some common threads which, to dispassionate psychologists, indicate obvious psychological and neurological patterns.

First there is the question of the emotional and sociological profile of abduction victims. According to the enthusiasts cases span all socioeconomic classes, professions and degrees of intellects. But they have to admit that there are a significantly greater number of female abductees. This is an interesting aberration because, in general, men are more likely to be out at night alone and therefore more vulnerable than women (it is important to remember that both male and female abductees are equally powerless in the face of alien interference, so physical strength is irrelevant). This must mean that statistically, there is an even greater slant towards women believing they have been abducted.

Another interesting aspect of abductions in relation to gender is that reports frequently have a strong sexual element. Often abductees are examined and sexually abused. In many cases the reports of experiencers have a marked similarity to the accounts of rape victims and even the most enthusiastic researchers are keen to highlight the fact that abductees often feel abused and violated. Abductees usually do not want to recall their experiences under hypnosis, but feel compelled to pour out what they had lived through.

The fact that experiencers are resistant to telling their stories even under hypnosis should not be surprising, and it certainly does not validate their supposed encounters with what they believe to be alien beings. Firstly, there is a social resistance to telling such tales. It may be that a few abductees have deliberately concocted their stories to make money or to gain their fifteen minutes of fame, but even they have to create a pretence of being resistant to the fact that they had been snatched and manipulated by extraterrestrials. Taking this further, if an experiencer shows resistance to their memories beyond the fear of ridicule, this is quite understandable because, if the experience was created in their own minds, they will have produced a barrier against the memory as a form of self-protection. If the false memory they have nurtured is painful, which almost all abductions appear to be, then they will try to submerge this false memory and they will have to be encouraged to speak about it.

Another possible explanation for the abduction phenomenon is that the individuals who come forward are merely satisfying a deep-rooted egomania or overcoming a powerful sense of inferiority. What more exciting and special experience could anyone ever have? To be abducted, no matter how unpleasant the experience, indicates that an individual is important, special, a notch above everyone else.

Often experiencers recount how they met the commander of the interstellar vessel they were taken to and engaged in a detailed discussion with the crew about the propulsion system of the craft, about the ecological dangers facing humankind, or on occasion, 'the meaning of the universe'. Remember, these are invariably ordinary citizens who have little knowledge of philosophy let alone high-powered physics. Is it reasonable that such people would be conversant with such things when they had just met an individual from another star?

There is also an element of one-upmanship within the UFO community, a clash of egos, so that experiencers are now trying to outdo each other. An American woman named Katherine Wilson has published a book called *The Alien Jigsaw* in which she describes her 119 abduction experiences spanning twenty-six years. In her book she tells of encounters with several different groups of aliens, about out-of-the-body experiences and time travel. She describes being privy to a meeting between Bill Clinton and George Bush shortly before the 1992 US election and how an alien ambassador negotiated a smooth transfer of power and 'arranged' the election, a tale which in itself weakens her claims – after all why should aliens be that interested in the politics of a single country?

To rival these claims there is the marvellous tale of one Peter Gregory, who claims to have been taken on board an alien craft and given a lecture on the perils of ecological mismanagement on Earth before meeting Oona, an adult alien-human hybrid, with whom he appears to have fallen madly in love. In Peter's tale he describes the control room of the alien craft including a 'viewing screen' and a control consul with an array of flashing lights, à la *Star Trek*, circa 1966.

But these are all outstripped by the testimony of an anonymous twenty-six-year-old businessman from West Virginia who claims to have been abducted no fewer than 1500 times.

A further explanation for the huge increase in the numbers of apparent abductions is linked with the social climate of the late twentieth century. It is clear that we are moving into a Godless age, particularly outside the US and the Third World. Church attendance in Britain is less than ten percent of what it was only fifty years ago and even in the far more religiously-inclined United States many people who cannot find a faith system based upon orthodox religion are turning to alternatives. The past two decades have seen a staggering rise in cult religions in the US and elsewhere. These range from suicidal groups who believe they are being contacted by aliens to those who follow Eastern religions and practice alternative health regimes and obscure meditative techniques. For such people, UFO lore and abduction is merely another tendril of a many-headed creature that offers an alternative universal view to orthodox religion – a different way to cope with existential fears and the corrosive angst many of us feel at one time or another.

Alien abduction offers a great deal to people who cannot accept institutionalised religion. It is fresh and different, it displaces the conventional 'God-like' figure with something tangible. It offers hope, excitement, it draws in the experiencer, drags them into a bigger world in which they play a significant role. Finally, it is more manageable than orthodox religion – after all, Christianity has been unable to offer a spectacular show for at least two thousand years and the faithful are expected to take their cue from a fallible clergy who are losing credibility by the day and who offer a doctrine based upon an ancient text facing its own credibility crisis.

The journalist Tom Hodgkinson puts the matter succinctly when he says: 'The UFO offers a satisfying blend of techno-futurism, religion and spiritual quest which is personally motivated and does not require a commitment to an externally imposed set of social rules. In a reason-based society, it is almost easier to believe in aliens poised to descend and save the earth at any moment, than it is to believe in God.'[7]

In other words, 'aliens are easy'. It is a simple matter to transfer one's anxieties, fantasies, fears and hopes onto an alien race and visiting flying saucers. Whatever your problem, you can always say: 'Aliens made me do it.' There are some who have become paid-up members of the newly-created Church of Elvis the Messiah in the United States. Should it come as any surprise that others have found a new religion in the lore of UFOs and abduction?

There is also the question of hysteria. We should not underestimate the power of public obsession and the way in which shared hysteria over something felt passionately can escalate almost out of control. The recent sad death of Diana, Princess of Wales presents a clear illustration of this phenomenon. For many people who had little time for the princess before her death, the circumstances of her passing were very sad and disturbing, but the reaction of the public verged on hysteria. The Royal Family and the Press were very quickly made scapegoats following a public outcry over the circumstances of her death and what was viewed as a cold response from her former in-laws. The public demanded that the Royal Family show remorse and the baying mob even insisted that the young Princes, William and Harry, be made to appear outside Buckingham Palace to inspect the thousands of floral tributes. Only then was the public anguish appeased.

And what was this anguish based upon? The vast majority of the mourners never even knew Diana and most of those gathered outside Buckingham Palace were not rabid Royalists. The reason for the reaction was angst, the individual's fear of death, of the abyss. And this is one of the key reasons for a belief in UFOs and alien abduction. The thought that we are being visited by aliens lifts us out of the parochial framework in which we live our daily lives, the limitations of being alone in the universe and restricted to this tiny planet. Abduction lore and UFO enthusiasm are every bit as potent as any religion and satisfy exactly the same needs.

Most abductees really do believe they have been taken aboard alien vehicles. This in itself is a fascinating neurological phe-nomenon and a number of possible explanations for it have been offered by psychotherapists and neurophysiologists.

The idea favoured by most psychologists is that abduction scenarios are created in the brain by stimulating the temporal lobes – an area of the brain in which we store memories. No one yet knows what may cause this stimulation and it may be the result of a collection of external (and perhaps internal) stimuli, but the effect has been shown to work in laboratory experiments. If the temporal lobes are artificially stimulated by the application of a magnetic field (using a specially-designed helmet), subjects recount experiencing many of the symptoms of an abduction.

Susan Blackmore, a psychologist from the University of the West of England is interested in the phenomenon of abduction and other paranormal claims and underwent experiments using the helmet. She described the experience as follows: 'I was awake throughout. Nothing seemed to happen for the first ten minutes or so. Instructed to describe aloud anything that happened, I felt under pressure to say something, anything. Then suddenly my doubts vanished. "I'm swaying. It's like being on a hammock." Then it felt for all the world as though two hands had grabbed my shoulders and were bodily yanking me upright. I knew I was still lying in the reclining chair, but someone, or something, was pulling me up. Something seemed to get hold of my leg and pull it, distort it and drag it up the wall. It felt as though I had been stretched halfway up the ceiling. Then came the emotions. Totally out of the blue, but intensely and vividly, I suddenly felt angry – not just mildly cross but that clear-minded anger out of which you act – but there was nothing and no one to act on. After perhaps ten seconds, it was gone. Later it was replaced by an equally sudden attack of fear. I was terrified of – nothing in particular. The long-term medical effects of applying strong magnetic fields to the brain are largely unknown, but I felt weak and disorientated for a couple of hours after coming out of the chamber.'[8]

Linked to this is the idea that abductions are the modern equivalent of what are known as *sleep paralysis myths*. During normal REM sleep (rapid eye movement sleep), the muscles of the body are temporarily paralysed. This is thought to be a defence mechanism because REM sleep is also the period in which most of us dream and it is believed that this muscular paralysis is triggered in order to prevent us hurting ourselves if we 'act out' our dreams. However, sometimes people become mentally alert while their body stays paralysed – the mind is awake, but the body is asleep. These experiences are often associated with sexual arousal.

Throughout the ages, people have reported vivid nocturnal experiences, sometimes of a sexual nature, but just as often they are frightening and vivid recollections of being chased or attacked by a monster and being powerless to do anything about it. These are the sleep paralysis myths reported by all sorts of people from young children to horrified nuns who believe their chastity has been sullied by a 'night caller'. The connection between this phenomenon, the effects of magnetic fields on mental processes and reports of alien abduction is striking.

Another suggestion, made by Albert Budden in his book *Allergies and Aliens*, is that the illusion of abduction is precipitated by what he calls 'electromagnetic pollution'. This pollution is created by the increased number of electronic machines in the environment which leak electromagnetic waves. A particular culprit is high voltage power lines and Budden points out that a great many cases of abduction occur near such power lines.

Other psychologists are more candid. For them the answer to alien abduction is a simple one. 'I have not come across the phenomenon of abductions by aliens except as a delusional belief of someone suffering from schizophrenia,' claims psychotherapist, Sue Davidson.[9]

For the sceptic, one of the most powerful arguments against alien abduction is the way enthusiasts dig their own traps. Recently, UFOlogists have begun to attempt to explain how alien visitors arrive here, how their technology works and even to discuss openly what they claim to be the physiology of alien races. These attempts have begun to appear thanks to what enthusiasts claim are leaks from government sources and relate directly to tales of captured alien technology and the possession of alien beings, both dead and alive.

The most famous example of this is the Roswell Incident and the supposed goings on at Area 51 – a military establishment in the Nevada Desert.

According to the United States authorities, there is no such place as Area 51, which is a flagrant lie and a misguided attempt at disinformation. The efforts of the military to deny the fact that there is a top-secret military establishment at the map reference corresponding to Area 51 is an unfortunate and typically heavy-handed attempt to disguise the truth. It has been a counterproductive move because the denials have simply attracted more and more interested investigators, who risk trouble for themselves in trying to probe the secrets of the establishment.

Area 51 is almost certainly a top secret military establishment where experimental craft are tested and cutting-edge research conducted, but the idea that a craft that crashed in nearby Roswell in 1947 and was taken to Area 51 along with a collection of dead alien occupants is far from substantiated. In fact the reports of those who claim to have leaked information about the aliens and their vehicle proves the very opposite and damages the UFOlogist's cause.

A few years ago what has been claimed to be a film of an alien autopsy was screened by television networks across the world. The film was purchased by a British film producer who claims to have acquired it from a man who was involved with the autopsy of the Roswell aliens in 1947. It shows what look like small humanoid figures on a slab, partly dissected and fitting the description of an alien that has since become almost a cliché – the archetypal 'grey' with large black eyes, an abnormally large bald head and long arms. However, even

UFO enthusiasts are beginning to suspect that the film is a fake and contrived merely to make money. Yet, in spite of this, ideas connected with this autopsy are widely accepted within the UFO community and discussed as if they are academically sound, established facts.

According to the enthusiasts, greys have a combined heart and lungs, and a combined pancreas and spleen. This, they claim, is a piece of information that has seeped out from places like Area 51 and is based upon close study of alien anatomy. The problem is, the idea is ridiculous, but it is easy to see the 'logic' behind this phoney anatomical description.

Those who make such statements obviously believe that alien visitors are more advanced than us technologically. This is perfectly reasonable and quite obvious because they can come here, but we cannot go there. However, they take this concept too far. They assume that alien bodies must have evolved further than ours and to those without a scientific training it would seem to make sense that a combined heart and lungs would be an improvement on separate organs.

But, actually, it would be the very opposite. It would be a great disadvantage.

We have a separate heart and lungs for a number of very good reasons, but most important is the advantage this arrangement offers as a defence against disease. If, for example, our heart becomes infected with a bacteria, the infection may not spread to the lungs and we have a better chance of fighting off the disease. If we had a joint heart-lungs organ then any attack would cause us far greater problems, we would have two infected organs in one.

In other accounts, UFO enthusiasts do not feel able to hold back with the application of pseudo-science to 'explain' how alien ships work or how travellers communicate. In one account entitled 'Aliens In Our Ocean' from a magazine called *Encounters*, the author discusses how human military forces can counteract alien weapon systems. She says: 'The question should be whether a rotating and oscillating high voltage, electromagnetic standing wave which changes gravitational phase, could be interrupted by cool longer waves ... Without being too technical, it is important to have specifics about phrases like, "The energy produced from this generator was to be concentrated so that it could be aimed and used as a weapon in order to destroy the alien craft and beam weapons." I do know that in radio astronomy, radio frequencies are measured in a beam of hydrogen atoms and that the vanished scientist in question had been testing particular [sic] his device beneath the water.'[10]

It is really anybody's guess what this is all about. It is a blend of scientific terms and contrived phrases used in an attempt to impress people who know little about modern science. For example, what is 'a cool wave'? Even more confusing is the last paragraph. The author says that radio astronomers measure radio frequencies 'in a beam of hydrogen atoms'. This is not a very precise description, but it would seem the author is confusing the fact that astronomers measure frequencies *against the standard of the hydrogen spectrum* using a technique called 'spectroscopic analysis'. This has nothing to do with 'beams of hydrogen atoms'. And what is to be made of the link made between this and the fact that the scientist in question was 'testing particular [sic] his device beneath the water'? Is the implication that the hydrogen spectrum used by radio astronomers is somehow linked with hydrogen because hydrogen is one of the atoms in the water molecule H_2O? If it is, then the author deserves an award for creative writing.

A further example is the often very mundane descriptions of the control rooms of flying saucers offered by experiencers. These are almost always descriptions straight out of B-movies or old-fashioned science fiction novels. Abductees use their experiences of television and cinema as reference points to describe the interiors of craft which are supposed to be designed by creatures thousands of years more advanced than us. Is it not reasonable to assume that the interior design and the gadgetry at the disposal of such aliens would be totally unrecognisable to an abductee? What would a layperson propelled from 1950 the bedroom of a late-1990s teenager know what to make of a Nintendo machine or even a PC?

There are many examples of flabby thinking in the UFO literature that have found fertile ground in this age of *X-Files* mania and what has been dubbed pre-millennial tension. Sadly such material undermines those who are interested in the idea of life on other planets and the serious search for extraterrestrial life. Because of the growing crank element, those in power and those with money to help fund serious research projects are put off assisting genuine scientists. There are even those who suggest that some of the more extreme ideas of the UFOlogists and particularly those who try to convince us of alien abduction are actually dangerous. UFOlogist, Jacques Vallee believes the phenomenon creates a loop of consciousness which escalates the idea far beyond its original foundations. 'Conventional science,' he claims, 'appears more and more perplexed, befuddled, at a loss to explain. Pro-ET UFOlogists become more dogmatic in their propositions. More people become fascinated with space and with new frontiers of consciousness.'[11]

An elevating of consciousness is a good thing, but unmanaged it leads to greater confusion and feeble reasoning. Any faith system, and UFO lore is simply that, which threatens to damage real science is a danger to society. The irony for the UFO enthusiasts is this: if aliens are visiting our planet they have managed this feat by the application of science. To accomplish something as amazing as this, many alien scientists would have had to work for many years refining their ideas and learning how the universe works. This may involve an holistic approach – incorporating what many would call 'alternative' mechanisms and thought-patterns combined with empirical and intellectual rigour, but there would have been no room on their world for the gullibility and the anti-intellectual stance epitomised by some within the UFOlogy community here.

Alien abduction is a product of human minds spurred on

by ulterior motives. These vary from sexual fantasy to the need to suppress a more painful experience. It is fuelled by a form of low-key public hysteria driven by a natural need for spiritual and emotional fulfilment in our modern age of spiritual frigidity and vanishing family security and a religious orthodoxy out of touch with the needs of modern people.

I genuinely wish aliens were visiting us on a regular basis, and that there was a great network out there in the galaxy of which we are a tiny part; but, not only is there no evidence, much more importantly, there is no logical reason for this to be true. This does not negate the fact that there may well be a network out there operated by advanced alien cultures, thousands of years in advance of us. Maybe one day we will join that most exclusive of clubs but, I'm sorry to say, we are not involved to any degree just yet, and one day we will look back upon the belief in alien abduction as an aberration symptomatic of the intellectual climate in which we all now live.

2

THE CULT OF THE CULT

'Kill a man, and you are a murderer.
Kill millions of men, and you are a conqueror.
Kill everyone, and you are a god.'

Jean Rostand

The scene that met the officers of the San Diego Police Department as they entered Rancho Santa Fe in a suburb of San Diego on 26 March 1997 was one of clinical horror. No bloodstained walls, no gore, no mutilated bodies, for this was a death scene from the final years of the twentieth century, but inspired by the twenty-third.

Inside the house the police found thirty-nine bodies. Each was dressed in overalls and new, previously unworn Nike trainers. Each of the former members of the cult group known as Heaven's Gate had a bag beside their death bed. The bag contained a change of clothes. In the top pocket of their tunics they had their passports and in their trouser pockets, a five-dollar bill and a roll of quarters. Over each head lay a metre square of purple silk.

They had, the investigators discovered, died in waves over a period of three days. Each had enjoyed a final meal, made a personal, upbeat goodbye video message, consumed a pudding liberally laced with phenobarbital, chased that with vodka and placed a plastic bag over their head. Those in the second wave removed the bags from the heads of those in the first and two women – the last to die – removed those from the heads of the second wave, tidied up thoroughly, deposited the bags and other detritus in dustbins and quietly killed themselves in the same way.

In some respects, the cult called Heaven's Gate that self-immolated in March 1997 bore a number of startling similarities to other suicidal cults, but in other ways it was very different. Although, like all other such groups, Heaven's Gate was lead by a mentally-damaged charismatic, a man named Marshall Herff Applewhite, who offered a prescription for an alternative reality, it was different because the cult members seemed to be entirely happy with their exit, and optimistic about their 'future' – there appeared to be no form of oppression or dictatorship within the cult.

Cult members were often seen in the neighbourhood. The women often gave away bourbon pound cakes which they were forbidden by their creed to eat. Both men and women had their heads shaved and wore plain tunics which disguised their gender. At least six of the men, including Applewhite, had been castrated long before their suicide.

One commentator has said that the cult members of Heaven's Gate 'died of kitsch'. This is actually a pretty accurate description. Fed on a constant diet of science fiction – from videos, TV, books, magazines and the Internet – the members of Heaven's Gate were actually living out a science fiction fantasy in which they were the lead characters, and for them, their mission was not to die but merely to enter the next stage of the plot – to, as they put it, 'shed their containers'. Ironically, one of the thirty-nine members was Thomas Nichols, brother of Nichelle Nichols who played Lieutenant Uhuru in the original *Star Trek* series.

The philosophy behind the group (if philosophy is what you want to call it) was of course a simple one – the simple script is always the most effective – and it came entirely from the mind of their leader, Marshall Applewhite.

Applewhite was a most modern guru, but as we will see

he fits neatly into the mould created by others through the ages. He was sixty-five at the time of the mass suicide and had lead a chequered life. His early years were spent with his family in Texas. His father was a Presbyterian minister and he was brought up in a strict, censorial environment. He went to college and then the University of Alabama, dropping out in the mid '60s. He was a talented musician with a good singing voice and he was physically attractive as a young man. He performed in university musicals and worked for a while in a small school in Houston where he produced several musicals before leaving under a cloud in 1970 after a scandal involving a sexual relationship with one of the boys in his charge.

From that time on, Applewhite seems to have gradually and deliberately retreated from the world. There followed bouts of alcoholism and drug abuse, he was committed to a succession of mental institutions and was seen by some who came into contact with him as a 'poor man's Timothy Leary'.

Towards the end of 1970 he met his soul mate, a woman named Betty Lu Trusdale Nettles, a nurse with a keen interest in the occult who had set herself up as an astrologer and 'spiritual guide'. Nettles was five years Applewhite's senior and soon after they met she left her husband and four young children and went into the wilderness with her new companion, never to return to her family.

Throughout the 1970s the pair travelled around the United States, spending a good deal of time in the South and forming a menagerie of obscure cults and groups who travelled with them. To show that given names were 'meaningless', they assumed pseudonyms such as Bo and Peep, and they collected minor convictions for car theft and drug possession. At one point their group was called HIM (Human Individual Metamorphosis), at another they dubbed themselves 'Total Overcomers Anonymous', then 'Undercover Jesus' followed by 'ET Presently Incarnate'. Later Nettles and Applewhite named themselves simply 'The Two'.

When Nettles died of cancer in 1985, Applewhite began

to remodel his 'philosophy' and to gather together a new group of devoted followers. His vision was a peculiar blend of Gnosticism and New Age/Cyber-tech fantasy, a doctrine in which the physical was scorned, most probably because he had been fighting inner sexual demons all his life. Applewhite was a homosexual and both he and Nettles repeatedly emphasised that their own relationship was completely non-sexual. The cult referred to the physical realm – everyday life – as *meatspace* and preferred to spend most of their time in cyberspace. Their ultimate aim was to actually leave this environment altogether, to progress to what they called 'the next level'.

The members of the cult were so calm and 'happy' about what they were doing because they believed they were merely going to step into a new and far better environment. They believed that an advanced extraterrestrial race was about to arrive near Earth and take them away to an alien world. Indeed, later they concluded that they were themselves alien beings who were merely occupying gross, human bodies. Their mission over, they were ready to return, to join 'Peep', a.k.a Nurse Nettles, and to live happily ever after.

This was the situation in early 1997; then the cult were pushed over the edge into affirmative action. This was precipitated by two things. Firstly Applewhite learned that he was seriously, possibly terminally ill. This meant that he had little to lose and was able to drag the other cult members to their own graves as he approached his – a form of ego-boosting sacrifice. More importantly perhaps, the group discovered what they adamantly believed to be a spacecraft approaching Earth.

In 1995 two astronomers, a professional, Alan Hale from New Mexico and Thomas Bopp, an amateur from Arizona, spotted a comet approaching Earth. It was named Hale-Bopp after the pair of them and when the news of this object made the Internet and later, the headlines of the world, the members of Heaven's Gate were convinced it was concealing a craft in its tail and that this was the signal they had been waiting for.

Comets have long been associated in lore with doom and destruction. The members of Heaven's Gate believed they were to be saved and the rest of humanity was to be destroyed by the arrival of Hale-Bopp – 'spade under' as they charmingly referred to it. Strikingly, this did not prevent one of the members joining after leaving her family and children including a seven-month-old baby.

Then, in November 1996 came the real clincher. An amateur astronomer named Chuck Shramek took a picture of Hale-Bopp which showed a bright disk-shaped object in its tail. It looked for all the world like a classic flying saucer hiding in the wake of the comet. Shramek's photograph became an overnight sensation and it was posted all over the Internet before journalists around the world picked up on it, propelling it into UFO legend.

The object was actually a star, SAO 141894, that lies many light years from Earth, but when viewed by terrestrial telescopes it appeared in the field of vision within the tail of the comet. It was actually nothing more than the poor quality of Shramek's optical equipment and imaging devices that had created the illusion that the object was in our solar system and shaped almost too perfectly like a 1950s image of a UFO.

The scientific explanation for this fell on deaf ears within Heaven's Gate. They knew what they wanted to believe – the original story as proclaimed by Shramek. It spurred them on and reaffirmed their ideas – it was quite irresistible and initiated what the cult called 'closure' – Heaven's Gate was about to close.

The cue was the comet's closest approach to earth, the night of the first deaths at Rancho Santa Fe. The members of the group believed they were to be transported aboard the craft and Peep (or Nettles) would be there waiting for them to take them home. Despite a thorough investigation of this entire story, to date no one knows what lay behind the need for purple silk scarves, rolls of quarters and five-dollar bills. One wit suggested the coins were needed for the cult

members to 'phone home' from the spacecraft; others have
suggested that it was done as a joke, a touch of black irony
from the members, a final gesture of rejection and contempt
perhaps. We will probably never know.

Heaven's Gate is just one example of the many hundreds
of cults that exist around the world today; a figure that is
growing steadily as we approach the millennium. Many of
these cults are benign and merely act as a safety valve for
many people who find it difficult to integrate within society.
Some cults and groups are what are called 'isolationist', they
seal themselves off from the world and retreat into their own
way of life. Some of these can become dangerous, some
become self-destructive. Others groups are outward-looking
and seen more as religious movements than alternative isolated communities of severely misanthropic individuals.

Cults have many shared traits. They usually consist of
young, well-educated people; they have a leader, often a
figure perceived as almost God-like; they have an idiosyn-
cratic language – deliberately created to isolate themselves
and exclude outsiders; and most importantly, they offer a
totally alternative and hermetically-sealed lifestyle.

It is this last factor that has drawn so many people to
cults in recent decades. Today there is a pervading sense of
dissatisfaction in Western post-industrial society, a feeling
that material gain and a standard of living vastly improved
since World War Two is not the be-all and end-all of a happy
life. Many people are seeking spiritual fulfilment and they are
not finding answers in orthodox religion. Cults and strange
belief systems are filling this vacuum and drawing a growing
number of people to an ever-increasing array of ideologies.

The group calling themselves Heaven's Gate shared many
of these characteristics. Its leader was as crazed as any other
leader of such inward-looking and ultimately self-immolating
groups even though their ideology was a little different to
the run of obsessive 'fire and brimstone' megalomaniacs the
world has witnessed in recent decades. Others have been far
more violent.

In November 1978, a cult comprising over nine hundred people, including two hundred and sixty children, drank a specially-prepared soft drink laced with cyanide. Their bodies were found scattered around a commune that had grown out of the jungle of Guyana, a place called Jonestown. The group had been settled there for almost four years and had grown steadily since the guru of the site, an American lay-minister named Jim Jones, arrived there in 1977.

Jones was mentally ill and, as we will see, he fitted precisely the template of the insane guru. Originally, life in Jonestown was considered by some as a rewarding experience, but gradually it turned into Hell on Earth. The cult members who saw Jones as a God were completely under his control. Jones gradually became more and more despotic, leading a double life as an absolute religious leader and a pseudo-head of a tiny, isolated state. His illusions of grandeur developed into a conviction that he could wield absolute power, that he was immortal and divine. He tortured and maimed children and murdered anyone who showed any signs of dissent. Almost unbelievably, he separated families and punished young children for minor offences in front of their mothers.

It is perhaps significant that when the authorities arrived in Jonestown they discovered that many of the victims had died of gunshot wounds, including Jones himself. No one knows what happened there during the last few hours of Jones's mad 'regime'. It could have been that the community finally turned against their leader but this would seem unlikely. It may have been that a small faction could not go along with the final stages of the plan and had to be 'helped'.

A man suffering a comparable psychosis and every bit as destructive as Jones was David Koresh, leader of a cult that called itself the Branch Davidians. In April 1993, he was the absolute head of a community of eighty-five people who went on to die in the fire that engulfed Apocalypse Ranch in Waco, Texas. Spurred on by delusions of divinity, he called himself 'Yahweh Koresh'.

David Koresh was born Vernon Howell in 1959. He had
lived through an unfortunate childhood. His mother was
fourteen when he was born and his father disappeared soon
after. He was raised by his grandmother and aunt, until his
mother married when he was five. He hated his stepfather
and left home as soon as he was able. Howell had been
bullied at school and was seen as retarded even though he
had an average IQ and was an able sportsman. In the late '70s
he joined the Seventh Day Adventists, but was expelled from
the church when he was caught in a compromising situation
with the sixteen-year-old daughter of his local pastor.

Koresh was obsessed with sex. Of the twenty-two children
who perished in the Waco fire, seventeen were fathered
by him. He married the fourteen-year-old daughter of an
Adventist Church official in 1983 and was soon sleeping
with her twelve-year-old sister. In the doomed Waco Ranch,
Koresh split up families and had men and women sleeping on
different floors of the building in order to make it easier for
him to seduce almost all the women who lived there.

Mirroring the events in Jonestown a decade earlier, Koresh's
deteriorating mental state meant that some of the cult members were desperate to leave before the final siege. Koresh
had specially-trained members of the cult posted as guards
on the inside of the building to stop anyone escaping,
and he too tortured and maimed, murdered and raped his
followers.

There are many other examples of such cults, and sadly
the list will grow still longer as the millennium comes upon
us. Some gurus, the likes of Koresh and Jones, are totally
destructive, akin to figures like Hitler and Stalin but without
the political intelligence, the opportunities and the advantage
of good timing. They are however motivated by different
variations of the same mental force. By controlling the minds
of susceptible individuals, they succeed only in destroying, in
snuffing out life.

Other gurus are less obvious. It has been claimed that both
Jung and Freud were gurus: they had a body of followers,

they created an alternative explanation for fundamental processes – in their case the functioning of the human mind –
and they also shared some of the mental characteristics and
even a few of what has been identified as the influences and
hallmarks of a guru's life.

In most cases, the cult of the guru dies with them. As
far as we know there are no serious followers of Koresh or
Jones left on the planet and it would be surprising to find any
existing believers in the cult of Heaven's Gate after the body
bags were removed from Rancho Santa Fe and the Earth
continued on its merry way untouched by the cataclysmic
interference of aliens. But there are some gurus whose ideas
continue after their death.

One example is the founder of the religion called Scientology.

Scientology is a fascinating example of a religion that has
grown out of its original cult status. Some point to the fact
that Christianity followed the same course – that Christ,
who incidentally also fits perfectly the guru template, was
originally a cult leader and is now perceived as one of the
great religious icons of Planet Earth.

Scientology is now officially a 'religion' or a 'church' – it
has been granted charitable status in Britain and claims to
have eight million followers world-wide, 100,000 of these in
Britain alone. But to many, Scientology is nothing more than
an elaborate con based upon fantasy and illusion. Indeed,
the British Home Office declared Scientology to be 'socially
harmful' as recently as the 1970s. Yet, to others, Scientology
is their religion and the church can point to several high-
profile members – including Hollywood stars, John Travolta,
Tom Cruise and Kirstie Alley.

Scientology was created by a man named Ron Hubbard
during the 1950s. Broke and drifting from one job to another,
Hubbard wrote a book called *Dianetics* which explained
his theory of life. It became an instant best seller and
has remained so ever since, selling principally to the ever-
growing numbers of new church members worldwide.

According to one version of Hubbard's life, he was an

all-action superhero, a great writer who worked on many Hollywood classics, was honoured and decorated as a war hero, was an accomplished scientist and charismatic leader. In the alternative version he was a con man *par excellence*, a hack who hit on an idea at the right time and followed it through to its logical conclusion.

It is interesting to note that Scientology may be seen as another influence in Marshall Applewhite's doctrine. Hubbard created the idea that we are all inhabited by the spirits of beings called *Thetans*. Most of us, he claimed, are unaware of this but we can become *operating Thetans* by a process of mental auditing or cleansing. This is done by exorcising painful memories. He devised a system for doing this (the basis of his famous book) and created a machine called an *electropsychometer* which helps to clear the mind of unwanted material – to enable followers to attain the enlightened state of being Operating Thetans.

Hubbard was certainly a guru. He fitted into the usual profile, but like Christ, Jung and others who are loosely joined together in this study, he did not enforce his will upon a small community, he did not turn inward and create a self-destructive ghetto. Instead, he projected his ideas, and in so doing he captured a far wider audience that flourishes still today.

So, given that gurus can encompass such diverse figures as Christ, Freud and Jim Jones, what is it that unites them, what lies behind the 'template of a guru'?

In his excellent study of gurus, *Feet of Clay*, the eminent British psychologist Anthony Storr has pinpointed the attributes common to almost all gurus. Firstly, they must preach and found a sect. Their style of preaching may vary depending upon the nature of their core belief – Applewhite traipsed around the southern States of America preaching self-enlightenment through suppression of natural drives, a doctrine spiced up enormously by his conviction that he was an alien trapped in a human body. Koresh preached fire and brimstone self-restraint (whilst indulging himself with unfettered enthusiasm). Bhagwan Shree Rajneesh, the guru from India who led a community of over 2000 in the late 1980s, extolled the belief that enlightenment could be attained through unlimited amounts of sex. Clearly, all gurus need a 'message' and a medium through which to preach and to gather a devoted following.

Gurus also need to be highly charismatic individuals. The word 'charisma' comes from the Greek and originally meant 'the gift of grace'. The psychologist Max Weber initially coined the modern usage of the word to describe someone who possessed special powers of attraction and who then acquired the belief that they were better than the run of people and in some way superior. The sociologist Eileen Barker has pointed out that: 'Almost by definition charismatic leaders are unpredictable, for they are bound by neither tradition nor rules; they are not answerable to other human beings.'[1]

Gurus are almost invariably self-taught. Each creates their doctrine, formulates an approach, a method to attain enlightenment which they then need to pass on to others. If we are to include figures such as Freud and Jung in the collection of gurus, the definition needs to be stretched a little because of course both men received a high level of training in their discipline. But each then rebelled against the establishment and produced their own framework, their own philosophy and their own methods. So in this respect, they too were self-taught. Jesus, is another example. There is no record of Jesus being taught anything. He is always perceived as the teacher, or at least an autodidact.

A third trait is intolerance of criticism. Almost all of us face criticism each and every day, for both minor and major errors, 'to err is to be human'. We take it as a basic aspect of all our lives.

Freud commented that: 'The man who is predominantly erotic will give first preference to his emotional relationships to other people; the narcissistic man, who inclines to be self-sufficient, will seek his main satisfactions in his internal mental processes.'[2]

All gurus are of the latter type. They are narcissistic in the extreme, turned inwards and totally incapable of accepting criticism, often reacting violently against it. Koresh killed people who opposed him, as did Jim Jones.

The Armenian guru and mystic, Georgei Ivanovitch Gurdjieff, was explicitly intolerant of any form of criticism and lashed out at any one who offered even measured critiques of his views. Jung and Freud were highly sensitive to criticism and indeed fell out irretrievably because they could not agree over their different approaches to psychology. When Jim Jones's wife Marceline tried to persuade their son Stephan to coerce his father into reducing his intake of narcotics, he is reported to have replied: 'You're talking about going to God and telling him he's a drug addict?'[3]

At the other extreme, there is no account of Jesus shunning criticism in the Bible, but then that should come as little surprise given the reverential nature of the written history of his life and times, and the sanitising of those accounts during the past two millennia.

Applewhite somehow managed to keep a certain balance within his community, but nobody really knows what went on in Rancho Santa Fe before death stalked the community. It would be safe to assume that Applewhite was as intolerant as all the other gurus I have ever considered. One clue lies in the way Heaven's Gate responded to the reaction they received when they began to emerge on the Internet some months before their mass suicide. Expecting to be received warmly by the cyber-community, they were instead 'flamed', insulted and treated with contempt. When they received this welcome the members of Heaven's Gate realised that their time had drawn near. As one former member, a man calling himself 'Jwnody' (who was left behind, apparently to spread the word, but has since recanted his faith) has put it: 'This was the signal to us to begin preparations to return home. The weeds had overtaken the garden and truly disturbed its usefulness beyond repair. It is time for the civilisation to be recycled – spaded under.'[4]

It follows from this that all gurus are elitist and totally undemocratic. Within all the enclosed communities known, there has only ever been one absolute leader; anyone who came close, anyone who posed the slightest threat to the leader's absolute position was discredited and expelled immediately, or more often, slaughtered.

The final pair of traits, also linked together through character and circumstance, is that all gurus are isolated and friendless. These two characteristics are common to what could be called 'positive' and 'negative' gurus – those who destroy and kill and those who merely enlighten.

Jesus had no friends, he had disciples who proclaimed they would lay down their lives for their saviour, but disciples are never friends. Friendship is a two-way process, a symbiosis. Gurus have to be above this arena, they cannot truly share their burden, nor do they wish to beyond the preaching of their doctrine.

For a guru, the greatest achievement is to engender devotion, and this then leads us to perhaps the most succinct and clear way of seeing what being a guru really means. A guru has sublimated love, sacrificed tender normal human relationships – for power. They have, for their own various reasons, and in their own different ways, nullified the instinctive drive to share, to love and be loved. Instead, they crave and sometimes find a different mechanism to get through life – they use power over others to gain satisfaction. The further they can push their disciples, the greater their sense of self-importance. By ultimately driving their followers to make the final sacrifice, to take their own lives, the guru gains the greatest of all emotional rewards.

But why? Why do some individuals need this? And how do gurus arrive at this stage in their sad lives?

The prevailing theory is that people who become gurus are trying to resolve an inner conflict. Many of us suffer in this way and it may be said that each of us has their own way of dealing with it. For some, immersion in the world of commerce, jobs, marriage, domestic commitment is a way of coping with this internal schism. Others, those with creative powers and enough drive, express their inner turmoil in various forms of art. Musicians, writers, painters, creative scientists share some of the characteristics of gurus. They have deep-rooted inner conflicts that need to find resolution. But an artist never truly believes that inner conflict can be resolved completely. An artist is constantly searching for resolution knowing that with each piece of work they only reach a partial conclusion, resolve only an element of their psychic disturbance.

A guru differs from an artist because they believe that they can find a resolution to their inner conflicts. A guru almost always passes through a period of mental breakdown, or schizophrenic episode. They find their way out of the maze of this severe mental or emotional eruption by settling on a 'solution'. This may take any number of forms, but it always comes from what psychologists refer to as the *Eureka Pattern* – a moment of great inspiration, of realisation – called 'divine fury' by Plato and understood in Renaissance times to be akin to the spirit of religious or mystical revelation. From this Eureka Pattern comes the realisation, the plot, if you like, for the new path, the new teaching, the new revelation.

For Jim Jones, a doctrine of severe antiracism was the key. He saw prejudice in everyone and in every aspect of society and created Jonestown on extreme antiracial principles. For Koresh it was the gaining of enlightenment through fundamentalist Biblical principles which he twisted and perverted at will. For Applewhite, it was a late-1990s counter-cultural idealism based upon science fiction, wish-fulfilment and emulation of cheap cable TV. For Gurdjieff, it was the idea that enlightenment could be attained through self-denial, intense physical discomfort and labour; for Rajneesh, Nirvana was hidden in the heart of total sexual liberation and complete immersion in carnal desires.

Another link between gurus lies with a recognised psychical condition called *folie à deux*. It has been known for some time that if two people live together and one of them is mad, the other will begin to accept and even adopt at least some of the other's delusions. In this way, Nettles and Applewhite would have reinforced one another's strange concepts, and within a community of believers this effect becomes marked and self-reinforcing; adding power to the guru and helping to perpetuate the ideology they expound.

Gurus are also insecure. In many ways they are even more insecure than their disciples and followers. The true difference between them is that the guru has the charisma or force of personality to impose their beliefs on others, beliefs which followers are able to accept wholeheartedly. For the guru, the follower is their salvation, their vindication, and they actually need the follower more than the follower needs the guru.

In some ways, all gurus of the isolationist type – the Koreshs, Joneses and Applewhites – are on a road to self-destruction from the moment of the Eureka Pattern. By forming a group and acquiring a self-supporting community around them, the guru is actually buying time. In almost all cases of isolationist communities, the leader's mental health is seen to go into rapid decline from the beginning of the group's formation, and the point where they seal themselves off from the outside world. It is almost as if the community is the guru's last-ditch attempt to save themselves, to find solace. When that support system is found to be insufficient for their egos and their insecurities, they have little room left for manoeuvre and the inevitable follows.

So what of the disciples? It is tempting to believe that followers of gurus are simple-minded, of low IQ and excessively gullible; but this is almost invariably not the case. The members of cults are usually from a range of socioeconomic backgrounds, different levels of education, IQ and age and are approximately divided evenly between the sexes. The composition of the Heaven's Gate community contained an unusually large number of older people. The average age was about fifty, the oldest member seventy-two.

Of course, cult members are unhappy with the 'normal'

world. Many are gullible and insecure, but the common thread is not stupidity or lack of intelligence, it is simply that some people are searching for fulfilment, seeking an alternative to what they see as the run-of-the-mill, the life of the average citizen. Many have gone through the standard course, followed the path of convention and for one reason or another have found it lacking.

What is astonishing about followers of extreme cults is not so much why they should join a group or a community, but the degree of devotion they then apply to this new platform. Mothers have left families, young babies and loved ones, fathers have walked out on wives, parents have allowed their children to be abused by the guru, some have watched passively as their loved ones have been butchered.

This obsessive devotion says a great deal about the power a guru wields, the level of corruption and the total abuse of this power. It also demonstrates how minds can be moulded and controlled, how some people are able to let go to the same degree that others can take command. History has demonstrated the horrors this symbiosis can produce – how else do we begin to explain why thousands came under such evil control in wartime Germany and participated in the horrors of the death camps? How else could US marines have been persuaded to slaughter innocent children in Vietnam?

The study of gurus and cults raises so many questions concerning the inner darkness of humanity and the points at which creativity and madness meet that we cannot yet hope to begin to understand many of the subtleties of this extraordinary power that crackles between the followers and the leaders, the sheep and the shepherds. But psychology is beginning to unravel many of the motivations, the hidden powers and the shrouded complexities of this fascinating psychic world. We can only hope that by studying the margins, the borders where insanity and art, sexual obsession and emotional desiccation meet, we may find solutions to problems of mental illness, schizophrenia and emotion imbalance. The study of gurus and cults is fascinating in itself, but such extremes of human character and behaviour may also provide answers to age-old questions such as: What is self? How do nature and nurture function in our mental development, and how does desire so often override rationality and reason?

3

MOJO RISING

'Also shall be qualified as attempted murder the employment which may be made against any person of substances which, without causing actual death, produce a lethargic coma more or less prolonged. If, after the administering of such substances, the person has been buried, the act shall be considered murder no matter what result follows.'

Article 249 of Haiti's Criminal Code.

In 1930, a French anthropologist named Dr Georges de Rouquct went on a field trip to the West Indian island of Haiti. He could speak fluent Creole and soon ingratiated himself so well with a local landowner that he was allowed to see what the Haitian told de Rouquct were genuine zombies. De Rouquct was not allowed to touch the zombies, but could observe them closely. He described the experience in his journal:

'Toward evening,' he wrote, 'we encountered a group of four male figures coming from the nearby cotton field where they had been toiling. I was struck by their peculiar gait, most unlike the lithe walk of other natives. The overseer with them stopped their progress, enabling me to observe them closely for some minutes.

'They were clothed in rags made from sacking. Their arms hung down by their sides, dangling in curiously lifeless fashion. Their face and hands appeared devoid of flesh, the skin adhered to the bones like wrinkled brown parchment. I also noticed that they did not sweat, although they had been working and the sun was still very hot. I was unable to judge even their approximate ages. They may have been young men or quite elderly.

'The most arresting feature about them was their gaze. They all stared straight ahead, their eyes dull and unfocused as if blind. They did not show a spark of awareness of my presence, even when I approached them closely. To test the reflexes of one I made a stabbing gesture towards the eyes with my pointed fingers. He did not blink or shrink back.

'My immediate impression was that these creatures were imbeciles made to work for their keep. Baptiste [the land-owner], however, assured me that they were indeed the zombies; that is, dead people resurrected by sorcery and employed as unpaid labourers.'[1]

The Haitian religion of Voodoo is an ancient one. It has its roots in the tribes of central and western Africa and was transplanted to Haiti with the slave trade of the seventeenth and early eighteenth centuries. The reason Voodoo is not better known on the mainland of the United States is that here the blacks were gradually assimilated into the population, whereas Haiti gained independence very early on (at the end of the eighteenth century) and its population of seven million is today made up almost entirely of the descendants of the slaves who arrived there centuries ago.

The fundamentals of Voodoo as a religion appear to be quite confused – a hotchpotch of different creeds and beliefs. There is even a name for this blending of religious ideology – *syncretism* (the same word used to describe how the language of Creole is derived from bits of other languages), and an old Haitian saying declares that Haitians are 95% Catholic and 110% followers of Voodoo.

Those who practice Voodoo believe in a God, a deity they call *Djo* or *Mawu*; but this God differs fundamentally from the Christian God because they think that Djo or Mawu is far too important to interfere in earthly matters. Followers of Voodoo believe that when a human is born they are mere animals but become infused with a spirit called the *lao* placed inside you as a guide during an initiation ceremony. Another aspect of your being is the *ti bon ange*, or 'little good angel', which is roughly equivalent to the 'will'. According to the Voodoo religion, at the initiation where the spirit imbues the body, the ti bon ange may be extracted and stored in a jar in the inner sanctum of the temple. When the owner of this life force dies, the jar is opened to allow their ti bon ange to hover over the dead person's grave for seven days. The purpose of leading a good life is to enrich the ti bon ange so that after sixteen incarnations, a human may return to God.

As well as these ancient beliefs, the Voodoo religion has incorporated randomly aspects of Catholicism. These ideas were picked up from the whites who transported the slaves to Haiti and from the Europeans who were already living in Haiti and the mainland of the United States in the sixteenth and seventeenth centuries. There seems to be no real pattern to these acquisitions from European religion, and visitors to Voodoo shrines in Haiti should not be surprised to see images of Catholic saints such as Saint James the Greater, or statuettes of the Virgin Mary amongst images of Erzuli, the female serpent/rainbow spirit or *loa* who symbolises love.

The term 'Voodoo', which derives from the African Fon language, comes from *voo* meaning 'introspection' and *doo* which means 'the unknown', and it means slightly different things to every practitioner of the religion. But aside from the basic tenets of the Voodoo deity and hierarchy of saints, there are other more exotic elements to the religion, many of which have been misinterpreted and misunderstood by non-believers.

Firstly, Europeans have an image of Voodoo as simply a rather nasty, even evil cultural phenomenon. They link it solely with zombies and sticking pins into dolls. These are indeed aspects of Voodoo, which I will explore later in the chapter, but Voodoo believers also insist that like all religions, there is a healing element to their faith. Not only is it a conduit for emotional and spiritual feelings amongst those who believe, it is claimed to be a mutual support system for what is a largely impoverished people. It should be remembered that the vast majority of Voodoo believers live on Haiti, a very poor island with limited resources. It is particularly important to the poorest of this poor community – those who live in the most remote parts, for they have little else but their religion.

It should also be recalled that another, far more wide-spread religion, Catholicism, is also followed most closely by those living in Third World countries. Many put this down to the fact that those living in poorer nations rely more heavily upon religious faith, particularly fundamentalism (as some would call the more controlling and divisive religions). Others have suggested that living in industrialised nations, better-educated people are less likely to believe in what some see as an outmoded faith system. It is perhaps significant that religion once played a far more important role in these same industrialised countries.

Equally, we should not lose sight of the fact that although there are undoubtedly cruel and barbaric aspects to Voodoo, in particular the creation of zombies and the infatuation with the power of *mojo*, what we would consider more orthodox religions also have their primitive overtones. Before we condemn outright the Voodoo priest, the *bokor*, it might be prudent to remember the Inquisition, regular sectarian killings in Northern Ireland, the pain and anguish caused by continued backward thinking on contraception and abortion in countries that consider themselves modern states, even countries that are fully-fledged members of the EC.

Putting aside the purely religious aspects of Voodoo and its comparisons with other faith systems, let us now look at the controversial elements of its practice and claims for the creation of zombies, and the power to influence matter at a distance purely by the power of the mind. There are two fundamental and supposedly powerful 'supernatural' angles to explore – the spirit world of the Haitian priests and their ability to raise the dead, and the power of mojo – the placing of curses, hexes and death wishes by the use of ritualistic magic.

The most important person in some Haitian communities, especially remote settlements that have little contact with the major towns of the island, is the *bokor*. Many Haitians live in fear of the *bokor*, who is considered a very powerful man never to be crossed. Whether or not you believe in Voodoo, there are some very good reasons to be afraid of the bokor, because, in one form or another, zombies do exist, and to become one fits perfectly the cliché of 'a fate worse than death'.

According to believers, a zombie is the resurrected body of a dead person – someone who has been reconstituted by a bokor in order to perform a specific task. Practitioners of Voodoo claim that the bokor is able to capture the soul or spirit of a dead person and separate it from the body. The spirit is then contained in a special jar and the body of the deceased is used for whatever purpose the priest chooses. To the believers, this is a purely super-natural process heavily dependent upon the skill of the much-feared priest. A particularly famous case will serve to illustrate.

On 2 May 1962, a young man by the name of Clairvius Narcisse 'died' in the Albert Schweitzer Hospital in the small town of Deschapelles. The cause of his 'death' was a mystery but he had developed a fever a few days earlier and then went into respiratory failure. Pronounced dead, he was buried within a few days. Then, eighteen years later his younger sister Angelina was shopping in the market of her home village, l'Estère, when from behind her she heard a voice she immediately recognised. She turned, and to her utter amazement saw a man she thought was long-dead, her brother, Clairvius.

When she had calmed down and taken the man, (who seemed confused and incoherent), back to his family, the story of his past eighteen years gradually came out.

His memory was hazy, but he recalled the scenes in the hospital almost two decades earlier. He remembered being short of breath and then slipping into a trance-like state. He could hear people talking and a doctor proclaiming him dead, but he had been unable to move or to say anything. It had been literally a living nightmare.

Checked by two doctors, one an American, the exact cause of Clairvius's condition was never ascertained, but because his skin was chalk white and his heartbeat had slowed to an imperceptible rate, he had been pronounced dead and subsequently prepared for burial.

Clairvius remembered the sound of the lid closing on his coffin. He recalled thinking that he really was going to die as one of the nails banged into the coffin pierced his cheek, and he could hear his sister weeping. After that he lost all track of time until he saw a light shining down on his face. He felt himself being dragged out of his coffin and then several men set upon him beating him almost to death before he was dragged away.

For the next two years he had been kept as a slave in the wild northern region of the country. He had been drugged by the bokor and regularly abused by him and the landowner who had enslaved him. Then, one day, one of his zombie companions had suddenly awoken from his trance and turned on the bokor, killing him. With the priest and controller dead, the effects of whatever it was keeping them sedated began to wear off and the entire group of slaves escaped. Clairvius wandered the island for another sixteen years until one day he heard that his brother had died and this had prompted him to return home.

At first the family were mystified by his account and especially the reason for Clairvius's decision to return when he had, but he explained that it had been his brother who had paid the local bokor to turn him into a zombie in the first place. The reason? Clairvius had crossed him.

Clairvius was eventually integrated back into his home village and accepted by the people he had known so many years before. He even became something of a national celebrity appearing on television shows, the first person to publicly claim they had once been a zombie.

To rational non-believers this entire story clearly has little to do with spirits being captured or 'undead' beings roaming the countryside of Haiti. But, if Clairvius was not one of the 'undead', what had really happened to him? Who were the zombies he encountered and how had the bokor exerted such power?

In the 1980s, an ethnobiologist, then working at the Harvard Botanical Museum in Boston, Dr Wade Davis, travelled to Haiti to make a detailed study of Voodoo and the practises of the bokors who live in remote parts of the country. He summarised his findings in two books, *The Serpent And The Rainbow* and *Passage Of Darkness*, which came up with scientific explanations for many of the phenomena we see in the ritualistic practises of Voodoo. One of Davis's key findings was that the bokors were in fact using a sequence of drugs to control people before, during and after what others perceived to be the subject's death.

The first stage is motivation for the action. Often, those who become zombies are victims of a hate campaign or are undesirable individuals that someone wants to get rid of. Clairvius Narcisse was a classic example. He had apparently become involved with a woman in whom his brother was interested and had made pregnant a number of other women in the village without any intention of marrying or supporting them. The brother had finally called upon the services of the local bokor to remove his wayward sibling.

The chemical route to becoming a zombie is rather delicate and requires the skilled use of very particular drugs. The bokor makes a powder called a *coup poudre*, the preparation of which is surrounded by ritual and hocus-pocus to add status to what is in essence a simple blend of a few potentially-lethal chemicals.

According to ritual, the coup poudre must be produced in June. To prepare it, the priest needs one 'thunderstone' or *pierre tonnerre*, which is a piece of rock that has been buried underground for one year before it is unearthed by the bokor. To this, add one human skull and assorted bones; two puffer fish (preferably female), one of which must be *crapaud de mer*, the 'sea toad'; one sea snake (the *polychaete worm*); vegetable oil; a sprig of a plant called a *tcha-tcha*; half a dozen pods of *pois gratter*, otherwise known as 'itching pea'; two blue agamont lizards; one big toad, *Bufo marinus*; and finally an assortment of tarantulas, white tree frogs and various insects according to taste.

These ingredients are to be used in the following way: the sea snake is tied to the leg of the toad, the *Bufo marinus*. The two are then placed in a jar and buried. The toad is said to 'die of rage' which, according to Voodoo lore, increases the power of the poison it secretes into the jar. At no time must the bokor touch any of the ingredients because some of the most potent elements can be carried through the skin and are deadly in concentrated form.

As the toad and the sea snake are doing their work, the bokor places the human skull in a fire with the thunderstone and a collection of other ingredients until the skull turns black. While this is being prepared, he grinds the vegetable and insect ingredients together and adds some shavings of the skull which had been taken before it was placed in the fire. The mixture should then be ground to a fine powder along with the skull and thunderstone and the poison exuded by the toad. The entire mixture is then placed in a coffin underground for three days. This is even more potent if the coffin is the one containing the body from which the skull was removed to begin the process.

After three days, the coup poudre is ready. Traditionally this is sprinkled in the shape of a cross on the doorstep of the targeted victim, but for a better chance of success it is more usually poured down the back or surreptitiously placed in a sock or shoe. The poison is then absorbed through the skin. Within hours, the victim will have problems breathing and will appear to 'die' soon after.

The active ingredients in this ceremony boil down to just two components. Firstly, the mix contains a chemical called *tetrodotoxin* which comes from the female puffer fish. This is both an anaesthetic and a poison. As an anaesthetic it is estimated to be almost 200,000 times more powerful than cocaine and as a poison 500 times more deadly than cyanide. The other essential ingredient is another powerful anaesthetic and hallucinogenic drug contained in the poisonous excretions of the *Bufo marinus*, a chemical called *bufotenine*.

Combined, these two compounds make a potentially lethal cocktail. In precisely the right doses, the preparation of which requires great skill, it can create the onset of symptoms that make the victim appear dead. The victim enters a trance-like state, their breathing becomes so shallow it is almost undetectable and they adopt a deathly-white pallor. This effect is even more pronounced in hospitals such as those on Haiti, (especially at the time Clairvius Narcisse was zombified in 1962), where highly sophisticated heart monitors are comparatively rare.

The rest of the components of the preparation are there largely for ritualistic purposes and their use has been refined over centuries primarily to add an element of the macabre and to instil greater fear into the minds of naïve country Haitians and those who want to believe.

So, with the first stage over, we now have someone presumed dead but actually clinging onto life with barely perceptible life signs. They are duly buried, grieved over and presumed to be left in peace. It is then that the bokor and his helpers return to their work.

The next stage of the process requires the reanimation of the 'dead' victim. Again, this requires precise timing.

If the victim is left buried alive for too long they really will die, but if they are dug up at precisely the right time they will be usable. This, incidentally, implies an almost unimaginable degree of cruelty on the part of those who pay for the bokor's services. Not content with having someone killed, they employ the priest to make their enemy one of the 'living dead'.

Returning to the graveyard, the bokor and his team remove the victim's coffin and lift out the limp body. They then viciously beat up the victim. This might seem like unnecessary cruelty, and it is, but there are two reasons for it. The occult reason given by the bokor is that they have to make sure that the zombies 'will', the ti bon ange is trapped and cannot return to the body so that the victim is under the complete control of the priest. Sometimes, a bokor will add an extra nasty twist to this scenario. If he and his helpers are feeling particularly cruel (or they have been paid extra), instead of trapping the ti bon ange in a jar, they will endeavour to transpose it into the body of an insect. According to the Voodoo faith, in this way the bokor is almost certain to destroy the victim's chance of resurrection and eventual union with God. In effect, the bokor is not only keeping a 'dead body' alive, but destroying the very soul of the poor victim.

In purely biological terms, the beating is necessary because the bufotenine that has put the victim into an hallucinogenic trance can have unpredictable side effects, and sometimes the intoxicated zombie can go literally berserk. The beating has the effect of sedating them just as the effects of the tetrodotoxin starts to wear off.

In this state, the zombie is of little use to anyone. However, the job of removing the person from the community has been fulfilled and the bokor has already earned his fee. But he has more work to do if he wants to earn a further fee for turning the zombie into a compliant slave via the use of another cocktail of chemicals.

After the beating, the victim is led to a cross and baptised with a new name. This is usually something insulting and humiliating. They are then force-fed a paste made from sweet potato, cane syrup and a drug called *datura stramonium*, commonly known as 'zombie's cucumber'. Datura is another hallucinogen which causes psychotic delirium. It also contains a drug called *atropine* which is the antidote for tetrodotoxin. So, this new chemical mix brings the zombie out of the catatonic state induced by the coup poudre and places them in a state of constant psychotic delirium, something like a permanent LSD trip in which the victim is able to walk, to carry out simple tasks such as working in a field, to eat and to drink. But zombies are unable to focus on reality, they cannot speak, and only understand vaguely what is happening to them.

As reported by Clairvius Narcisse, there have been cases where a zombie has snapped out of this condition, usually because the landowner to whom the zombies are enslaved forgets to administer the drugs at the appropriate time or erroneously allows the zombies certain forbidden foods. Most important of these is salt. At no time should a zombie be allowed salt because, according to tradition, this will allow them to return to the real world. This is actually because of the metabolic breakdown of the datura. Large quantities of salt will metabolise the drug into a less potent form and as a result of the delirium will gradually fade. Understandably enraged, the zombie, who is more often than not a disreputable individual or criminal, will then turn on their keepers and murder them before escaping.

This scenario accounts for the way in which the vast majority of zombies have been produced by bokors in Haiti. No one knows how many people have been zombified, but over the centuries it may run into many thousands. It is thought that people in this state do not usually live very long, since they are worked hard and the constant application of hallucinogenic drugs severely damages the brain, leading eventually to cerebral haemorrhaging and true death.

Recently, other explanations for the existence of zombies have been suggested.[2] Professor Roland Littlewood of the department of anthropology and psychiatry at University College, London has studied a number of Haitian zombies and reached an altogether different explanation to the biochemical process described above. He claims that many zombies are actually mentally ill members of the community. He speculates that in remote communities some people suffering from mental illness (most usually paranoid schizophrenia), are dealt with by being sold into slavery. Whether or not these poor souls are also fed a constant diet of hallucinogenic drugs is still unknown.

It is most likely that the zombie community of Haiti is made up of a mixture of victims. Some bokors no doubt conduct their rituals on the mentally ill and in this way lay claim to creating the undead. Other zombies are probably criminals and ne'er-do-wells who have fallen prey to what amounts to a long-drawn-out assassination.

However zombies are formed, the threat of zombification is very real in the minds of many Haitians. Sometimes families deliberately mutilate the bodies of their dead relatives just before burial to render them useless as slaves even if the bokor resurrects them. And, throughout their time as leaders of Haiti, the Duvaliers, 'Papa Doc' François and 'Baby Doc' Jean-Claude regularly employed Voodoo imagery and occult ideas whilst officially outlawing its practice. Papa Doc even went so far as to let it be known that he was a powerful bokor, and he named his private Mafia *tontons macoutes*, after the most powerful of Voodoo sorcerers. Although Baby Doc was deposed in 1986, a belief in Voodoo was never dented by the Duvalier's strictures and lives on after Haiti's former rulers have disappeared utterly from the political scene.

The other major aspect of Voodoo to be considered is the black art of harming or even killing victims by suggestion, by action at a distance using ritualistic black magic. This is the art of mojo.

Mojo is a curse or magic spell used to bring harm to others.

The traditional idea is of a Voodoo priest sticking pins in waxen images of the victim which then produces excruciating pain or even death. But there are other methods employed by various practitioners of black magic around the world. The Aborigines use a technique called *bone-pointing* which involves no physical contact with the victim. Instead, during a carefully-contrived ritualistic ceremony, a priest merely points a special bone at the victim and they are treated by the others as though they are already dead. Soon they are ostracised by the community and often despair leads to suicide. Other priests use wooden effigies, the power of the magic enhanced by applying curses over cuttings of hair or nail clippings taken from the victim.

Again, to many Haitians mojo is a very real and potent aspect of their faith. When American marines landed on Haiti during a brief occupation of the island in 1994, it was widely believed that there were groups of bokors working to thwart the military effort by the use of curses and hexes. The same year, an American judge actually jailed a man on Haiti whom he believed was preparing a curse against him because this well-known Voodoo priest had been found mixing a lock of the judge's hair into a specially-prepared elixir.

Quite naturally, emotive rituals such as those performed by Voodoo priests are easily exaggerated by believers and practitioners alike. The believers want to believe and are fearful, and the priests manipulate hysteria and anxiety for their own ends. As a result, there is no shortage of graphic tales that appear superficially to support fantastic claims that there is real magic at work when the priest points a bone or impales an image with a needle.

During the 1930s, the anthropologist Dr Herbert Basedow was one of the first to introduce Europeans to stories of priests applying the black arts and conjuring the evil of mojo. He included what was then a startling account of such a ritual in a book about Aboriginal tribes called, *The Australian Aboriginal*. In it he wrote:

'A man who discovers that he is being boned by an

enemy is, indeed, a pitiable sight. He stands aghast, with his eyes staring at the treacherous pointer, and with his hands lifted as though to ward off the lethal medium, which he imagines is pouring into his body. His cheeks blanch and his eyes become glassy, and the expression of his face becomes horribly distorted . . . he attempts to shriek, but usually the sound chokes in his throat, and all one might see is froth at his mouth. His body begins to tremble and the muscles twist involuntarily. He sways backwards and falls to the ground, and for a short time appears to be in a swoon; but soon after he begins to writhe as if in mortal agony, and covering his face with his hands, begins to moan. After a while he becomes more composed and crawls to his wurley [his hut]. From this time onwards he sickens and frets, refusing to eat and keeping aloof from the daily affairs of the tribe. Unless help is forthcoming in the shape of a counter-charm, administered by the hands of the *Nangarri* or medicine man, his death is only the matter of a comparatively short time. If the coming of the medicine man is opportune, he might be saved.'[3]

As with the zombification of victims, there are two crucial elements in this series of events that go some way to explaining how such seemingly grotesque and frightening phenomena could occur. The first is the fact that the victim is almost invariably a troublemaker. This entire ritual can be interpreted as a court dishing out a punishment. These people live in small isolated communities in which the only law is that the strong dominate the weak. Equally, in some cases, those hurt by a troublesome member of the community can rely upon the medicine man to intervene. The 'victim' in the above account is basically ostracised by everyone he knows and falls into a deep depression. This is fuelled by guilt and the fear of the medicine man, a fear that has been instilled into the members of the community since early childhood.

The other factor to consider is the liberal use of hallucinogenic drugs. Although Basedow made no specific mention of this in his account it is well known that most tribal people around the globe use some form of recreational drug which finds use during ritual. This might be alcohol, mescalin, or other less well known but often very powerful agents. It is not at all surprising that a combination of drugs and community pressure should be so effective.

Such a potent blend should not be underestimated. The ethnobiologist Wade Davis has suggested that the victim of a hex actually becomes a threat to the community and that the community actively conspires in the eventual death of that victim. In some cases, they deliberately mourn in front of the victim, as though they were already dead.

This conspiracy activates and encourages what scientists have dubbed a *giving-up complex*. They describe this as being similar to the frame of mind sometimes adopted by people who are terminally ill – they 'lose the will to live'. It is easy to imagine how anyone could adopt the giving-up complex after a terrifying ceremony in which they are cursed and have their former friends and family treating them as if they were already dead; especially if this treatment is combined with the use of mind-altering drugs.

Wade Davis describes this as a form of 'total social rejection'. 'Although physically the victim still lives,' he says, 'psychologically he is dying and socially, he is already dead.'[4]

Crucial to the success of this process is total belief in what is happening both within the mind of the victim and in the community as a whole. Professor Gottlieb Freisinger of the John Hopkins University in Baltimore, USA has declared that: 'Special circumstances and beliefs in a community must exist before an individual can die by hex.' And psychologist Stanford Cohen working at Boston University, USA believes that: 'Hexing can be fatal when it implants a mixture of fear and helplessness in the victim.'

Wade Davis rightly points out that: 'Even doctors of the most traditional sort admit the role psychology plays on our well being.' And that: 'If one believes strongly enough then it is more likely to happen.'[6]

To demonstrate that the power of suggestion is greatly influenced by the total commitment to a belief in what is happening, Professor William Sargent, an expert in brain-washing techniques, used electric-shock therapy on a woman who was convinced she was being cursed. He persuaded the woman that the electric shocks had removed the hex and she duly recovered.

But is this the entire answer? Surely there are some individuals who would be resilient to the pressure of those around them? This may be true, especially if we consider that many of the so-called victims of hexes are themselves actually rather unpleasant individuals, including in their number, thieves, murderers and rapists or those who have crossed others seriously enough to have become subject to the attentions of the medicine man. But no matter how tough they may be, they would face serious practical problems because of the treatment of the community.

Firstly, if the community is treating the victim as though they were already dead then presumably the hexed individual would find it hard to continue daily life, to eat or drink, to find shelter or gainful employment. Their only option would then be to leave, but they would probably be prevented from doing so. Inevitably their health would suffer and they would fall into rapid decline. But even then, there may be purely biochemical reasons for hastening this fall.

During the 1920s, doctors treating soldiers who had returned shell-shocked from the trenches, discovered a new syndrome precipitated by a process called *vagal inhibition*. This is caused by an over-stimulation of the adrenal system. If the blood is flooded with adrenaline, the blood supply to the extremities of the body is reduced so that blood can be concentrated in the muscles. The reason for this is simple: adrenaline is pumped into the body to stimulate the muscles ready for 'fight or flight'. However, with the supply of blood to the extremities reduced, the cells in these parts of the body become less infused with oxygen and the tiny capillaries that carry blood (and oxygen) to these regions become more permeable to blood plasma. The blood plasma then seeps into the tissue surrounding the capillaries further reducing blood pressure.

This vicious circle of events causes a continued drop in blood pressure and if left unchecked, the victim will die. The process takes a few days and is almost certainly a major factor in the gradual 'fading-away' so often described in mojo stories.

So, it appears that the ability of bokors to produce the 'undead' and the power of the medicine man or the priest to cause the death of someone by suggestion are both real and powerful phenomena. However, neither are 'supernatural' – each can be explained using the accepted laws of science. In the case of the zombification of victims, the bokor utilises a complex amalgam of drugs mixed with ancient rituals to generate fear in the community over which he already commands a powerful position. The use of mojo or hexes is a blend of sociological factors that work strongly against the victim, combined with the liberal use of drugs. In each case, fear lies at the heart of both ritual and practice. In the case of hexing, this element of fear may be the crucial factor that sets in motion an elaborate chain of biochemical events ending in death.

In Haiti there is a proverb that sums up precisely the many-layered complexities of this ancient, elemental and highly divisive religion. It says: 'The closer you get to Voodoo, the more vulnerable you are to its power.' A scientific explanation for the work of the bokors does nothing to diminish the truth and the power of this aphorism.

4

MIRACLES AND WONDER

'A cask of wine works more miracles than a church full of saints.'

Italian proverb.

What constitutes a miracle?

In one sense, the concept of miracles lies at the heart of the paranormal. We may think of ghosts as 'miracles' or even the arrival of alien beings in shiny flying saucers as 'miraculous'. This is because, as Arthur C. Clarke has so cogently put it: 'Any sufficiently advanced technology is indistinguishable from magic.'[1] In other words, the reality and the meaning of 'miracles' are really built upon the perception of the witness. If the witness to a miracle has sufficiently detailed knowledge, the event is no longer miraculous. Some would therefore argue that miracles are not just for the gullible but only meaningful to those *without* knowledge.

Miracles, as we understand the term, are also more closely linked to orthodox religion than many other aspects of the paranormal. The Scottish, eighteenth century philosopher David Hume knew this and was being as sceptical over the matter as any latter-day scientist when he wrote: 'The Christian religion not only was at first attended with miracles, but even at this day cannot be believed by any reasonable person without one. Mere reason is insufficient to convince

us of its veracity: and whoever is moved by faith to assent
to it, is conscious of a continued miracle in his own person,
which subverts all the principles of his understanding, and
gives him a determination to believe what is most contrary
to custom and experience.'[2]

There is little to be said about telepathy, abominable
snowmen or spontaneous human combustion in the Bible
or other holy works (although some would claim there is
plenty written about alien visitation and abduction in ancient
religious texts), but there are many references to 'miraculous
happenings'. In fact such events have a category of their own
in the litany of the paranormal, they are called *Biblical miracles*
and include such things as turning water into wine, parting
the Red Sea and raising the dead.

There are also latter-day 'miracles'. They are called this
because of their modernity, and because they impact with
both the occult and conventional religious faith. Perhaps the
most important of these are the phenomena of *stigmata* and
claims of *incorruptibility*. It is these, and the canon of biblical
miracles, that will be considered in this chapter – paranormal
phenomena that have a strong religious connection.

Both the Old and New Testaments of the Bible contain
dozens of stories of miracles, and, to the cynical, it is these
stories that have been used to give weight to the faith system
at the foundation of Christianity. Although most religions
preach the concept that faith should not be based upon
evidence, that the true believer does not *need* miracles, there
do seem to be a substantial number of such tales sprinkled
throughout the gospels and in earlier parts of the Bible to
consolidate events and teachings. The devout would argue
that these need not be there and that the Bible and the basis
of Christianity would be just as sound without them.

When reviewing some of the miraculous tales recounted
in the Bible and other ancient holy texts it should be remembered that these stories come from a time when humans had
little knowledge of how the universe worked. To people from
these ancient times, domestic life as well as the observed

grander sweep was a mystery; they believed that nature was controlled by a personal God, or Gods, and they had no concept of physical laws describing the fundamental natural forces we now understand through science. To these people, life was ruled by supernatural forces forever beyond the control of humankind. Within such an intellectual climate, the idea that the sea could be parted, that plagues and pestilence were controlled by a wrathful deity, or that individuals could be struck by a lightning bolt or reduced to a pillar of salt was unquestionably within the power of the Almighty.

Old Testament miracles are grand in scale, whereas those related in the New Testament are more personal and focus on the deeds of Jesus Christ. But although both of these lie at the heart of Christian literature and teaching, what does the dispassionate scientist think of them?

One of the grandest of grand Old Testament miracles is the parting of the Red Sea. This tale describes how the Egyptians had enslaved the people of Moses, and the great prophet leads them to safety after parting the sea, allowing them to reach freedom before the waters return to engulf the pursuing Egyptian soldiers.

To the rationalist, this sort of divine favouritism has no basis in logic – why should God be on the side of one tribe of humans rather than another? It all smacks of race ego, the idea that a benign God looks after us (although even this is in itself contradictory, after all this God was obviously not so benign towards the Egyptian soldiers in this old tale). But even putting these objections to one side, let us consider the details of the story of Moses parting the Red Sea.

To make the trip described in the Old Testament, the fleeing slaves would have journeyed close to a region called *Per Rameses*, which is made up almost entirely of papyrus swamps. This is negotiable on foot, because small groups with an able guide can skirt the most treacherous areas. However, soldiers unfamiliar with the terrain and with chariots and carts laden with supplies may well have run into serious trouble. It would seem likely then that Moses used very human earthly skills to guide his people through dangerous terrain that became the graveyard for the soldiers in hot pursuit. This version of the story is also supported by the fact that the Hebrew name for the region through which Moses lead his people to safety is *yam suph*. The true translation of this is not Red Sea but Reed Sea.

Similar clinical analysis can also help to explain the torrid tales of plague and pestilence wrought upon parts of humanity by God in order to help out other groups. The most vivid and detailed of these stories again involves Moses and is known as the *Ten Plagues*, which God is supposed to have inflicted upon the Egyptians to persuade them to release the Hebrew slaves. The Ten Plagues were a particularly nasty collection of punishments. First, the Nile was turned to blood, then the country was invaded by frogs, followed by a plague of mosquitoes, then flies. Next, the cattle perished, men fell ill with boils all over their bodies, and hail rained down. Then, the country was beset with a plague of locusts, darkness fell for three days, and finally, all the first-born children died.

Now of course, this is a rather calamitous series of events for any one nation, but the account of these terrible misfortunes is rather short on specifics. It does not give an accurate timescale for these events and what we may now see as a succession of natural interlinked misfortunes is enwrapped in a description filled with horror and portrayed with relish by the partisan authors.

To begin with, the Nile has been known to 'turn red' on many occasions. This is caused by pollution washed down from the highlands of Ethiopia. This pollution is mainly stagnant water that has collected in slow-moving pools during dry spells, combined with reddish sand and silt. This pollution would cause frogs to leave the Nile. Then later, when the water receded, the land that had been flooded would have retained many of the micro-organisms that had been living in the polluted water. This would then have acted as a breeding ground for mosquitoes and flies. These pollutants could also precipitate a number of serious local diseases, in particular anthrax, which would infect animals, killing cattle and bringing humans out in boils. The most susceptible to the disease would be the old and the very young. Of these, the most important to the community would have been the babies and young children. The fact that many young children died would have been given greater emphasis in any account of events so that, from the viewpoint of those looking back, it might seem that only the first-born had died.

Finally, such a succession of disasters would have inevitably created the effect desired by the Hebrews – they would have been freed by the Egyptians. It could be argued that, from the perspective of the Egyptian rulers, the Hebrews would have represented a further drain on a society already on the edge of destruction precipitated by what was actually a series of interconnected natural problems.

Similar cataclysmic events recounted in the Old Testament can be explained using a degree of detachment and clear reasoning based upon a greater amount of information than was available to the ancients. The fall of the walls of Jericho may be explained by the fact that the site of the city is now known to have stood in an area plagued by frequent earthquakes. Likewise, the Dead Sea lies in a rift valley ravaged by earthquakes and it is thought to have been a particularly violent quake in 2350 BC that destroyed five cities that once lay on the rim of the sea. These were: *es-Safi*, *Khanazir*, *Numeria*, *Bab-edh-Dhra* and *Feifah*. Two of these are thought to have been the Old Testament cities of Sodom and Gomorrah, which were, according to the Bible, destroyed by fire and brimstone wrought upon them by an angry God. Again, to simple people who knew nothing of seismology, an earthquake would be seen as an act of God. Indeed, even today we call natural disasters 'Acts of God' – just look on any insurance policy.

In the New Testament, the reported miracles are more to do with individuals and small-scale situations. The turning of water into wine has been explained by analysts as either an illusion – the skilled application of sleight-of-hand, or else Christ was able to add something to the water that made its taste approximate that of wine. One suggestion is that he merely added sugar to the water to liven up the flavour and the tale became elaborated later.

Christ's documented skills of raising the dead are harder to explain away, but analysts have tried. Explanations range from the use of suggestion or illusion to the idea that in all cases those who were apparently dead were in fact merely catatonic or unconscious for a variety of reasons and that Christ was sufficiently knowledgeable to know how to snap them out of this state. It has also been claimed that the greatest miracle of the New Testament – the resurrection of Christ himself – was again a grand deception, that Jesus did not die on the cross but was taken down before he expired and healed by a group of his followers.

Naturally, the devout will ignore all these ideas and stick to what they believe. This should come as little surprise, for the power of faith is incredibly strong and even the sceptic can only offer alternatives to what they consider the unpalatable and unacceptable idea that miracles do happen. Again, David Hume has much to say on this matter. Almost two hundred years ago he pointed out that: 'When anyone tells me, that he saw a dead man restored to life, I immediately consider with myself, whether it be more probable, that this person should either deceive or be deceived, or that the fact, that what he relates should really have happened. I weigh the one miracle against the other; and according to the superiority, which I discover, I pronounce my decision, and always reject the greater miracle.'[3]

This is all well and good and sound reasoning about which any sceptic would heartily approve, but it takes no account of what people *want* to believe. Hume is absolutely right in a purely empirical logical sense, but most people allow their feelings, or their beliefs, to cloud the issue so they can no longer see which is the 'superior' notion.

As I said at the start of this chapter, to the atheist and the dispassionate observer, a miracle is only such to someone with a certain, rather narrow, perception of the events; someone who does not question too deeply. Even so, those who probe and conduct as thorough an investigation as possible can only offer alternatives. Because the events described in the Bible occurred so long ago and have come down to us via complex and meandering paths, it is extremely difficult to say for certain what really happened. The best the sceptic can do is to offer what should be more logical and clear-cut explanations based upon analysis rather than blind faith.

Because of this it is in some ways more rewarding to consider modern day 'miracles' and to see how they could be accounted for using fundamental scientific principles. Interestingly, orthodox religion, and most especially Catholicism, has little patience with most modern miracles and has made it very clear (quite properly) that these events should not be articles of faith and should not be presented as 'evidence' of God's existence or in any way as validating the teachings of the Church. Indeed, the Catholic Church has rigorously investigated many of these accounts in an effort to find flaws in them and only after intense scrutiny have they considered some to be of interest, but still not intrinsic to religious doctrine.

The cynic would argue that the Church has been forced into this approach by their need to accommodate science and that it would be dangerous for them to support claims of paranormal happenings such as those made by stigmatics, believers in apparitions of the Virgin Mary or those who claim that the bodies of saints have remained physically uncorrupted after death.

Probably the most sensational modern-day miracles are those known as *Marian apparitions*, claims that the Virgin Mary has appeared to the faithful. Such claims have been made by hundreds of witnesses and may be traced back centuries. Interestingly, a high proportion of the witnesses, especially in recent times, have been children.

In some cases the vision interacts with the witness. There have been reports from those convinced they have seen the Virgin Mary and that she spoke to them, extended her arms as though to embrace them, to leave them messages given seemingly by telepathic means.

The most famous case of visitation comes from the experiences of a young girl named Bernadette Soubirous who at the age of thirteen in 1858 is said to have witnessed a vision of the Virgin Mary at Lourdes in France. According to Bernadette's own testimony, the Virgin Mary appeared to be a young girl no bigger than herself and dressed in white. She witnessed the vision a total of eighteen times, and gradually the apparition revealed more information about herself and the purpose of the visitation.

The vision informed Bernadette that a chapel should be built on the site. Later, she was told to wash her face in a stream, but there was no water nearby. Before witnesses, Bernadette then scrambled in the earth and water flowed forth. Apparently, soon after, a blind man was made to see after bathing his eyes with the water, and before long, the site at Lourdes became the most important shrine in the world, visited by hundreds of thousands of pilgrims each year.

A visitation almost as famous occurred in 1917, at Fátima in Portugal. Three young children from a peasant family saw the figure of a woman surrounded by a bright light floating above a tree in an isolated field near their native village. The woman told them that she was from heaven and that she would appear on the thirteenth day of each month. At the appointed time the following month, the children again saw the vision and gradually, during the next few months, the story leaked out and adults began to accompany the three children to the site.

Eventually, by October 1917, a crowd of over 70,000 people was attracted to the spot in the field near Fátima to witness the spectacle. However, no one but the three children ever saw the image of the Virgin, although many in the crowd that October afternoon claimed they had witnessed the miracle of the sun 'wobbling' in the sky after a downpour had soaked them. According to reports, immediately after the sun performed this trick, the clothes of the soaked crowd were found to be completely dry.

So, what is to be made of these claims?

The first effort at explaining these events is to suppose that the original witness or witnesses have become hysterical or self-deluded and that they have been able to subvert the thinking and the emotions of others.

The phenomena of mass hysteria and contagious hysteria are actually common occurrences and have been studied extensively by psychologists. It is an idea we have already encountered in the scientific investigation of alien abduction (Chapter 1). The human mind is a very powerful instrument with great (and in many cases still hidden and little understood) potential. If an individual wants to believe strongly enough or has suffered an intense emotional disturbance, the mind can play very powerful tricks. It is then a question of the deluded creating further delusion in others who may themselves be susceptible to suggestion. In the case of apparitions, these susceptible individuals have an intense religious faith.

It is certainly no coincidence that such experiences are frequently linked with religious events. Intense religious feelings are often the strongest that any human being ever feels and may be even more powerful and deeply rooted than personal love for another human being. With this sort of force at work in the human psyche, other more mundane ulterior motives may be perverted by the subconscious mind.

In the case of Bernadette, there is a strong possibility that her deeply-held religious convictions were exaggerated at a time when she would have been experiencing the natural chemical imbalances associated with puberty. If she believed intensely enough, perhaps the two forces fed off one another. Displaying profound faith is infectious in the right environment and she could have convinced others the vision was genuine. From thereon the myth became self-perpetuating.

The children at Fátima may have had other reasons for the strength of their conviction. Perhaps they formed a pact to try to become famous and gradually began to believe in their own piece of fiction. The fact that no one else, not one of the 70,000 witnesses who were eventually drawn into the net, could claim with conviction that they were seeing what the children saw, is strongly suggestive that there really was nothing to see. As for the strange events surrounding the behaviour of the sun, odd meteorological incidences in which anomalous lighting conditions produce the illusion that the sun is moving unnaturally are more common than one might expect. The fact that the crowd had been soaked by a rainstorm only moments before the sun was supposed to wobble adds weight to this claim because such conditions – bright sunlight through a wet atmosphere – are exactly those most likely to generate optical illusions and mirage-type effects.

It would seem likely then that visitations of the Virgin Mary are a combination of powerful self-delusion combined with a high level of mass suggestion all within a highly-charged atmosphere of religious fervour and exaggerated by a profound willingness to believe. A startling example of this occurred as recently as 1997 and precipitated a slightly different version of the apparition story; unusually, one not directly associated with religion.

When Diana, Princess of Wales died and her coffin was positioned in a private room in St James's Palace, crowds queued around the block for days to write comments in a series of books placed on long tables in the public hall of the palace. The atmosphere amongst the patiently waiting crowds was charged with intense emotion. The population of Britain had been drained by the media coverage and the various twists and turns in the unfolding saga of the princess's tragic end. But for some people it seems that the emotionally-charged atmosphere simply became too much to take.

On the third day, as the queues lined up in the September warmth, someone claimed that they saw Diana's face in a painting in the great hall. The word spread, and within hours dozens of people swore they too could see the face of the princess. Then others announced they had seen her in the glass windows along the corridor leading to the hall. People in the queue were interviewed by TV crews and newspaper journalists, all declaring that they had seen a vision. But what was most striking about this incident was how the story became elaborated almost like a game of Chinese whispers. What began as an outline of Diana's head seen in a painting, grew to become a full-length glowing vision, an image of the 'divine' Diana enshrouded in celestial light. The only surprise was that no one ended up claiming that they had seen the Princess standing beside them in the queue, alive and well, resurrected on the third day after her death!

An alternative to the religious experience of visitation are the many reported cases where statues of religious figures have been seen to bleed, secreting or absorbing other liquids, and even in some rare cases, to move.

Weeping Madonnas have been reported all over the world. Many have been explained easily as trickery. More often than not the fake is crude – a pump is placed inside the Madonna and the porous material of the statue absorbs what is often genuine human blood, this then eventually finds its way to a part of the statue where the enamel has been scratch away – often the tear ducts or sometimes the palms of the hands.

More sophisticated fakes involve allowing the liquid to be absorbed by the porous material of the statue, then removing the pump and allowing capillary action to suck the liquid to the desired spot.

A few years ago, a new idolatry craze hit the headlines. According to reports, statues in Hindu temples in India were observed to drink milk from a spoon placed at the mouth of the idol. News spread and within days, worshippers in temples as far afield as East London and New York were feeding milk to the images of their gods. As expected, the scientific community quickly came up with simple explanations. The high absorbency of the material used in making the statues soaked up the milk. Indeed, the liquid need not have been milk at all, any liquid would have done the same.

More difficult to explain is a famous case from Naples, Italy.

According to its guardians, for over 600 years, the blood of St Gennaro has been preserved in a vessel used in an annual ceremony in the city. The ceremony involves a procession through part of Naples during which the vessel of blood is swung on a ceremonial chain. At the beginning of the procession, the vessel is seen to contain what can only be described as a congealed brown gloop, but after the vessel has been swung around by the priest for an hour or two the brown gel turns into a red liquid that flows as easily as blood.

Many devout Catholics believe this to be a miracle, but the church does not officially recognise this annual event and it is certainly not sanctioned or deemed an article of faith by the Vatican.

In 1902, the blood was analysed by scientists who were only allowed to investigate the liquid through the glass (indeed even today, the local church authorities will not allow even a tiny amount of the liquid to be removed from the vessel). Using a technique called *spectroscopic analysis* in which light is passed through the glass vessel and the result-ant spectrum studied, scientists were able to reach certain conclusions about the chemical make-up of the mixture. They found that the vessel indeed contained blood, but it was mixed with other unidentified contaminants.

Oddly, this conclusion seems to have comforted the believers, and even modern writers appear to think that this discovery somehow adds weight to claims this is a miraculous process. The investigator of the paranormal Jenny Randles has written: 'This quashes some assertions that it is purely a chemical concoction.'[4]

What is meant by this is unclear. Blood is, after all, a concoction of chemicals. A more recent investigation conducted in 1991 by Italian chemist Professor Garlaschelli has confirmed the results of 1902. But, Garlaschelli has also constructed a theory to explain what may be happening in the vessel during the procession. He has produced a blend of chemicals which exhibit what is called *thixotropy*, this is a property possessed by some substances which allows them to turn from solid to liquid when exposed to external forces.

Non-stick paint is a material which exhibits thixotropy. When the brush applies the paint to a surface it is in the liquid state because of the movement of the brush and the force applied by the painter. When the force is removed, the paint quickly solidifies and does not run.

In the case of St Gennaro's blood, the devout have erroneously concluded that the prayers of the faithful in some way change the chemical consistency of the blood of a long-dead saint. In reality, a purely physical process changes the chemical composition of a complex blend of materials. The substance in the vessel may well comprise in part the blood of St Gennaro, but combined with other substances in the vessel it has taken on the rare property of being able to change consistency via thixotropy.

Closely linked to the experiences of those who claim to see visions of religious figures (usually the Virgin Mary) are the surprisingly large number of cases involving stigmata – spontaneous manifestations of bloody wounds more often than not related to what Jesus Christ may have suffered during crucifixion.

The earliest documented case of stigmata is attributed to St Francis of Assisi. These began to appear shortly after he had a vision in the year 1224. Like modern-day stigmatics, St Francis produced wounds in the palms of his hands and in the middle of his feet which bled profusely. According to legend, St Francis's stigmata was so powerful real nails could be seen in the wounds on his hands until after his death. These were apparently witnessed by the many hundreds of pilgrims who saw him lying in his coffin. Of course, such tales are difficult to verify 700 years on and it is quite possible that the detail of the nails was faked by self-interested custodians of the St Francis enigma.

Today, investigators of the phenomenon of stigmata have pinpointed five common locations for them. Known as the *typical stigmata*, these appear on the two hands, two feet and in the side. The last of these is supposed to represent the point of entry of the spear stuck into Christ's body during the torture of the crucifixion. Sometimes, but less commonly, wounds appear above the eyebrows and around the head of stigmatics which represent the placement of the crown of thorns on Christ's head.

There have been more than 300 documented cases of stigmatism since St Frances of Assisi. Until recently there were far more women displaying stigmata than men, but the gap is closing. This is thought to be because men are becoming less inhibited and more able to discuss what may be viewed as their feminine side, including (in admittedly rare cases), discussion of their own stigmata experiences.

The most famous modern stigmatic was Padre Pio, an Italian Roman Catholic priest who first received the stigmata whilst praying in September 1915. By 1918 he had all five of the typical stigmata and was observed bleeding profusely from his wounds on many occasions and by large numbers of witnesses.

Another stigmatic, a Bavarian woman named Therese Neumann, born in 1898, experienced dramatic stigmata in all five places as well as across her eyebrows every Friday for many years. Each Friday she would lose as much as a pint of blood and, according to reports, up to 3.5 Kilos (8 lbs.) in body weight. Even more miraculous was the fact that witnesses swore her wounds were always completely healed by Sunday, thus mirroring the three-day passion of Christ.

Before considering some possible physical explanations for these experiences it is important to consider the psychological aspects of such cases.

Again, we return to the theme of hysteria, and the enormous energy of religious devotion. With proper training, the mind can control the physical actions of the body. Adepts can overcome pain and accomplish the most amazing feats of endurance. And, in one sense, we can perceive religious obsession and the regime some religious fanatics follow as a form of 'training' or preparation for physical endurance. Constant denial is really a way in which certain individuals can achieve astonishing results which those who lead 'normal' comfortable lives could hardly contemplate. It should not be surprising then to discover that these same individuals may be able to spontaneously generate odd effects within their own bodies.

This is supported by one glaring fact unearthed by research into this phenomenon – that stigmata first appeared (possibly with St Francis) within only a few years of the earliest graphically painted representations of Christ's crucifixion. Until the beginning of the thirteenth century, artists did not show accurate anatomical details surrounding Christ's suffering; it was only around the year 1220, three or four years *before* the stigmata appeared on St Francis's body that the first vivid representations of nails driven through flesh were seen by the faithful. However, even more striking is the fact that in those early representations, the wounds were always shown to be in the palms of the hands and the centre of the feet. Yet it is now known that the nails that pinned Christ to the cross were driven through the wrists and ankles and not the places where stigmatics regularly display their wounds.

This does not imply that St Francis or any of the other 300 cases of stigmatism are fakes (although some may well be), but does it suggest that the wounds have been generated by some strange mechanism in the tortured and obsessed mind of the devout? That stigmatics produce these wounds in the places they believe they should appear?

Some researchers are convinced that many of the wounds displayed by stigmatics are merely self-mutilation. Dr Eric Dingwall of the Society for Psychical Research conducted extensive studies of the phenomenon in the 1920s and reached the clear-cut conclusion that all stigmatics were victims of their own lifestyle. He cited in particular St Mary Magdalen de Pazzi who was apparently a stigmatic during the last years of her life in the 1580s. Dingwall found that St Mary frequently starved herself and her nuns and went in for exhaustive self-flagellation. Many of the nuns under her care also suffered physical torture both applied by others and self-inflicted during their devotions. He concluded that such a regime could quite naturally lead to definite physical signs of abuse.

But Dingwall's conclusions do not satisfy modern research-ers and there have been cases of stigmatism involving people who had lead an otherwise normal life. One example is the first case of a black stigmatic – a Californian girl named Cloretta Robertson who first showed signs of stigmata when she was ten years old in 1972. Cloretta was not a devout Christian and came from a family who were not particularly religious. However, it is significant that a week before the bleeding wounds appeared in the palms of her hands, she had seen a television programme about the crucifixion that had moved her deeply.

The implication from this, and some other modern cases such as that of Therese Neumann, is that there is a strong psychological element in the precipitation of spontaneous wounds.

Professor John Cornwell of Cambridge University has put forward the theory that stigmata may be caused by a psychosomatic disorder called *psychogenic purpura*. This is a rare disease in which patients bleed spontaneously without displaying wounds. In some cases, visible wounds appear later. However, the apparent link with stigmata goes fur-ther, because patients suffering from psychogenic purpura usually show symptoms after experiencing severe emotional trauma. Cases have also been known in which patients have been observed to bleed spontaneously following hypnotic suggestion.

There is little doubt that the majority of stigmata are self-inflicted injuries, produced for effect – a physical manifestation of devotion, a fashion accessory for the psychotically pious. But, it would also appear that some rare cases are genuine. However, they are not produced by 'divine intervention'. Instead, they appear to be the result of intense emotional involvement with the *image* and emotional wellspring of religion. In some rare individuals, a biochemical abnormality blends with powerful emotional forces to produce a physical manifestation of their obsession.

Perhaps even more mysterious than stigmata is the final 'miracle' to be considered in this category – the phenomenon of *incorruptibility*.

This is a rare phenomenon and involves the apparent preservation of dead bodies by purely natural means. Almost all documented cases of incorruptibility involve the remains of important figures in the Christian church, particularly saintly figures. The reason for the predominance of accounts involving saints or beloved religious figures is that these people are the most likely to be reinterred and there physical condition studied after burial.

One investigation, conducted during the 1950s by the Jesuit researcher of paranormal phenomena Father Herbert Thurston, involved analysis of the physical remains of forty-two long-dead saints. Father Thurston found that twenty-two of these were in a better condition than would be expected for their age.

Probably the best documented case of incorruptibility is that of St Bernadette (Bernadette Soubirous), the young girl who claimed to have seen the Virgin Mary and established the shrine at Lourdes. After her vision, Bernadette became a nun and died young, at the age of thirty-four in the convent of St Gildard in Nevers, France. In 1909, thirty years after she died, Bernadette's body was exhumed, and, according to an eyewitness: 'Not the least trace of corruption nor any bad odour could be perceived.[5]

Often incorruptibility is associated with other strange phenomena. Sometimes, instead of producing the rank smell of a decomposed body, the saintly corpse is said to give off a pleasant odour, usually described as 'fruity'. In some cases it has even been known for oils to exude from the skin of the dead body. Indeed, the body of Marie Marguerite des Anges is said to have produced so much oil that it was used to burn the lamps in the chapel of her convent. Ironically, before her death, she had prayed that her body would be burned as a sacrifice to the blessed Sacrament.

Incorruptibility has been observed outside the circle of religious figures. In Kiev there are seventy-three very well preserved bodies naturally mummified and laying in open coffins. In a set of catacombs in Palermo, Sicily, hundreds of bodies have been exposed to the air, in some cases for over two centuries, yet none have decomposed to anything like the degree they should have done, and none are skeletal.

Although dramatic, the phenomenon of incorruptibility can be explained using basic biochemistry. A major clue to the mechanism at work here is the reports of fruity odours emanating from the dead bodies. Religious fanatics often submit themselves to extremely rigorous lifestyles and the most usual way in which they do this is to starve themselves. Because of this, the fat content of their bodies is exceptionally low. When any animal dies, the bacteria that live naturally in the animal's body begin to breakdown the structures in the body. The first materials to be broken down are fats and then the bacteria move on to the body's proteins. In the case of a very thin person, there is little fat to breakdown, so the bacteria quickly move on to the proteins. This is called the *deamination* of proteins. The chemical product of this break-down are chemicals called *ketones*, and ketones have a fruity smell.

Another significant series of biochemical events explains how the bodies of some saints appear to be remarkably well preserved even many years after their death. When the bacteria decompose the body, they begin in the intestines and move outwards. But, in the case of someone who has starved themselves, the bacteria have very little to feed on and many die or go into a dormant state. Meanwhile, the skin of the corpse starts to dry out and gradually hardens. Over a period of time, if the atmospheric conditions are appropriate, the skin dries to the point where it is almost leathery in texture and the surviving bacteria cannot break through. The eventual result of this is that the corpse appears to be perfectly preserved, but inside, it has completely decomposed, the organs and connective tissue digested by bacteria.

So what is to be concluded from this analysis of miracles?

Certainly some cases of individuals suffering stigmata are genuine. Equally, incorruptibility, or at least outward, *apparent* incorruptibility is also a well-documented and quite genuine phenomenon. Visions and apparitions are almost certainly due to hysterical responses and suggestion exaggerated by religious fervour. Descriptions of Biblical 'miracles' are unreliable because they have been handed down to us after generations of revision and reworking, delivered from an ancient time when the universe seemed to be beyond the understanding of mere mortals. Almost all the extraordinary events described in both the Old and New Testaments can be explained by applying simple scientific ideas, a sprinkling of logic and common sense, all viewed with a healthy degree of detachment. As soon as emotional commitment or 'faith' come into the equation, any hope of a realistic solution is destroyed.

The universe harbours many secrets, and happily humanity is on an endless journey to unravel these secrets; it is the excitement of solving the mysteries of life that make it worth the effort of investigation. But, as we have seen with many of the phenomena described in this book, most of these mysteries require knowledge to unravel them properly. Any mystery can be easily explained if we are not discerning or if we are obsessed with a notion, but these are not true answers in the universal and most profound sense. They are merely self-satisfying solutions.

Such a false process can be illustrated by the old joke about the researcher who wanted to discover how spiders could hear sounds. He placed a spider in a box and made a loud noise at one end, causing the spider to run in the opposite direction. Next he took the spider out of the box, cut off all its legs, placed it back in the box and again produced the loud noise. When the spider did not move, the researcher concluded that the spider's ears were in its legs.

5

SEARCHING FOR THE
SECRETS OF LIFE

'A most wonderful majesty and archmajesty is the tincture
of sacred alchemy, the marvellous science of the secret
philosophy, the singular gift bestowed upon men through
the grace of Almighty God – which men have never
discovered through the labour of their own hands, but
only by the revelation and the teaching of others.'

Thomas Norton, *The Ordinall of Alchimy*, 1477.

Strands of long grey hair protrude from the base of the old
man's cap. His sweaty face looks incredibly thin as golden
light from the fire dances across his features. He stokes
the fire and peers through the haze into the receptacle
which glows iridescently amidst the flames, then steps back
and sits on his stool staring into the light. The rest of
the smoke-filled room is gloomy, the dim light of early
morning hardly illuminates rows of glassware, metal tools
and jars of mercury laying in shadow upon wooden shelves.
Beneath the jars are rows of books and in the half-light,
handwritten hieroglyphics can just be seen covering pages
tinged in brown.

For many weeks the alchemist has worked alone, always at
night. So often he has fallen asleep only to awake suddenly to
see demons at his throat, beasts suspended in the air mocking
him before they disperse and fade.

Then suddenly, in the fire, he sees it; there, lying at the bottom of the receptacle, a nascent glow, a glimmer of treasure. He leans closer, his fingers avoiding narrowly the flames. Suppressing his excitement, he studies the globule of shining metal at the bottom of the container. With a pair of metal tongs, he pulls the glass vessel from the fire and holds it up to the glow of the flames and looks through it. When he is satisfied he has made no mistake, he moves his stool to a low bench at the back of the room and, leaning over the empty page of his notebook, begins to describe the technique which has enabled him to fulfil his dream. He scribbles fitfully about his findings staring as he does so at the ingot of material laying in a puddle of pure gold at the bottom of the crucible – the dreamed of *Philosophers' Stone*.

Alchemy has been practised for thousands of years and it still has its followers today. Some say that the art has its roots in truly ancient times before recorded history and that such figures as Moses were adepts. However, this is almost certainly an example of the exaggerated claims that is all part of the alchemist's stock-in-trade.

The first known alchemical work was probably a book called *Phusika kai mustika (On natural and initiatory things)*, written by one Bolos of Mendes which contains instructions for the making of dyes and the working of precious metals and gems. When exactly this was written is uncertain, but it probably dates from around 250 BC. It does not describe transmutations or processes to produce what has become known as the *elixir of life* (these were later obsessions), and so, in many respects it is atypical of the material alchemists studied in translated form in Europe some fifteen hundred years later.

Most alchemists from the Dark Ages to the beginning of the scientific era were inspired by a belief in the notion that alchemical wisdom extended back many centuries to ancient times and that their roots could be found within a collection of ideas known as the *Hermetic tradition*.

The literal meaning of this is 'body of occult knowledge' and it was believed to have originated in the mists of time and to have been 'bestowed' to humanity through supernatural agents. The very title 'Hermetic tradition' derives from the god Hermes, and a mythical figure known as Hermes Trismegistus (Hermes the Thrice Great) is credited with the composition of some of the most important early alchemical works. Venerated by alchemists throughout history, it was said of Hermes Trismegistus that he '. . . saw the totality of things. Having seen, he understood. Having understood, he had the power to reveal and show. And indeed what he knew, he wrote down. What he wrote he mostly hid away, keeping silence rather than speaking out, so that every generation coming into the world had to seek out these things.'[1]

Naturally, it was in the alchemist's own interests to further the misconception that their art had mysterious, ancient foundations because it added even greater exclusivity and importance to their ideas. Furthermore, it became an essential feature that their techniques were hidden or, as this writer describes it: 'every generation coming into the world had to seek out these things.'

In reality, almost all the techniques used by the alchemists of Europe and indeed their most sacred texts did not date back to the era of the Old Testament times but originated instead in the city of Alexandria around 200–300 AD.

The earliest theoretical basis for alchemy in the West stems from Aristotle's notion of the four elements and the concept that one element may, under the correct conditions, be *transmuted* into any of the others. Aristotle also believed that each element had special properties that were related to human emotions and characteristics. According to this philosophy, Fire is related to the blood and therefore passion; Water is manifest in phlegm, too much of it produces laziness. Earth is found in black bile, which is associated with melancholy, whilst Air is present in yellow bile and is linked with the emotion of anger. According to this set of ideas, all matter can be transmuted into any other by changing the proportions of the four basic elements from which it is composed. For example, relatively valueless lead could be changed into precious gold simply by realigning the proportions of the four elements, Fire, Earth, Air and Water present in the lead.

In terms of technique, alchemy was greatly developed by the Arabs following the fall of Alexandria at the end of the fourth century AD. So much had been lost in the destruction of the city's great library that a mere outline of the subject survived, but from this a slightly altered form of alchemy developed. Early Syriac texts, which constituted the majority of the elementary works in alchemy, were soon translated into Arabic and this teaching spread beyond the Near East. But, the most important changes to alchemy came not so much through development of processes or special laboratory methods as from the 'spiritual' and metaphysical foundations of the subject.

We may think of alchemy as being based upon two central themes – the search for the *Philosophers' Stone* and the production of a supernatural *elixir of life*. Both of these concepts came not from the ancient texts supposedly handed down by figures such as Moses; but from ancient China. The Chinese, who may actually have been the first alchemists anywhere in the world, were certainly the earliest to try to produce a 'magical' material with the power to change 'base' metals into gold. They were also the first recorded seekers of a potion which could restore life or endow eternal youth. In fact they were so enthusiastic that they conducted experiments with various concoctions on convicted criminals – the original lab rats!

The search that probably began in Alexandria and was pursued by the Arab philosophers of later centuries eventually led to Europe. With the fall of Rome, Western Europe descended into the Dark Ages and it was not until the eleventh century that learning started to return via the migration of Arabic philosophy and science and the beginnings of trade between East and West. As a result, many of the early alchemical works originating in Alexandria and later modified by the Arabs, were translated into Latin and this spread the art throughout the Continent.

In European history many innovations are attributed to the great thirteenth century philosopher Roger Bacon. In some ways Bacon was a man born far ahead of his time, and is believed to have rediscovered gunpowder (probably first developed by Chinese alchemists over a thousand years earlier). He also drew designs for a telescope several hundred years before the Dutch astronomer Hans Lippershey reinvented it in 1608. Although he followed many traditional teachings, particularly conventional Christian doctrine, he was a practising alchemist and wrote a treatise entitled *Speculum Alchimiae* (*The Mirror of Alchemy*), which was finally published in 1597. He is also known to have been one of the first to see the usefulness of experiment and wrote three far-sighted tracts: *Opus Majus, Opus Minor* and *Opus Tertium* which outline his philosophy and his experimental techniques in a range of disciplines, much of which we would now recognise as alchemical. Bacon's work established his reputation for posterity, but others viewed his ideas as too close to the occult and anti-Establishment (which in those days meant they did not agree with Aristotle's accepted ideas about Nature).* Seen by the then pope, Nicolas IV, as a subversive, for all his efforts, Bacon was imprisoned for life as a heretic.

Other famous adepts who mixed what would now be considered 'respectable' science with magic were two contemporaries of Bacon – Albertus Magnus and his pupil Thomas Aquinas. As well as developing notions of natural philosophy such as the aphorism 'like seeks like' and

---

* A note here to alleviate any misunderstanding – although I mentioned earlier that early alchemical reasoning was based upon Aristotle's idea of the four elements of Nature, Aristotle himself should not be thought of as an alchemist. Indeed, his ideas about science (which were almost without exception wrong) were the bedrock of orthodox Natural Philosophy (science) for about 1400 years and the polar opposite of many concepts held sacred by the alchemists.

ideas about the nature of fire which were worthy for their time, Magnus and Aquinas were also said to have produced automatons that could speak and acted as domestic servants by use of the Philosophers' Stone and a mysterious *elixir vitae* (elixir of life). But typically for commentators of the time, it was not enough that a philosopher should have the ability to understand how things worked, they had to perform tricks, feats of 'magic' in order to prove themselves. Albertus Magnus was believed to be capable of controlling the weather and to influence the seasons. It was a spirit of wonder and a belief in occult properties at work in the world that dominated philosophy, and within this climate the ideas of the alchemists flourished.

Instead of being content to help develop a coherent philosophy or a 'science', alchemists pursued their own fantasies and desires and helped to quell any attempt to formalise their art by following these dreams in their distinctly individualistic ways. Only rarely do alchemical tracts agree upon any method or technique.

Later, during the fifteenth century, the pursuits of the alchemist were given a huge boost by the rediscovery of lost Hermetic texts given the collective title *Corpus Hermeticum*. This treatise was written from the viewpoint of a seeker of truth who is led to the wonders of the universe by an omnipotent being and began: 'Once upon a time, when I had begun to think about the things that are, and my thoughts had soared high aloft, while my bodily senses had been put under restraint by sleep – yet not such sleep as that of men weighed down by fullness of food or by bodily weariness – I thought there came to me a being of vast and boundless magnitude, who called me by name, and said to me, "What do you wish to hear and see, and to learn and to come to know by thought?" "Who are you?" I said. "I," said he, "am Poimandres, the Mind of the Sovereignty." "I would feign learn," said I, "the things that are, and understand their nature, and get knowledge of God."'[2]

In 1460, Cosimo di Medici had sent emissaries around the

world in an effort to track down ancient manuscripts about the Hermetic arts. A monk came to him claiming that he had in his possession a work written by none other than Hermes Trismegistus himself and dating from the time of the ancient Egyptians. It was not until 1614 that the manuscript was found to be no older than the second or third century AD, but during the intervening period it inspired several generations of alchemists throughout the Continent and beyond and was probably the single most important factor in the massive growth of interest in the Hermetic tradition and the occult during the Renaissance.

By the sixteenth century, there were literally hundreds of wandering magi who found sponsors amongst impressionable wealthy merchants and European nobility. Others who became enamoured of the art were already rich – the sons of wealthy men, who actually lost the family fortune chasing dreams of making unlimited amounts of gold. Often these seekers died in abject poverty having succeeded only in wasting their lives trying to hunt down their fantasies.

An example is the case of one Bernard of Treves. Born in Padua to a wealthy noble family in 1406, he succeeded in squandering his entire inheritance during a lifetime dedicated to alchemical fantasies. Chasing one crazy method after another, tricked by a succession of thieves and fraudsters during a lifetime of travel through Europe, Bernard ended his days as a beggar on the island of Rhodes aged eighty-five.

However, many of the great names of European Mediaeval and Renaissance philosophy have also been associated with alchemy and during this pre-scientific era the distinction between what would later be refined into 'science' and what was clearly 'magic' was blurred. It is also clear that many early technologies and elements of pre-Newtonian scientific knowledge were intermeshed with some of the more bizarre notions of the Alexandrian magi.

For almost five hundred years, from the early twelfth century to the middle of the sixteenth, Europe was the new centre of the alchemical world, a place where sages and 'wise men' travelled freely from state to state in search of elusive but greatly-prized wonders. Many alchemists wrote of their adventures and their experiments, but almost always their recipes were encoded so that others could not copy them without first gaining insights into the art and undergoing special initiation. Some spent their entire lives attempting to decode the works of others and adding their own interpretation to handed-down wisdom.

In some countries and at certain times, alchemists were tolerated, even encouraged and financed by the ruling monarch; in other states, alchemists and magicians were reviled and their practices deemed illegal.

In England, alchemists received mixed fortunes. In 1404, Henry IV made the practise of alchemy a capital offence because it was thought that if an alchemist could succeed they would disturb the *status quo* by producing vast amounts of gold that would destabilise the economy. However, Queen Elizabeth I employed alchemists in an attempt to boost the royal coffers. One of her favourites was John Dee, a gifted natural philosopher as well as a deluded alchemist and occultist.

Another alchemist, John Aurelio Augurello, who lived in Italy during the fifteenth century, presented the then pope, Leo X, with his latest alchemical work, *Crysopeia*, which described the process of making gold. Having dedicated the book to Leo, Augurello was hopeful the pope would return the favour with a reward. He did – Leo recalled him to the Papal Court and with great pomp and ceremony he drew from his pocket an empty purse and presented it to the penniless alchemist saying that because he was such a great magician and could make gold, he would need a purse to keep it in.

Other rulers were more extreme, both as supporters and avengers. Frederick of Wurzburg maintained special gallows for hanging alchemists and used them frequently, whilst Pope John XXII, himself a practising alchemist, actively encouraged others in the art.

Hundreds of alchemists wrote books about the techniques

they used, but they deliberately obscured their meaning with codes or poetic language so that other alchemists could not copy their work. A good example is the writings of a female alchemist from the second century AD, one Kleopatra, which begins: 'Take from the four elements the arsenic which is highest and lowest, the white and the red, the male and the female in equal balance, so that they may be joined to one another. For just as the bird warms her eggs with her heat and brings them to their appointed term, so yourselves warm your composition and bring it to its appointed term.'[3]

Of course, the other reason they hid their findings in this way was to cover up the fact that they were totally unsuccessful in finding what they were after – unlimited amounts of gold. Quite simply, most alchemists were chasing sunbeams in their attempts to transmute matter.

Alchemists could never have hoped to succeed because they were attempting to transform the basic fabric of matter by using nothing more powerful than a furnace and a mixture of simple chemicals. Transmutation is only possible today in the heart of nuclear reactors where large atoms are split into small elements in a process called 'nuclear fission'. It is now possible to produce gold from other metals, but the amount of energy needed (and therefore the cost involved) in doing this would be far greater than the value of the material produced by the end of the process.

The methods of the alchemists were very basic. During the fifteenth and sixteenth centuries, when alchemy was at its most popular in Europe, they usually began by mixing in a mortar three substances – a metal ore, usually impure iron, another metal (often lead or mercury) and an acid of organic origin, most typically citric acid from fruit or vegetables. They ground these together for anything up to six months, to ensure complete mixing, and the blend was heated carefully in a crucible, the temperature allowed to rise very slowly until it reached an optimum and kept there for ten days. This was a dangerous process that produced toxic fumes and many an alchemist working in cramped, unventilated rooms succumbed to poisoning from mercury vapour, while others went slowly mad.

After the allotted period of heating was completed, the material in the crucible was removed and dissolved in an acid. For many generations, alchemists experimented with different types of solvent and in this way nitric, sulphuric and ethanoic acid were all discovered (possibly by fourth and fifth century Arabs). This dissolution process had to be conducted under polarised light (light which vibrates in only one plane), which they believed they could produce by using sunlight reflected by a mirror or working solely by moonlight.

After the material was successfully dissolved in the solvent, the next step was to evaporate and reconstitute the material – to distil it. This distillation process was the most delicate and time-consuming stage of the whole operation and often took the alchemist years to complete to his satisfaction. It was also another highly dangerous phase – the laboratory fire was never allowed to go out, and claimed many lives through the centuries.

If the experimenter was not consumed by flame and the material was not lost through poor control, then the alchemist could move onto the next stage, a step most clearly linked with mysticism. According to most alchemical texts, the moment when distillation should be stopped was determined by 'a sign'. No two alchemical manuals agreed upon when or how this should happen and the poor alchemist simply had to wait until he deemed it the most propitious moment to stop the distillation and to move onto the next stage.

The material was then removed from the distillation equipment and an oxidising agent added. This was usually potassium nitrate, a substance certainly known to the ancient Chinese and quite possibly to the Alexandrians. However, combined with sulphur from the metal ore and carbon from the organic acid, the alchemist then had, quite literally, an explosive mixture – gunpowder.

It was by reaching this stage that Roger Bacon probably made his discovery of gunpowder in the thirteenth century, and many an alchemist who survived poisoning and fire ended his days going up with his laboratory.

Those who managed to master all these stages of the complex and time-consuming process were then able to continue to the final stages where the mixture was sealed in a special container and warmed carefully. After cooling the material, a white solid was sometimes observed which was known as the White Stone, capable, it was claimed, of transmuting base metals into silver. The most ambitious stage – producing a red solid called the Red Rose by an elaborate process of warming, cooling and purifying the distillate, could lead eventually, so the alchemist believed, to the production of the ultimate substance, the Philosophers' Stone itself, the fabled material that could transmute any substance into pure gold.

All of these stages in the process were described in the literature allegorically and were enveloped in mystical language and secret, esoteric meaning. So the blending of the original ingredients and their fusion via the use of heat was described as 'setting the two dragons at war with one another'. In this way the male and the female elements of the substances symbolised by a King and a Queen were released and then recombined or 'married'. This was the concept behind one of the most famous of all alchemical books, the allegorical romance, *The Chemical Wedding*, which, on one level, has been interpreted as describing the transmutation process.

As well as this physical aspect of alchemy, we should consider the psychological element, the purely 'spiritual' dimension to the work of the alchemist.

The spiritual element of the experiment was also the key to the alchemist's philosophy. It is this which has led some writers on the subject to the suggestion that, for many alchemists, it was the practical process that was a side issue and their search was really for the elixir or the Philosophers' Stone *within them*. In other words, by conducting what seems a mundane set of tasks, they were actually following a path to enlightenment allowing *themselves* to be transmuted into 'gold'. For this reason, the alchemist placed great store by the concept of 'purity of spirit' and often spent many long years in preparation for the task of transmutation before even touching a crucible.

Carl Jung was fascinated with alchemy and wrote a great deal on the subject. He was particularly interested in the motivation of the alchemist as well as what it was they were really seeking and came to the conclusion that alchemical emblems bore a close relationship to dream imagery. This observation eventually led him to one of the most important breakthroughs in his thinking, the concept of the 'collective unconscious'. In this theory, Jung speculated that at a deep level of the subconscious mind, the psyche of a person merges with the collective psyche of humankind, so that all individuals share a common heritage of symbols or images. These he called *archetypes* and they manifested, he believed, in our dreams and affected waking thought patterns subconsciously. Jung was very interested in his own dreams and studied them carefully. In some he saw alchemical imagery. 'Before I discovered alchemy,' he wrote, 'I had a series of dreams which repeatedly dealt with the same theme. Beside my house stood another, that is to say, another wing or annex, which was strange to me. Each time I would wonder in my dream why I did not know this house, although it had apparently always been there. Finally there came a dream in which I reached the other wing. I discovered there a wonderful library, dating largely from the sixteenth and seventeenth centuries. Large, fat folio volumes, bound in pigskin, stood along the walls. Among them were a number of books embellished with copper engravings of a strange character, and illustrations containing curious symbols such as I had never seen before. At the time I did not know to what they referred; only much later did I recognise them as alchemical symbols. In the dream I was conscious only of the fascination exerted by them and by the entire library.'[4]

The alchemists, Jung believed, had been inadvertently tapping into the collective unconscious. This led them to assume they were following a spiritual path to enlightenment when they were actually liberating their subconscious minds through the use of ritual. This is not far removed from other ritualistic events – those exploited by faith healers, the ecstasy experienced by ritualistic voodoo dancers, or charismatic Christian services. Jung said of alchemy: 'The alchemical stone symbolises something that can never be lost or dissolved, something eternal that some alchemists compared to the mystical experience of God within one's own soul. It usually takes prolonged suffering to burn away all the superfluous psychic elements concealing the stone. But some profound inner experience of the Self does occur to most people at least once in a lifetime. From the psychological standpoint, a genuinely religious attitude consists of an effort to discover this unique experience and gradually to keep in tune with it (it is relevant that the stone is itself something permanent), so that the Self becomes an inner partner towards whom one's attention is continually turned.'[5]

To the alchemist, the most important factor in the practice was participation of the individual experimenter in the process of transmutation. The genuine alchemist was convinced that the emotional and spiritual characteristics of the individual experimenter was involved intimately with the success or failure of the experiment. And, it is this concept, more than any other aspect of alchemy, that distinguishes it from orthodox chemistry – the scientific discipline that began to supersede it at the end of the seventeenth century. The alchemist placed inordinate importance upon the spiritual element of his work and for many sceptics it was this which pushed the subject into the realms of *magic* and left it forever beyond the boundaries of 'science'.

Enthusiasts of alchemy claim there are many parallels between modern physics and the traditions of alchemy and refer especially to what they see as the anthropomorphic dimension of some of the latest ideas at the forefront of quantum mechanics. But, these claims are quite unjustified.

The main point of confusion comes from the idea that,

according to some versions of quantum theory, the experimenter plays a role in the experiment – that the experimenter can affect the outcome of an experiment. But although this may appear to be a link with the beliefs of the alchemist, there is no direct comparison between this result and the idea of the alchemist influencing the contents of his crucible.

Quantum theory is an exact, mathematical science based upon a collection of fundamental concepts which show rigorous consistency and relate closely and cohesively with other scientific disciplines. Most importantly, *quantum theory works*. Without it, we would have no lasers, television, satellite communications – the entire catalogue of modern technology. The practicality of quantum theory is unquestionable, the usefulness of alchemy in pushing back the barriers of cutting edge science is nonexistent. Modern physics is demonstrable, but most importantly for this argument at least, *it is repeatable*. Although to the uninitiated, the language of science is indecipherable (much like that of the ancient alchemists some declare) it is nevertheless a common and very strict language, consistent and communicable – unlike that of the alchemists of lore. And, unlike those intrepid adventurers, the modern seeker of Truth, the physicist, does not hide behind a facade of mystical code and they work independently of religious feeling or emotional character.

Put simply, modern chemistry is very different to alchemy because it is not based upon a faith system, but is a unified subject with shared rules and mathematical integrity which sticks to empirical knowledge and logical experiment.

Having said this, it is important to remember that all the efforts of the alchemists down the centuries, from ancient times until it began to wane in the seventeenth century, did actually pay dividends. The alchemists invented many techniques including heating methods, *decanting*, *recrystallisation* and *evaporation* and pioneered the use of a vast range of chemical apparatus, including heating equipment and specialised glassware.

Successive generations of alchemists also refined the technique of *distillation* based upon the earliest form of the method practised by the magi of Alexandria almost two thousand years ago. Today, no chemical laboratory would be complete without distillation apparatus, alcohol could not be produced in large quantities without a still and the same equipment on a much grander scale lies at the heart of an oil refinery allowing crude oil to be separated into its components.

These practical applications of alchemy are very useful and have made a difference to the practice of modern science, but there is another aspect to alchemy that provided even greater real benefits. Alchemy had an enormous impact upon several important scientists during the seventeenth century, including Isaac Newton, Isaac Barrow and Robert Boyle. Of these, the most important was Isaac Newton who was so obsessed with alchemy that he wrote a secret collection of over 1,000,000 words on the subject – more than he composed on pure science.[6]

Newton was no mere dabbler in the art of alchemy but actually derived his famous laws through his obsession with the occult. Quite simply, modern physics, which has its foundation in Newton's work, is not based purely upon scientific experiment and mathematics but came about largely through Newton's alchemical experiments.

Newton was obsessively secretive about his interest in the occult because his enemies would have used it to illustrate a conflict with his conventional scientific work, and because officially at least, alchemy was still illegal and carried the death penalty. But, by the time biographers came to consider his life, Newton was dead, and the need to hide his interest in the occult had gone; but what confused his early biographers was a body of incriminating evidence to be found in Newton's vast library and within his huge collection of papers and notebooks. This material made it very clear that the most respected scientist in history, the model for the scientific method, had spent a greater portion of his life intensely involved with alchemy than he had researching pure science. This material also confirmed what a few of Newton's close friends knew during his lifetime – that he had expended a vast amount of his time studying the chronology of the Bible, prophecy, investigating natural magic, and most of all, attempting to unravel the Hermetic secrets – the *prisca sapientia*, all of which had greatly influenced his scientific thinking and the evolution of his epoch-making discoveries.

After studying the contents of Newton's secret papers (those documents, manuscripts and notebooks ignored by early Newton biographers), in 1936, the great economist and Newton scholar, Maynard Keynes, delivered a Royal Society lecture in which he concluded that Newton was: '. . . the last of the magicians, the last of the Babylonians and Sumarians, the last great mind which looked out on the visible and intellectual world with the same eyes as those who began to build our intellectual inheritance rather less than 10,000 years ago. Isaac Newton, a posthumous child born with no father on Christmas Day, 1642, was the last wonder-child to whom the Magi could do sincere and appropriate homage.'[7]

At the time of his death, his library contained 169 books on alchemy and chemistry, including works by some of the most important names in the history of the subject, and it was said that he possessed the finest and most extensive collection of alchemical texts ever accumulated up to his day. Amongst these books was to be found a copy of the Rosicrucian Manifestos published in *The Fame and Confession of the Fraternity R.C*, an English translation by the alchemist Thomas Vaughan in 1652 which is heavily annotated by Newton himself.* He also read two important books about

---

* The Rosicrucians were a secret society who believed they possessed supernatural powers. They caused quite a stir in seventeenth-century France, Germany and England, but gradually faded from the scene. However, some believe that they continue to exist today and play a key role in guiding world political affairs. One can only assume they are by now rather weary of the task!

the Rosicrucian movement by a famous alchemist named Michael Maier, *Themis aurea* and *Symbola aureae mensae duodecim* and made extensive notes on all three works.

In all, Newton possessed nine works by Maier, eight by the celebrated Spanish alchemist Raymund Lull, who was a contemporary of Roger Bacon, and four volumes by a Benedictine monk named Basilius Valentinus (who was a peer of the unfortunate Bernard of Treves). Along with these were works by Thomas Vaughan under his pen-name of Eirenaeus Philalethes, texts by the well-known sixteenth century English alchemist, George Ripley, those written by the great Polish adept, Michael Sendivogius and, perhaps most importantly, one of Newton's first and most used purchases of alchemical literature – the six-volume collection *Theatrum Chemicum Britannicum* by another key English alchemist, Elias Ashmole.

An important figure in these books was the alchemist Paracelsus, a man whose name has become almost synonymous with early medical practice. Born near Zurich in 1493, he travelled around Europe searching for the secrets of the Ancients, squandering much of his talent and any money he earned along the way. Like most of his fellow seekers, he died in poverty, discredited by the intellectual Establishment. What made him unusual was his interest in applying alchemy to medicine.

'[Alchemy's] special work is this,' he wrote. 'To make arcana [a celestial power Paracelsus believed to be contained in metals], and direct these to disease . . . The physician must judge the nature of Medicine according to the stars . . . Since medicine is worthless save in so far as it is from heaven, it is necessary that it shall be derived from heaven . . . Know, therefore, that it is arcana alone which are strength and virtues. They are, moreover, volatile substances, without bodies; they are a chaos, clear, pellucid, and in the power of a star.'[8]

Another key figure from alchemical lore prominent in Newton's library was Cornelius Agrippa. He was said to possess extraordinary powers of the mind and body but he too was misled by impossible dreams and never managed to bring to reality these hypothetical abilities. A contemporary of Paracelsus, he travelled widely, working in turn for the Emperor Maximilian, King Francis I and Margaret of Austria and had, along the way, turned down a generous invitation to join the Court of Henry VIII. He wrote a number of books in his lifetime, some of which appeared in Newton's library in translated form or as part of collections. His most important book was the *Vanity and Nothingness of Human Knowledge*. Other works considered various means of transmutation and it is these that probably interested Newton most when he began his own alchemical researches.

By comparison with the earlier practitioners, the alchemists of the sixteenth and seventeenth centuries, men such as Michael Maier, Thomas Vaughan, Robert Fludd, Elias Ashmole and others, were far more realistic in their approach and ideals.

Maier, who was born in Germany in 1566, was another academic who for many years held a respectable position as physician to Emperor Rudolph II. After the death of the Emperor in 1612, he travelled Europe establishing a network of contacts with other alchemists and philosophers. He came to England and for a time was a close associate of the English alchemist and Rosicrucian, Robert Fludd. Later, between 1614 and 1620, he embarked on writing a collection of books which proved to be highly influential in the alchemical world. These included a book of alchemical emblems or symbols called *Atalanta fugiens* which contained esoteric text relating to a blending of alchemy with rationalism and orthodox religion. Some see this as one of the earliest models for the ethos behind the establishment of the Royal Society.

As well as owning the largest private collection of occult books in the world at the time, when Newton died, the million or so words on the subject of alchemy he left behind served as a clear indication that he not only read and researched but was himself an active experimenter and chronicler. But what did he actually achieve in the art?

Newton's greatest contributions to science began early in his career. According to the history books, his great achievement – the elucidation of the theory of universal gravitation – came in 1666 when he was living at his mother's house in Woolsthorpe. It is true that Newton, along with the rest of the academic community, had fled Cambridge during the plague years of 1665/6 and he did indeed return to live with his mother at their rural home. It is even possible that Newton did one day sit under an apple tree as he mused upon the meaning of gravity and could have seen an apple fall. This may have pushed his thinking along, but it is ridiculous to believe that the whole concept of universal gravitation came to him then in one great rush. Today it is recognised that Newton probably made up this story to conceal the fact that he had used alchemy to help derive his famous theory.

The discovery of the theory of universal gravitation took Newton almost twenty years and did not really take shape until he wrote his great book, the *Principia Mathematica*, between 1684 and its publication in 1687. And during the twenty years taking us from the garden in Woolsthorpe to the appearance of this work, there were many influences that shaped the theory. Most important was mathematics. As a student, he formulated a simple relationship between the distance between two bodies such as planets and the force of gravity between them, called the *inverse square law*. However, this was only the first step to creating the theory of universal gravitation, the idea that all matter has a gravitational effect upon all other matter.

In the seventeenth century, the idea that an object could influence the movement of another without actually touching it was unimaginable. This behaviour is now called *action at a distance*, and we take it for granted. But people in Newton's day could not understand this and saw it as magic or an occult property. Through his experiments in alchemy Newton was able to approach gravity with a more open mind than most of his peers.

Newton began investigating alchemy in about 1669, after he had returned to Cambridge and around the time he was appointed Professor of Mathematics there. He travelled to London to buy forbidden books from fellow alchemists and carried out his private experiments, hidden away from the authorities and his rivals within the scientific community. His earliest experiments were very basic but after reading everything he could about the practice he soon pushed the art beyond the limits set by his predecessors. In true scientific fashion, he approached experiments logically and with great precision, meticulously writing-up what he had discovered. Whereas the alchemists of lore fumbled around for years not really knowing what they were doing, Newton approached his work systematically.

Another great difference between Newton and his predecessors was that Newton was never interested in making gold. His sole purpose in studying alchemy was to find what he believed were hidden basic laws that governed the universe. He may not have realised that he would come to a theory of gravity through alchemy and other occult practices but he did think there was some basic law or hidden ancient knowledge to be found from his researches.

The breakthrough came from alchemy when Newton observed materials in his crucible and realised that they were acting under the influence of *forces*. He could see particles attracted to each other and other particles repelled by their neighbours without there being any physical contact or tangible link between them. In other words he saw action at a distance within the alchemist's crucible. He wrote to his friend Robert Boyle about his discovery describing what he saw as a '... secret principle in nature by which liquors are sociable to some things & unsociable to others'.[9] Soon, he began to realise that this might also be how gravity worked and that what happened in the microcosm of the crucible and the alchemists fire could perhaps also happen in the macrocosm – the world of planets and suns.

These influences came to fruition in the *Principia*, seen as probably the most important scientific treatise ever written, ironically a book that came not just from Newton's genius for science but his obsession with the occult and the arcane lore of the Ancients. And, from the *Principia* came the Industrial Revolution, modern science and much of the everyday technology we take for granted today.

And that is really where alchemy and its uses come to an end. Yet, some refuse to accept this. Surprisingly perhaps, at the end of the twentieth century, there remain believers in alchemy. Although discredited by the advent of empirical science, alchemy has survived and maintained a following throughout the Enlightenment, circumventing Victorian rationalism, the succession of technology and the atomic theory.

As a final refuge for those who insist the world is flat and that NASA faked the Apollo moon-landings, the ancient art of alchemy is a warm haven, with a hall of fame filled with fellow eccentrics, and men of great intellect. Ironically, these great men of previous ages produced something workable almost by default, and in so doing created some of the most important science in the history of human civilisation.

6

WE ARE MADE OF STARS

'Thank your lucky stars . . .'

Of all paranormal concepts, astrology probably touches the lives of more people than any other. It is also the single most respected and documented supernatural idea amongst those inclined towards New Age or alternative philosophies. Yet, at the same time, to the scientist, astrology is the most vague and archaic pastime, rooted in primitive thought and misguided in the extreme.

To rationalists, astrology is an irritating puzzle. When those whom we believe to be otherwise rational, intelligent people let slip at dinner parties that 'there may be something in astrology', or that 'maybe there are secrets about astrology that we do not understand', the rationalist begins to wonder if they have chosen the right friends. Yet astrology is incredibly popular: How many times have any of us been at a gathering when the subject of astrology comes up and someone has declared that they can tell the star signs of others in the room?

According to some statistics, 99% of people know their star sign, and an estimated 50% of the population consult horoscopes regularly. One company that has set up a horoscope telephone line, called 'Astroline', claim they have in excess of one million calls per year. The reason for the huge public interest in astrology and these frankly disturbing statistics is a complex issue, but one worth addressing.

Astrology is now a mass-market phenomenon. Ironically, during an age fascinated with the occult in all its manifestations, the Victorians were not terribly interested in astrology or horoscopes and it was only revived with the advent of mass media. Originally the newspaper horoscope, the favourite of all modern tabloid newspapers, was created in the 1930s to boost circulation, and at one point in the 1980s, the horoscope page of the late mass media astrologer Patric Walker was said to have increased weekly sales of the British newspaper, the *Mail On Sunday*, by a staggering 200,000.

I will look at the differences between this form of astrology and what the serious practitioners deem the real 'science' of astrology later in this chapter, but, it is clear from the success of modern-day popular astrologers such as Russell Grant and Mystic Meg that there remains a great public need for such people.

Part of the appeal is, of course, entertainment. Horoscopes are about everyone's favourite subject: 'me', and therefore they generate an undying appeal. Newspaper astrology is dynamic – it keeps offering new stories for the readers and it is always, always comforting. In an ever-changing world in which many people feel they have become less than a number, horoscopes offer a personal touch, something in which they can immerse themselves, something with which they can feel comfortable.

And, like many aspects of the paranormal, astrology is also undemanding. Real science, the sort that moves civilisation forward, the sort that has made all our lives infinitely better than it was for our ancestors is, to many people, hostile, frightening and difficult. To understand the universe via science requires either traditional training or the dedication to read books. Astrology is an easy route to what some feel to be an enlightened view, it is thought to bestow 'mystical secrets', which many people believe to be the real 'keys to the universe'.

Even orthodox religion presents problems for those searching for something beyond science or beyond the 'difficult' intellectual world. Religion makes just as many demands as science, but these are emotional and spiritual rather than intellectual or rational. Most orthodox religions require commitment to a complete bundle of ideas or faith-system, and many parts of this package may not appeal. To complete the problem for religion, at the turn of the millennium religious orthodoxy is perceived, especially by the young, as distinctly uncool. Western religion appears to ignore the flow of modern life, it does not seem to incorporate the needs of many people today and is a doctrine that has been marginalised by the broader sweep of history. To those who believe this, but still seek a spiritual aspect to their lives, astrology offers an easy path that is directed straight to the self.

Celebrities seem particularly attracted to astrology. The Queen Mother is said to have consulted astrologers, and the late Diana, Princess of Wales, is reported to have had long discussions with a clairvoyant and astrologer only days before her death and to have employed an astrologer regularly for years. Pop stars, Hollywood actors and television personalities have also recently 'come out' as fans and users of astrology, and belief in astrology has become something of a fashion statement. To cater for this need and to fuel the flames, the bookshop shelves creak under the weight of books on the subject in all its possible permutations – 'love signs', 'astrology and the body', 'your horoscope', 'sex and the stars' – all of it geared to massage the ego and calm the nerves of stressed-out modern people – a quite understandable need.

So, given the very real, human reasons for the enduring popularity of astrology, what is the basis of the subject? And is there anything in what the enthusiasts claim categorically to be a 'science'?

Astrology is a truly ancient practice. No one is certain when or where it began. Practitioners assign overwrought significance to its supposed origins placing it in the ancient realm of Atlantis and suggesting that the ancients bestowed astrological knowledge on the Sumarians and the Babylonians. The truth is probably more prosaic: the original seed of astrology was cultivated about 10,000 years ago, but exactly where remains a mystery. Some theories suggest that monuments such as Stonehenge, which are around 5000 years old, could have been constructed for astrological purposes, others place the first astrological dabblings earlier and in the Middle East.

The oldest relic linking humans with astrology comes from a document called the Venus Tablet or the *Enuma Anu Enlil*, which has been dated to the age of the Babylonian civilisation sometime between 1800 and 800 BC, and contains astrological references and talk of 'omens'. 'In month eleven, 15th day,' the tablet reads, 'Venus disappeared in the West. Three days it stayed away, then on the 18th day it became visible in the East. Springs will open and Adad will bring his rain and Ea his floods. Messages of reconciliation will be sent from King to King.'

Early Greek civilisation adopted astrology and it was placed in high esteem by the philosophers of the time. There was no delineation between astronomy and astrology from the era of the Greeks almost until the time of Galileo, and the same mathematical tools were employed to study the movement of the stars as those used to help astrologers make prophesies and personal star charts.

As we saw in the last chapter, modern European culture was spawned at the end of the Dark Ages by the arrival in Europe of Arabic philosophy and science in the eleventh and

---

* Galileo was, incidentally, a practicing astrologer as well as one of the first modern astronomers. However, historians believe that he 'played' with astrology simply to help pay the bills and thought little of it as a 'science'.

twelfth centuries. It was wrapped up with a fascination with alchemy and the ancient mysticism or Hermetic secrets, the *prisca sapientia*. By the Renaissance, around the beginning of the fifteenth century, interest in the ancient teachings and the writings of men such as Aristotle, Archimedes, Galen, Democritus and others had reached a new peak as ancient texts were discovered in monasteries and private libraries and a new learning based upon the old ideas of two millennia earlier flourished. Our modern preoccupation with astrology had begun.

In one form or another an abiding interest in astrology survived the Age of Reason, but it fell into decline during the late eighteenth and early nineteenth centuries, partly, it is believed, because of the vogue for everything 'modern' – the desperate and quite laudable clamour towards the Age of Technology. Isaac Newton and others had crystallised the concept of the universe as a mechanical thing – the planets held in orbit by gravity – indeed, a mysterious force it seemed, but one that could be understood using human ingenuity and mathematics. Suddenly the ancient Gods and the daily flux of Nature no longer seemed all powerful and beyond our understanding. As human civilisation rushed headlong though the Industrial Revolution and into the era of modern medicine, modern astronomy and a world ruled by Darwin, Marx and Einstein, belief in astrology became unfashionable, an embarrassment.

Many scientists and rationalists would wish things had stayed that way. Richard Dawkins has called astrology 'meta-twaddle' and has declared that: 'There's a thing called being so open-minded your brain drops out.' Immediately after the Industrial Revolution the upright citizens of the Western world were content with their faith in God and machine, they had no urgent need to find spirituality elsewhere, and indeed, they would have considered the modern disrespect for orthodox religion as blasphemous and the search for solace in Eastern religion, alternative philosophies and astrology as fickle.

Today, the art of astrology is experiencing something of a renaissance, but there is astrology and astrology and if we are to appraise the subject properly we must have clear definitions of what it is all about.

To the serious astrologer, newspapers' gurus of the subject, (the Russell Grants and the Mystic Megs) are nothing more than charlatans who are merely in it for the money. To them, the nonsense we see spouted out on television shows and in the tabloid press demeans what they consider to be a serious subject based upon very strict and highly-complex rules. So effectively, for the moment, we can ignore this aspect of astrology, consign it to the intellectual wastebin; which is actually nothing more than the 'serious' professional astrologer would demand of us.

However, just because the high-powered astrologers who claim to be masters of a complex craft say that their work is based upon ancient and elaborate mathematical concepts, it does not make it true. Indeed, constructing a complete birth chart for an individual requires an element of skill unnecessary for a tabloid columnist. But actually, even this so-called technical expertise requires little more than GCSE-level mathematics. To draw up a birth chart, a half-dozen factors need to considered – fewer than a simple engineering task such as building a wall.

The astrologer needs a basic grounding in geometry and a little trigonometry, as well as a smattering of simple astronomy. But this is nothing a reasonably intelligent twelve-year-old could not manage. To coin a popular but quite apt phrase: 'It's hardly nuclear physics.'

As well as this quite minimal mathematical ability, the professional astrologer employs a strong element of interpretation based upon ancient handed-down wisdom. Although the 'serious' astrologer surrounds their trade with a veneer of expertise and frankly makes too much of the mathematical skill involved and the training required to master the art of astrology, there is also the question of motive. Expert astrologers and critics are united in condemning tabloid astrology and Fleet Street horoscopes, but surely the motivations and the drives of the highbrow practitioners are little different. Do they not offer fantasies wrapped up in what they like to think is complex mathematics? The only real difference between them is the market to which they appeal. Self-proclaimed elitist astrologers such as Shelley Von Strunckel and Sally Brompton (who is a graduate of something called the Faculty of Astrological Studies in London), write books aimed at the top end of the popular astrology market and act as personal consultants for the rich and the famous.

Such divisions in a single practice produce an amazing range of beliefs and subsets. It is possible to see more rival disciplines within the broader sweep of astrology than any other aspect of the paranormal. So, not only do we have the up-market practitioners and the 'lowbrow' tabloid horoscope hacks, but there are those who believe astrology is the overriding power that shapes us, determines who we marry, what careers we take up and our state of health. Yet, others see astrology as merely a means of interpretation, a little like Tarot or the use of the *I, Ching*.

Some astrologers believe that the stars influence our health. This was an idea first popularised by the alchemist, astrologer and all-round mystic Paracelsus, who believed there was an intimate connection between the elements (the four substances of which, according to Aristotle, all matter was made) and the stars in the heavens. He linked the behaviour of the elements, the movements of the stars and the wellbeing of his patients in a triumvirate that led to an astrological-alchemy which some modern astrologers believe valid even today.

Others totally disregard the advances of the past century and place far greater significance upon the influence of the stars than they do upon factors such as psychological development, genetics or environment. An example comes from a book called *Life Cycles* by an American astrologer named Rose Elliot, in which she claims that child development has little to do with mundane factors such as nurture or nature but is controlled by astrological influence. According to Elliot, the child's behaviour when they first experience 'separateness' from their parents (often referred to as 'the terrible twos') is not moulded by anything so prosaic as the relationship between child and parent, the presence of a younger child, the personality of the child, the genetic characteristics of the child and parents or the environment in which the child is raised. No, it is because the planet Mars returns to its birth position in the child's star chart at the age of two, and, because Mars is identified with war and aggression, it exerts a disturbing effect on the mood of the child. Obvious, really.

So, this is the background to astrology. It is a much-divided subject, split into elitist and popularist groups. Like many subjects and enthusiasms it is quite naturally studied by people with very different opinions and views and those who place different emphasis upon certain aspects of the art. It is also a very ancient practice and has its roots in the mists of history, a practice that has been manipulated and moulded for different ages, but one which has at its heart a set of ideologies that have remained unchanged since ancient times.

The astrologer believes that the planets of our solar system and the stars themselves play a fundamental role in the way we develop as individuals and what happens to us in our daily lives; that celestial objects can control our destiny and that of the world at large. To the astrologer, world events are not governed by chaos theory, a succession of random events upon which we humans try to impress our individual wishes and desires with varying degrees of success, but are instead predetermined and set in motion and maintained in equilibrium by some intangible force exerted by the planets and stars.

Let us for a moment suspend disbelief if we are sceptics,

and contain our desires and wishes if we are ardent enthusiasts. How could astrology work?

Unless the influence the stars have upon our lives is due to
some as-yet-unknown force, we only have conventional forces
we already know about to explain it. There could possibly be
other forces at work in the universe, but as science builds a
clearer picture of the way the universe works, the room for
new forces and strange mechanisms diminishes (although it
would be extremely arrogant of any scientist to assume that
all forces and all mechanisms are known). However, for the
purposes of trying to work out how stars and planets could
have an affect upon our lives and personalities, postulating
some unknown force gets us nowhere. So, if we say then
that if astrology is a true mechanism controlling the way in
which we as individuals interact with the universe, we have
a limited number of options.

The most popular idea has long been that some form of
gravitational force is at work and responsible for the claims
of astrology, that in some way the gravitational force
between distant planets and ourselves causes a mysterious
link so that we are all subject to this mechanism. In other
words, as the stars and planets move in their paths, there
is a *flux* or force, or a 'system of energies' that makes
us what we are and dictates what we do. This then
leads to the actions of the individual and the future of
nations.

The major flaw with this idea is that the force of
gravity is extremely weak. In fact it is the weakest of the
four types of natural force (the weak nuclear, the strong
nuclear, the electromagnetic and gravitational force). It
has been calculated that the gravitational force between
a baby at the moment of birth and the midwife in the
delivery room would be a million times greater than the
gravitational influence of any planet in our solar system
and an astronomically larger influence (literally) than the
distant stars.

To see why this is so, we need only a brief consideration

of Newton's discoveries about gravity made over three hundred years ago. Newton created a grand theory, the law of universal gravitation which demonstrates that every single material thing in the universe exerts a force upon any other material thing. So far, so good for the astrologer. The problem is, not only is the force of gravity weak, it depends upon the distance between two pieces of matter and diminishes in power the further apart the objects are.

Newton showed that the way the force of gravity between pieces of matter changes over distance may be calculated using what is called an *inverse square law*. For example, imagine two planets A and B, orbiting a sun. Suppose A and B are of equal size, but the distance between A and the sun is half the distance between B and the sun.

This means that the force of gravity between A and the sun will be four times greater than that between planet B and the sun. Similarly, a third planet C (of equal mass to A or B) which is three times further from the sun than A will experience a gravitational attraction one-ninth of that between A and the sun.

Everything in the universe adheres to this inverse square law. This is why the midwife (a relatively small object, but much, much closer to the new-born baby) actually exerts a far greater gravitational influence upon the child than a planet hundreds of millions of miles away.

Often astrologers and enthusiasts who want to believe in astrology, try to use Newton's law of universal gravitation to produce what they like to believe are explanations for the power of planetary influence, but they miss the point completely. The most familiar argument goes something like this: 'The moon creates tides on earth because of the gravitational interaction of the two objects – the Earth and the Moon – why then shouldn't the Moon and the planets also effect the human brain? After all, we are made up almost entirely of water.'

The first part of this argument is quite correct. The gravitational forces that act between the Earth and the Moon (and indeed the Earth and the Sun) creates the effect of tides*. However, this is because we are dealing here with very large masses. There is no comparison between the gravitational effect between the Moon and such a small mass as a single human and that between the Moon and the entire planet Earth.

So, what other forces could we consider as candidates to explain the claims of the enthusiasts? Well there are actually very few. There is a force called the *tidal force* between any two objects. This is linked to gravitational forces, but the effect of distance between objects in calculating its influence is even greater, so this force would have even less impact upon us.

Aside from these possibilities there are the other three fundamental forces, the weak and strong nuclear forces and electromagnetism. But each of these operate over short distances compared with the force of gravity. The weak nuclear force is responsible for the decay of unstable nuclei, electromagnetism requires bodies to be charged for there to be any form of interaction between them and accounts for electrical interactions and a large proportion of chemical processes. The strong nuclear force operates between subatomic particles which are in the order of 10^{-12} cm apart and has infinitesimally small influence at any greater distances.

However, these problems have not stifled the creation of many imaginative ideas to explain how astrology could work. The exciting idea that there may be an explanation

---

* It is also interesting to note that there is such a thing as *land tides*, again caused by gravity. But, because these are created by the gravitational force between solids these are much weaker effects. It is also worth noting that the Moon presents the same face to the Earth at all times because of gravitational effects – the Earth being the larger body long ago 'despun' the Moon. This has happened to all large moons in the solar system.

for existence or meaning of life in the stars and the allure of finding how that could operate has even drawn some otherwise respectable scientists into the net.

Professor Peter Roberts, author of the book *The Message of Astrology*, has suggested that the human body can somehow act as a conduit for a mysterious form of what he describes as *resonant planetary interaction*. This is a pseudo-scientific term conjured up to describe what Roberts believes is the influence of planets acting via some mysterious force which travels across space using a wave with a frequency sympathetic with some sort of 'life-force' or energy within all of us. Unfortunately he does not explain where this resonance originates, how it operates or how it impacts on human beings using anything other than the vaguest terms. So in effect, it leads us nowhere. Roberts is joined by another scientist, an astronomer named Dr Percy Seymour, author of a New Age tract called *Astrology: The Evidence of Science*.

The problem is, this account is again terribly vague and takes us little further than the astrologers who talk about some strange energy coming from the planets and stars. Using similarly muddled ideas based upon the notion of resonant planetary interaction, Seymour even has the temerity to try to dismiss the scientific objection to talk of external forces emanating from the cosmos influencing us at birth. In a recent newspaper article, the journalist (who was clearly on the side of astrology) says: 'Trotted out by detracting scientists time and again, the standard objection [to any form of force such as gravity influencing our lives at the moment of birth] is that the magnetic resonance of the planet is so slight that it would be swamped by the electrical equipment in the hospital, or at home by the likes of storage heaters. By way of rebuttal, Dr Seymour proceeds as if ripping through a rather dim first-former's test paper. "Firstly bear in mind the old trick of an opera singer shattering a wine glass. It only works when the voice resonates at the same frequency as the atoms of the glass. So, in the hospital, there's no question of planetary resonance being swamped because the electrical equipment will be operating at different – that is, the 'wrong' – frequencies. If your radio is not tuned to a sole station, you won't hear it.""[1]

These are neat analogies, but this 'explanation' actually answers nothing and certainly is not an argument that rips through 'a rather dim first-former's test paper'. Dr Seymour assumes that the frequencies generated by the machinery nearby would be the 'wrong' frequencies, but how does he know? Where is the evidence? What single scrap of proof can he or any other enthusiast for astrology show to demonstrate irrefutably that there is a strange resonance that effects all our lives? Let alone at which frequency it operates. It is pure speculation – something I can only assume he would never allow in his official work as an astronomer.

Furthermore, what does 'magnetic resonance' really mean in the sense these authors use it? Has anyone ever noticed the work of this mysterious force other than when it acts on an atomic level during interactions between particles at the heart of a very useful laboratory devise called a *nuclear magnetic resonance spectrometer* (NMR)?

As Professor Seymour's description shows, magnetism is one other possible contender from the armoury of the enthusiast often used in an effort to define the force which is supposed to enable planetary influence. But again, magnetism is an incredibly weak force that only operates over short distances – try it yourself with a compass and a small bar magnet.

In reply to this, enthusiasts point to the fact that migratory birds are known to be able to navigate using the lines of magnetic force around the earth; why then, they argue, could magnetism not lie at the root of planetary influence in astrology? The answer is similar to that used to counter the astrologer's hijacking of Newton's law of gravitation. Migratory birds do not make interplanetary journeys! The lines of force which they mysteriously and fascinatingly employ are powerful magnetic lines of influence that are produced by the huge iron core of *our planet*. Besides, if astrologers really want to insist that there is some sort of magnetic effect at work, then that influence would be dominated overpoweringly by the magnetic field of the Earth itself. In a sense, this is analogous to the comparison between the influence of the midwife and the planets, the impact of the magnetic field of the Earth would be vastly greater than any intangible magnetic force that has somehow reached us from the other planets of the solar system.

This then is a summary of the ways enthusiasts of astrology suggest the planets could influence us and the counter-arguments of the scientists, but there is much more to the debate between science and astrology. Consider the use of experiment and the advances in astronomy during the past three hundred years.

Let us look at the first of these. What has been gleaned from scientific experiment?

The most famous attempt to quantify what the enthusiasts claim and to use statistical analysis in an attempt to reach conclusions about astrology comes from the work of the psychologist and statistician, Michel Gauquelin, who summarised his endeavours in a book called *Dreams and Illusions of Astrology*.[2]

Gauquelin was interested in the idea that celestial influence may, according to the believers, play a major role in the personality of individuals and decided to see if this was apparent by matching star signs to profession. To do this, he took the birth data of 576 members of the French Academy of Medicine. To his surprise, he found that, in what he considered to be a statistically significant number of cases, the individual's birth charts had either Mars or Saturn just risen (this is called the 'ascendant') or those planets were at that moment in the midpoint of the sky (the mid-heaven). To see if there really was anything in this, Gauquelin next repeated the process with a similar sample of professions chosen at random. He found no correlation between the birth charts and the careers these people had followed.

Now intrigued, Gauquelin followed the experiment through with other groups to see if there was an emerging pattern. He found what he claimed was a disproportionate number of sports champions who were 'Mars people', in other words, those who had that planet prominent in their birth charts. Meanwhile, he found that artists and writers tended to be dominated by the Moon, and that Jupiter was prominent in the natal data for military leaders, journalists and politicians.

Michel Gauquelin, who died in 1991, was never an advocate for astrology but came to the conclusion that there was some unknown scientific principle at work here, some odd link between humanity and the mathematics of nature. He certainly never subscribed to the view that the apparent connection he had stumbled upon was anything to do with the direct influence of these planets via some mysterious force operating over interplanetary space. Of course, the astrology fraternity has lionised Gauquelin and adopted him as one of their own. Time and again the man's findings are paraded as 'proof' that astrological principles are correct, that in fact we are mere creatures without any self will or independent thought.

The reaction of the scientific community has been to marginalise Gauquelin and today his results are treated with contempt. Some even refer to it using the jargonese term 'non-robust', which means it does not really stand up to intense scrutiny. And indeed, it would seem the reliability of his findings may be brought into question.

The subject of statistics is a notoriously slippery customer and many believe it can never be relied upon to show clear evidence for anything unless it is backed up with other experimental proof or independent analysis. One of the crucial aspects of the discipline of statistical analysis is the need for a correct *sample size*. What this means is that statistical analysis of anything is utterly useless unless enough material is involved in that analysis. For example, imagine we had no idea of the chance of obtaining a 'head' or a 'tail' when we toss a coin. We decide to find out, but we're in a hurry, so we can only toss the coin 10 times. As chance would have it, that day, we toss the coin and find that it lands 'heads' 7 times and 'tails' 3 times. We might then conclude (quite wrongly, of course) that the chances of heads is always 70% and tails, 30%.

A more rigorous experimenter, or statistical analyst, would spend a few days doing the same experiment and toss the coin say, 5,000 times. They would certainly obtain a very different result to their colleague and, within perhaps a one percent deviation, they would get 2,500 'heads' and 2,500 'tails', showing the probability of each to be 50%.

The only difference between these two experiments is the sample size. The same principle applies in any statistical analysis. If pollsters sampled ten people before an election they would almost certainly get a very different result to that obtained if they interviewed 100,000 voters the same day. The same applies with Gauquelin's work. In each of his studies he analysed the natal charts of about 500 people. This is not enough and would be considered an inadequate sample to give any truly meaningful result.

Furthermore, in the case of the first trial, he also allowed for four separate criteria – he matched medics with four planetary events: Mars in the ascendant or in mid-heaven and the planet Saturn in the ascendant or mid-heaven. This further reduces the significance of the results.

And this is not a trivial objection on the part of sceptical scientists. If paranormal investigators want to be taken seriously and want their claims to be accepted as supportable and verifiable, they have to stick to the same rigorous rules science applies to itself, or else their ideas remain mere speculation and guesswork. But even ignoring this, further doubt now falls upon Gauquelin's work because of more recent statistical analyses that contradict it. An analysis of 1 in 10 returns from the 1971 British census (some 3 million people) showed absolutely no correlation

between professions and star signs. Even more embarrass-
ingly for the believers of astrology, the then president of
the Astrological Association, Charles Harvey, made some
predictions before the results were published. He claimed
that most nurses would tend to be born under feminine signs,
while union leaders would have been born under masculine
ones. Professor Alan Smithers from Manchester University,
who studied the results, found that this was actually borne
out, but also announced that there was a disproportionate
number of miners born under Scorpio and Capricorn – both
feminine signs.

As a final piece of evidence in this debate, it is conveniently
forgotten that Gauquelin himself also produced results that
completely contradicted his initial findings. Based upon his
earlier findings, Gauquelin expected a test involving 2,000
army generals to show them to have a predisposition towards
the star sign Aries. In fact, the generals were found to have
been born within a random range of signs. Furthermore
it is significant that this time the sample was larger (and
therefore statistically more sound), and the test was based
upon linking a single rank with a single star sign.

Coupled with this is a very simple study which has looked
at the personalities of individuals who had all been born
at the same time in the same hospital. It was found that
each of them developed into quite different individuals
and pursued very different careers, married very different
people (themselves born under different star signs from
those predicted by astrology) and suffered different physical
illnesses.

More prosaic experiments have also produced very revealing
results. Analysts long ago noticed that many horoscopes contained a large number of very vague statements. Examples
include such waffle as: 'you have considerable hidden talent
that you have not yet used to your advantage' and 'while you
have some personality weaknesses, you are generally able
to compensate for them'. Critics of astrology have dubbed
such declarations 'Barnum statements' after the American

showman who coined the phrase 'there's one born every minute'.

Most strikingly, surveys have shown that when a sample of people are shown Barnum statements from horoscopes, 90% of them believe the statement applies to them and can link what is said in even the most crass tabloid horoscope to events in their lives or their hopes and aspirations. The fact that, on occasion, these horoscopes have been either deliberately fabricated or written by hard-pressed journalists makes no difference at all to the readers. One research scientist, Geoffrey Dean, has also noted that when horoscopes contain succinct, but slightly more specific, personality references such as: 'you have a good imagination', they are seen as less relevant to individuals reading them than the horoscopes full of Barnum statements.[3] The reason for this is clear: with a Barnum statement anyone can make of it what they will.

Other experiments have been, if anything, even more revealing. In a set of tests relating to his work on linking personality with properties of natal charts, Michel Gauquelin placed an advert in the magazine *Ici Paris* offering free horoscopes to anyone who responded to the ad. He received 150 requests and duly posted the horoscopes. He then followed this up by asking each applicant what they thought of the horoscope they had been sent. 94% of them said that they believed the horoscope accurately fitted their personality. What Gauquelin did not tell them was that they had received the same horoscope ... that of Dr Petroit, an infamous French mass murderer.

So much for experimental and statistical analysis of what astrology claims; but what of the so called 'science' of astrology. Here, I'm afraid, this arcane study again fails to deliver.

Firstly, we have to consider the fact that the constellations as we see them from earth are pictures primitive humans contrived in order to help them understand the universe a little better. The stars that make up these constellations are not really grouped together; indeed most are hundreds or thousands of light years apart and it is only from the perspective of someone here on earth that they seem to take on patterns such as the Plough or the Great Bear.

The second anomaly in the arguments put forward by astrologers is the matter of when exactly the mysterious 'astrological force' is supposed to take effect. Is it not obvious that in terms of impacting on the character of the embryonic human, the moment of conception would be far more significant than the moment of birth – the point at which this new human being simply leaves one environment to join another?

But, even if we ignore these problems, what is to be made of the fact that ancient astrology, which has remained ostensibly unchanged for many thousands of years, is based upon the premise that there are only six planets in our solar system? The ancients observed only Mercury, Venus, Mars, Jupiter and Saturn. The other three planets of the solar system have all been discovered during the past 250 years – Uranus was discovered by Sir William Herschel in 1781, Neptune in 1845 and the most distant planet, Pluto, was first observed as recently as 1930.

Astronomers point out that if these three planets were unknown, then surely all natal charts drawn up before 1930 were incorrect, even if the celestial influence claimed by astrologers is real. When questioned about this, astrologers become strangely tight-lipped. If anything, their most common response is to say that the discovery of these planets makes no difference. When pushed on the matter, the popular astrologer and author of many books on the subject, Linda Goodman has claimed intriguingly that 'a planet does not have any astrological influence until it is discovered.'[4] A statement one would have thought rather undermines the entire premise upon which astrology is built.

Clearly, astrology should not call itself a genuine science. Typically it played no role in the detection of Uranus, Neptune and Pluto and it has offered not a scrap of useful material towards the discovery of *anything* tangible.

In fact, many practitioners of astrology are proud of the fact that the central tenets of the subject are rooted in ancient understanding. Linda Goodman has stated: 'Alone among the sciences, astrology has spanned the centuries and made the journey intact. We shouldn't be surprised that it remains with us, unchanged by time – because astrology is truth – and truth is eternal.'[5]

Sadly for the enthusiast, astrology cannot be both 'a science' and 'unchanging'; the two are mutually exclusive. The essence of science is experiment and a willingness to question even long-established tenets of the subject. Without this, science would be a dead subject, as dead as astrology.

Two further points reinforce this view. Firstly, there is the matter of the planet 'Vulcan'. During the 1850s the co-discoverer of Neptune, Jean Joseph Leverrier, calculated that there should be another planet within the orbit of Mercury – the closest body to the Sun. He accounted for this by noting that the orbit of Mercury was not what would be expected if it was the only planet in the vicinity. We now know that there is no such planet as Vulcan and that the effect Leverrier had observed is actually a consequence of general relativity and not the presence of another celestial body within the orbit of Mercury. But this has not stopped astrologers getting it wrong again.

Perhaps because they had realised they had been wrong-footed over the discovery of Uranus, Neptune and Pluto, they overcompensated. Hearing about the imaginary planet Vulcan, it was quickly incorporated into their false science. Take for example Linda Goodman again, this time in her *Star-Signs* for 1968 (long after scientists had dispatched Vulcan to the land of Nod), 'It's important to mention here the still unseen planet Vulcan, the true ruler of Virgo, since its discovery is said to be imminent ... Many astrologers feel that Vulcan, the planet of thunder, will become visible through telescopes in a few years.'[6]

The final thing to consider in this discussion of the

foundations of astrology is the question of the relevance of the twelve star signs. Astronomers have long known of a phenomenon called *procession*. This is another name for 'wobble' and is exhibited by any rotating body. As the Earth rotates, it *processes*, which means that for observers on the Earth, the relative position of the Sun and the constellation changes over a period of a few centuries. Now of course, this relative position of the Sun to the constellations is the essence of astrology – a star sign is literally the constellation in which the Sun was positioned at the moment of birth. The constellations and the dates of the calendar were fixed 2000 years ago, giving us certain dates for certain star signs. For example, Sagittarians are born between November 23rd and December 21st.

But, during the past 2000 years, the relationship between the dates and the star signs has shifted by at least one star sign, so that Sagittarians are actually Scorpians, Aquarians are really born under Capricorn, and so on. What this means for the personality profiles which many astrologers gleefully link to star signs I'll leave the reader to wonder.

Astrologers ignore this latest blow to the art and claim it is irrelevant; which, if we needed any further proof, demonstrates that astrologers are certainly not scientists. Scientists do not ignore verifiable, repeatable experimental evidence.

Those astrologers willing to defend the issue do so by suggesting that the signs 'remember the influence of the constellations that corresponded to them two thousand years ago.'[7] But, how do these 'scientists' explain why it is that the old correspondence of constellations did not remember the relationship between stars and dates that would have existed longer ago than 2000 years? After all, the Earth did not start processing only two millennia in the past.

So, what are we to make of all this? Clearly, the scientist and, to be honest, anyone else who places their world view in the realm of reason and logic, observation and experience, cannot take astrology seriously. Putting aside the matter of how astrologers view themselves, how they delineate between what they like to believe are serious astrologers and commercially-minded pundits and hacks, there is no rational basis to astrology and it simply does not work. Despite what one's friend may claim after a few glasses of wine, there is absolutely nothing to astrology. The world does not operate in the way astrologers fantasise about. Our individual characters are moulded by two things – nature and nurture (genetics and environment).

And that is how the world should be. We have no need for anything more esoteric – genetics and environment (experience) are amazing enough in their own right and give the world all the variety, excitement and wonderful differentation we could ask for. Together, they give us a very colourful world full of individuals, good, bad, ugly and beautiful. With this, who needs astrology?

But, beyond even this is a set of ideas and facts far more inspiring than anything irrational astrologers can offer – 'real astrology'. For, yes, in one sense at least, we are linked to the heavens, but in a way no astrologer would have ever discovered or be able to explain.

The stars that fill the cosmos, the tiny furnaces we can see each clear night, were not all made at the same time. Some, like our Sun, are stars in their prime. Others are forming at this moment and there are many, many stars older than our Sun.

Some stars have long-since expired. When a star dies it can do so in different ways depending upon what type of star it was in the first place. Some swell up, then explode, spewing out vast quantities of matter and energy into the universe. These events are called *supernova* and they, in part, account for why we have a wide variety of different elements in nature. Some material from ancient supernova ended up in the gas ball that made our Sun, and the Earth was formed as a globule of plasma (super-hot gas) that broke away from the cooling sun some 4.5 billion years ago.

So, some material that had once been in another star

found its way into the material that made our earth. And, for all our grand ideas about ourselves, we are, in essence, the physical matter from which we are made, and we are made from elements and compounds derived from the Earth – we are all part of an ecosystem. Except that this ecosystem is not self-contained and restricted to the material that is within our immediate environment; there is a constant flux between the Earth and the Sun, the Earth and the creatures living here and between creatures on the Earth.

Inside you and me are atoms that were once in the heart of a star perhaps thousands of light years from earth. And one day, a tiny part of you or me, or the book you are reading, will find its way into the heart of another sun and from there to the body of an alien being, an alien book, perhaps even the equivalent of this full stop.

7

FIRE FROM THE SKY

'I would rather believe that Yankee professors lie than
that stones fall from heaven.'

Thomas Jefferson, 1807.

The wasteland of the Tunguska region of Siberia is only
sparsely populated today, but nearly a century ago its thousands of square miles was home to no more than a handful
of people. That is why, on a fresh June evening in 1908, there
were very few witnesses to the most powerful explosion in
modern times. That evening, an object about one hundred
metres in diameter and weighing around 100,000 tonnes
exploded some 6 km above the ground.

Of the few eyewitness accounts, most came from a trading
post seventy kilometres from the epicentre of the explosion.
One report reads: 'I was sitting on the porch of the house at
breakfast time and looking towards the north ... suddenly
the sky was split in two, and high above the forest the whole
northern part of the sky appeared to be covered with fire.'
Another eyewitness recounted: 'Suddenly before me I saw
the sky in the north open to the ground and fire pour out.
We were terrified, but the sky closed again and immediately
afterwards bangs like gunshots were heard. We thought that
stones were falling from the sky, and rushed off in terror,
leaving our pail by the spring.'[1]

No one really knows what the object was. The most likely

explanation is that it was the nucleus of a stray comet that had crossed the path of the Earth as we make our journey around the Sun. Another explanation is that it could have been a meteorite – a large chunk of rock, or possibly a small asteroid, that had originated in our solar system. There are even those who find it necessary to add this event to the UFO conspiracy theory and suggest it was a large alien craft that exploded that night.

Whatever it was, it caused enormous devastation. Estimates of the power of the explosion vary, but when the region was explored a few years later it was found that in a few seconds over 2000 square kilometres of forest – that's about the area of Greater London – had been totally obliterated. Seismographs around the world recorded the event and tremors were felt thousands of kilometres away on the other side of the continent. Estimates vary, but it is safe to say that the explosion was the equivalent of at least a twenty megaton bomb, or about 1000 times more powerful than the atomic device dropped on Hiroshima in 1945.

As it stands, the Tunguska Incident, as it is commonly known, serves as a warning for what could happen; and illustrates how, when it comes to collisions with extra-terrestrial objects, our fate as a race is in the lap of the Gods. But, as John and Mary Gribbin have pointed out in their study of near-earth collisions, *Fire On Earth*, we should not simply consider only the catastrophic outcome of such events. If the explosion at Tunguska had occurred 4000 kilometres to the west, in St Petersburg, human history may have been very different, for the population of the city would have been killed in an instant including in their number a young political activist, one Vladimir Ilyich Ulyanov-Lenin.

Thankfully, such events as the Tunguska Incident are very rare, but not so rare that we can all feel completely safe – we have experienced too many close encounters in recent decades to be complacent, and, according to some scientists, we should be doing more to protect ourselves. Just this century there have been at least five close calls – in 1937, 1968, 1989, 1993 and most recently in 1996. We have no defence system against the possibility of another such disaster and we remain wide open to impacts.

The energy released by such an explosion is truly awesome. It is an easy matter to calculate the energy contained in an approaching asteroid or comet. The material from which the object is made is irrelevant, its energy would be the same if it was made of ice, iron or French fries. The kinetic energy can be calculated using the equation:

$$K.E. = \tfrac{1}{2} MV^2$$

This is:

The kinetic energy of the object = ½ x the mass of the object (m) x its velocity (v) squared.

So, a relatively small object weighing a mere million tonnes (1,000,000,000 kg) and travelling at a leisurely 50,000 k.p.h. (14,000 metres per second) would produce:

K.E. = ½ x 1,000,000,000 x 14,000
K.E. = 7,000,000,000,000 Joules of energy.

That's seven thousand *billion* joules of energy, or the heat produced by a two-bar electric heater for every man, woman and child on Earth radiated from the point of impact in a fraction of a second ... And, such an object would be considered a small asteroid.

So far in recent years no meteorite, comet or asteroid has landed in a densely populated area, but as humanity spreads into almost all corners of the Earth, it is thought to be only a matter of time before a catastrophe greater than any earthquake, eruption or tidal wave could befall us. And, if the object was large enough it would not be a mere local disaster (a few million people killed), it could mean the end of civilisation itself.

The threat comes from three main sources – comets, meteorites and asteroids. Comets are celestial wanderers, but that does not mean they travel randomly around the universe. In fact, they follow very definite paths. Some, such as Halley's comet, travel through orbits around our sun that bring them back into the inner solar system with relative frequency – in the case of Halley's comet, every seventy-six years. Others have much longer orbits so they come round every few thousand or every few tens of thousands of years. It is these that could account for the many known close encounters the planet has experienced in the past. There is even a suggestion that there might be a gigantic 'doomsday' comet that has an orbit bringing it into the solar system after long intervals and may account for some of the great disasters of legend – the Biblical flood and the sinking of Atlantis to name but two.

Using current technology, such a comet could not be detected from Earth until it had approached within a few weeks journey time. The Hubble telescope may be able to detect such an object if we knew where to look, but at present it would be like trying to find a specific individual grain of sand on a beach – an impossibility.

Although comets have been observed since ancient times and astronomers since the eighteenth century have been able to plot the orbits of a few of them, it was not until the 1950s that a theory began to emerge describing their origin. There are two 'belts' or 'regions' where there are high concentrations of comets. The *Oort Cloud*, named after its discoverer, lies about 100,000 Astronomical Units (or AUs) from the Sun. An astronomical unit is the distance between the Sun and the Earth – 93 million miles. The Oort Cloud is thought to contain several billion comets, most of which stay within the vague limits of the belt and travel at only a few hundred kilometres per hour. During the long history of our planet, one of these comets has occasionally strayed much closer and entered the inner solar system.

Another belt begins close to the orbit of one of the outer planets of the solar system, Neptune, and stretches outwards to about 100 AU. This belt contains an estimated billion comets and may account for many more of those that stray close to the Earth from time to time.

Comets mainly comprise of a chunk of ice and frozen carbon dioxide, ammonia and methane, along with grit and dust. The mass is concentrated in the nucleus and as the comet approaches the Sun and warms up, some of the nucleus sublimes and forms a gaseous tail.

The second type of extraterrestrial object to cause trouble are meteorites. These are just chunks of rock which sometimes contain organic matter. As they hurtle through space they are known as 'meteors' and only acquire the name 'meteorite' when they enter the atmosphere. Like all celestial objects, as they approach the Sun and come under its gravitational influence, they take up a regular orbit. If this orbit crosses that of the Earth then the meteor may enter the atmosphere and if it is large enough, it will survive the huge heat generated upon entry, and may reach the ground.

Scientists estimate that something in the region of 75 million meteors of different sizes enter the Earth's atmosphere each year. Most of these are tiny, grain-sized pieces of rock that burn up very quickly. But between 1975 and 1992 there were 136 airbursts caused by meteors several metres across. All of these exploded before they reached the ground but if they had survived the heat and reached the ground intact they would have been powerful enough to devastate a town or part of a city. And, once in a while a far larger object will cross our orbit around the Sun and the resulting meteorite has the potential to be a 'city-crusher' or even a 'civilisation-killer'.

But, more worrying than meteorites are asteroids. Like comets, asteroids lie in a belt, but their orbits are generally far closer to us than those of comets. The asteroid belt is concentrated between Mars, which occupies an orbit with an average distance of about 85 million kilometres from Earth (200 times the distance between the Earth and the Moon), and

Jupiter which orbits the Sun at a distance of about 550 million kilometres from Earth, and contains several million asteroids. But of more relevance to those worried about near-Earth encounters, there are almost one hundred asteroids, called the *Apollo asteroids*, known to occupy a region far from the main belt, and many of these intersect the orbit of the Earth.

New asteroids are being discovered all the time but most are relatively small. Although there are only a few larger than one hundred kilometres in diameter, around half a million are more than one kilometre across – certainly large enough to cause widespread devastation on earth.

So, having reviewed the sort of objects that can come into close contact with the Earth, what has happened in the past to suggest that we may be in danger from these things in the future?

The most famous example of a collision site is the Barringer Crater in Arizona in the United States. This is a massive hole 1200 metres wide and 180 metres deep that was produced about 25,000 years ago by a meteorite or a small asteroid sixty metres wide and weighing around a million tons. The explosion that produced the hole would have been of about the same power as the explosion at Tunguska. But rather than it being a twenty megaton air burst, this was a twenty megaton ground-level explosion.

The Barringer Crater is one scar among many on earth. The evidence of meteorite and asteroidal collisions is to be seen everywhere in the solar system – the craters of the Moon and similar marks on the surface of all the inner planets have been produced over aeons of time when meteors, undiminished by their surfaces burning away in an atmosphere have created vast impact marks. On Earth, many meteorites and asteroids have landed in the sea and left marks thousands of feet below the surface of the ocean. It has been suggested that many 'rim' features have been caused by collisions. Examples include huge 'pockmarks' like the Wash in Eastern England, the Gulf of Tarentum in the heel of Italy and the vast Hudson Bay in Canada.

However, the most important collision in history may have been one which occurred sixty-five million years ago and precipitated the extinction of the dinosaurs, allowing mammals to become the dominant species – opening the evolutionary road for *Homo sapiens*.

The notion that the dinosaurs may have become extinct because of a collision between the Earth and a large celestial object had been considered for some time but there was no hard evidence for it, it was merely a neat idea. Then, in 1978, oil prospectors discovered a massive geological structure 4000 feet beneath the Gulf of Mexico called the Chicxulub structure. This crater dwarfs Barringer and analysis of what may have caused it and the effects it had, makes for chilling reading. The sixty-five million-year-old Chicxulub structure is 110 miles across. Reaching out from the centre are ripples of solid rock deposited there by the impact, and around the Gulf are to be found large deposits of minerals commonly associated with meteors; in particular there are high concentrations of the element iridium. These mineral deposits would have been dumped on the Mexican shoreline by a tidal wave the height of the World Trade Centre in New York – over 1300 feet.

The fact that the meteorite that caused the impact crater at Chicxulub landed in the sea would actually have made little difference to its destructive power. If you think about the dimensions of the oceans it becomes clear that from the perspective of an incoming meteor, the oceans and the seas are a wafer-thin covering and they would make little difference to the power of the collision. The tidal effects would also be a secondary destructive force after the initial impact.

The probable scenario that destroyed the dinosaurs began with such a monumental impact. The shock would have jolted the planet on its path around the Sun, but even such a tremendous explosion would have caused only a relatively minor orbital disturbance. The greatest damage would have been caused by the fact that dust and water vapour thrown into the atmosphere by the force of the collision would have altered the climate of the planet. The actual effect would have been a shift of perhaps only a few degrees in temperature, but this would have been enough to wipe out many cold-blooded species, most especially the lumbering dinosaurs.

Geologists describe five major extinctions in the history of the Earth – what they dub 'the Big Five'. The extinction of the dinosaurs was the most recent and it is suspected that some earlier known extinctions were also precipitated by similar catastrophes.

In more recent times there have been some serious catastrophes that seem to have been initiated by collisions between the Earth and extraterrestrial objects. One astronomer who specialises in asteroidal and meteorite collisions, Duncan Steel of the Anglo-Australian telescope in New South Wales has pointed out that: 'On average there is one impact capable of causing global catastrophe with a very large fraction of humankind perishing about once every 100,000 years.'[2]

It is no mere idle speculation to suggest that asteroidal or comet impacts could have caused the destruction of at least one ancient civilisation even if evidence for such events are circumstantial. One example is the destruction of Mycenaean civilisation, the precursors of the Greek city states. An account of the destruction comes down to us from Solon, a lawgiver of sixth-century BC Athens via the historian Plutarch. Solon described the destruction of the Mycenaeans as having: '. . . the air of a fable, but the truth behind it is a deviation of the bodies that revolve in heaven round the Earth and a destruction of things on earth by a great conflagration. Once more, after the usual period of years, the torrents from heaven swept down like a pestilence . . .'[3]

Although this could be dismissed as romantic fiction of the time, there are actually several pertinent points in this brief passage. The notion of a 'deviation of the bodies that revolve in heaven' shows a remarkable grasp of celestial mechanics because although it is not necessarily a 'deviation' that causes a collision, more a crossing of paths, the essence of what happens is there in the description. Perhaps more significant is the last sentence beginning: 'Once more, after the usual period of years . . .' Not only does this show that the ancient Greeks had some understanding of the idea that meteorite showers and the passage of comets across the skies follow a regular pattern and reappeared at intervals, but that other catastrophes dating back further than the destruction of Mycenaean culture could have been attributed to similar conflagrations. The entire notion of cyclical disaster is a strong thread in many ancient texts including the Bible. This could be accounted for by superimposing quite natural climatic and even seasonal rhythms upon the development of civilisations and their ability to ride out lean times, but this pattern could also be attributed to a long record of disasters precipitated by 'fire from the sky'.

Moving closer to our own time are the events of the mid-fifth century. In their book *The Cosmic Winter*, authors Victor Clube and Bill Napier suggest that there was a series of disasters between the fifth and sixth centuries that wiped out cities and killed tens of thousands. They suggest that the period, prominent in legend as the time of Arthur and the Knights of the Round Table, is remarkably lacking in lasting chronicles. This is particularly odd because the period immediately preceding it – the departure of the Romans from Britain – is extremely well documented and the era after Arthur is equally well covered by historians including the Venerable Bede who wrote the *Ecclesiastical History*.

Tales from the Arthurian period were first brought to general attention by Thomas Malory writing in the fifteenth century with his *Le Morte d'Arthur*, whereas a chronicler who would have been a contemporary of Arthur, one Gildas, who wrote a treatise called *The Ruin of Britain*, did not even mention the man who was supposed to be the king of a significant portion of what soon after became England.

The supposition is that Arthur did not actually exist but was created by the writers of the time to give the public some good news to counteract the catastrophes that were befalling them. And the times were indeed hard. There are several accounts of major catastrophes involving what we would attribute to collisions with celestial objects. From Gildas we have: 'The fire of righteous vengeance, kindled by the sins of the past, blazed from sea to sea. Once lit it did not lie down. When it had wasted town and country, it burned up the whole surface of the island until its red and savage tongue licked the western shore. All the greater towns fell. Horrible it was to see the foundation stones of towers and high walls thrown down bottom upward in the squares, mixing with the high alters and fragments of human bodies.'[4] And from contemporaneous Chinese chroniclers we have an account of a destructive comet that caused 'the Sun to become dim', and created a darkness that 'lasted for eighteen months'.[5] At the very time Arthur was meant to be fighting his battles for supremacy over England, in some regions of China eighty percent of the population were dying and the capital of the Northern empire, the Wei civilisation, was deserted in the year 534 AD.

Moving forward in time to the twentieth century there have been several frighteningly close encounters. In 1937 an asteroid called Hermes, a chunk of rock weighing some 400 million tons and travelling at an estimated 80,000 k.p.h., missed us by a little under 750,000 kilometres. That may sound a safe enough distance but it is only about twice as far as the Moon. If the asteroid had struck you would not have ended up reading this, because the impact would have had the force of 20,000 megatonnes of TNT or one million Hiroshimas, producing a crater thirteen kilometres in diameter.

In 1968, another asteroid, Icarus, passed within 6.4 million kilometres – still in our own backyard. In February 1989 a similar object to Hermes passed within a million kilometres of our planet. When this asteroid was discovered by Dr Henry Holt, an astronomer working with the gigantic Mount Palomar optical telescope in California, he was quoted as saying: 'If this one had appeared only a few hours earlier, it would have nailed us.'[6] This is absolutely accurate: the impact would have occurred because the orbit of the Earth would have been crossed by the trajectory of the asteroid. If the rock had travelled a little slower, or if its trajectory was only slightly different, it would have arrived at the same point in space as the Earth at the exact same moment – with catastrophic global consequences.

Four years after this close encounter, in 1993, there was an even closer and potentially even more deadly one. An asteroid, estimated to be between ten and fifteen kilometres wide, passed within 140,000 kilometres, half the distance to the Moon. A collision with such a monster would have almost certainly have meant the end of civilisation. An object this large would have made a crater fifty kilometres wide and thrown trillions of tonnes of dust into the atmosphere. The few who would have survived the impact, the aftershocks and earthquakes would have been subjected to a 'cosmic winter' lasting many years.

And there has been another since then. In May 1996 a meteorite some 1200 metres in diameter passed us at a distance of 400,000 kilometres, a little beyond the orbit of the Moon. Travelling at an estimated 85,000 k.p.h., its impact would have been the equivalent to the detonation of several hundred thousand Hiroshimas.

These close encounters are not only terrifying because of the fact that the objects involved came so close, perhaps even more disturbing is the fact that none of them were observed before they arrived in our region of space. In relative terms these asteroids and meteors are tiny pinpricks of rock hurtling through space at tens of thousands of kilometres per hour so they are virtually impossible to track and appeared as if from nowhere and completely without warning. It is a chilling thought that if one day such an object does arrive at a point in space at precisely the same moment as the Earth, we will not know about it until it happens.

So, what are the real chances of such an event? Are we worrying unnecessarily or is it something that we should take seriously? Statistics are often suspect and applying them to this problem is every bit as flawed as trying to judge the outcome of elections or guessing the flow of lottery numbers over a year of draws, but at present there is little else we can do. It might come as a surprise to learn that, statistically, any one of us is more likely to die from the consequences of a collision between the Earth and a celestial body than in an air crash or a usual natural disaster such as an earthquake or a flood. But, how sound is the reasoning that gives us this result?

I mentioned earlier that statistics show that, on average, there is an impact capable of causing a global catastrophe every 100,000 years. No one can say for certain when the last big one occurred. The Barringer Crater was caused by a relatively small impact 25,000 years ago. If it occurred today it would not be the end of civilisation but would probably kill millions of people. The same can be said for the comet collision in Siberia in June 1908. An impact that has caused a mass extinction has not occurred since the monumental event that destroyed the dinosaurs, sixty-five million years ago. So, taking one line of reasoning we are certainly living on borrowed time. But, as the astronomer Duncan Steel has pointed out: 'These objects do not follow timetables like buses, so the question "When was the last one?" is of no significance. All we can say is that the probability of a catastrophic impact is one in 100,000 per annum.'[7] What bumps up the statistics to make death by asteroid more likely than other more prosaic means is the fact that when these impacts do occur they are totally devastating. So, although they are mercifully very rare, collisions between the Earth and large celestial objects are all-embracing.

But, how real does this make the danger? The answer to that depends upon how you view statistics. The fact that there is more chance of an asteroid destroying civilisation on Saturday night than you or I winning the national lottery that evening is one way of looking at it. On the other hand, the fact that we have not had a civilisation-killer collision for sixty-five million years perhaps means our luck will hold out for many more millions of years.

Recently, a growing number of scientists have begun to think there may be a very real danger from asteroids and comets. Questions have been raised in Congress in the US and in Parliament in Great Britain and committees and groups have been organised to investigate the phenomenon.

In Britain, an army officer, Major Jay Tate, has compiled a report on the question of near-Earth objects and comet encounters and there are plans to establish a small investigative team to look into the phenomenon and to compile a report suggesting possible practical solutions.

An international group called Spacewatch, created to monitor observable objects, concluded that there were hundreds of times more asteroids crossing Earth's orbit than was suspected prior to a survey they conducted in 1991. These asteroids, they claim, are part of Earth's own mini-asteroid belt – a group of asteroids that orbit the Sun following relatively erratic paths but within a few million miles of the course of our planet.

David Morrison, who was one of the founders of the Spacewatch programme, firmly believes that governments must investigate the problem of Earth collisions and set in motion some form of protective system. After an exhaustive study of the phenomenon and a workshop held at NASA in 1992, Morrison and his colleagues proposed a scheme called the Spaceguard Survey. Their plan is to utilise a network of six new ground-based telescopes each with an aperture of 2.5 metres – about half the size of the huge telescope at Mount Palomar (which was until recently the largest in the world). These telescopes would be able to plot the course of all celestial objects within the inner solar system and afford a warning time of a few months. The scheme would cost no more than $50 million to establish and have running costs of up to $10 million per year.

Perhaps it should come as little surprise that when the Spaceguard scientists took the idea to Congress they received short shrift. The warning time – a mere few months – was the sticking point. For Congressmen without technical know-how and living with a heavy burden of complacency, such protection was as good as useless.

This decision was, many believe, misguided. Any warning, they say, is better than nothing and the cost would be equivalent to a small fraction of a dollar per US citizen, per year – a tiny percentage of what most people spend on life insurance. But at present, the scheme remains ignored, with the US government vouchsafing a paltry $500,000 per year to investigate the phenomenon. This, Morrison points out, leaves the study of near-earth objects (NEOs) conducted by 'fewer people than it takes to run a single McDonald's'.[8]

It is possible to see where the scepticism derives and why those holding the purse strings are less than impressed by the potential dangers. To a politician, the short term is everything. He or she may have a niggling fear for themselves and their descendants over the issue of whether there is a real danger from extraterrestrial objects, but the demands of balancing the books and getting re-elected override these.

There is also a degree of 'techno-complacency' in all of us. We are the dominant species on planet Earth. We have constructed a great civilisation, we can put humans on the Moon, live in space for months, conquer most diseases, generate energy from the fundamental particles of which the universe is made – how could we possibly be obliterated by a lump of rock? Deep in the hearts of most people, especially those without the benefit of a scientific or technical training, is the conviction that we are indestructible, that somehow our technology could cope with such an event. The brutal fact is: the last close encounter came like a bolt out of the blue, unnoticed until it had skimmed past us.

Hard as it may be to accept, we could do absolutely nothing about an object that was on collision course with us unless we had at least a year to prepare. There have been suggestions that the human race could turn the nuclear weapons we once pointed at each other towards space to create a genuine 'space guard' against incoming objects. That may be feasible one day but there are no plans to use the stockpile of weapons left over from the Cold War in this way just yet. Others have talked vaguely about using a form of 'Star Wars' weaponry to defend ourselves. That again would be feasible within a few years given endless supplies of cash and manpower. The Star Wars Project was halted during a Republican administration with the Cold War still very chilly. It is hardly likely that it would be resurrected to fight an invisible enemy which may not present any tangible danger for millions of years. If the US government cannot be persuaded to part with a relatively trivial sum to create Spaceguard, as already proposed by Morrison and his colleagues, then neither they nor any other power would be inclined to spend a substantial percentage of their GNP on a defence system against asteroids and comets.

So, this is where we find ourselves today. Many believe there is a real threat from space, others dismiss the danger and point to far more pertinent problems – world famine, disease, illiteracy, AIDS, wars and other relatively frequent natural disasters. Perhaps one day the human race will be lucky enough to experience a near-miss so tangible that governments are shaken out of their complacency and made to realise the potential horrors. Until then, we just have to sit with our fingers crossed, and hope our luck holds out.

8

OUR BRETHREN AMONG THE STARS?

'Evolution is the law of policies: Darwin said it,
Socrates endorsed it, Cuvier proved it and established
it for all time in his paper on 'The Survival of the
Fittest'. These are illustrious names, this is a mighty
doctrine: nothing can ever remove it from its firm
base, nothing dissolve it, but evolution.'

Mark Twain, *Three Thousand Years Among the Microbes.*

To many people, scientists and non-scientists, the question of whether or not there is life on other planets is one worth little consideration. To them the answer is clear: 'Yes, of course there is life in great abundance – we live in a universe over-brimming with all manner of alien beings.'

In this chapter, I want to start with the assumption (false or otherwise) that this is true and to move onward, to an investigation of what forms alien life might take and what we now understand could govern the evolution of extraterrestrial life.

This is a legitimate area of scientific study and one pursued daily by genuine, salaried scientists, men and women who call themselves exobiologists.

What we know of alien life is, of course, based upon pure conjecture but guided by the laws of science we already understand and apply regularly to more common matters.

The only model we have is life on Earth, for this is the only world we are sure harbours life. This is of course a limitation, and we will not know whether the theories of the exobiologists are even close until we encounter other life in the universe in one form or another. But I think anyone who has reached this far in the book will agree that the exploration of this subject is at the very least great fun and may lead to some interesting ideas.

To cover this subject we need to ask the questions exobiologists ask and try to formulate sensible answers based upon the very latest information available. To do this we will need to bring together a collection of disparate disciplines, just as exobiologists do, and try to sift ideas to see whether they are 'right' or 'wrong'. Sadly, we will not be able to reach any definite conclusions, just probabilities based upon what is presently known.

The first question we need to ask is the most fundamental of all: what is life?

At a glance, the answer might seem obvious. But actually, 'life' is a tremendously difficult concept to define.

We can start by suggesting that all living things grow and move, but this does not help much. Crystals grow, producing regular patterns and repeated simple units which might be compared to cells; any liquid can flow. So, in themselves, these abilities are not enough to distinguish between animate and inanimate, or living and non-living.

Perhaps a more sophisticated answer is to say that all life uses energy. But this too is inadequate. All machines use energy. A slightly more useful definition might be to say that all living beings can *control* energy; but then so do some advanced machines such as those developed in recent years that use 'intelligent' software.

Is the argument that only living things process and store information an alternative? The answer is 'no', because this is exactly what even the simplest word processor does.

So, how can we pin down the quintessential factors that separate living things from inanimate objects?

Using the old-fashioned school-book definition – that all living things exhibit the three 'f''s – fight, flight and frolic – leads us into further difficulties. Lightning might be seen as capable of 'flight' – it is repelled by certain matter and attracted by others – and the word 'frolic' really means 'to reproduce', which is certainly not limited to living things; after all, flames 'reproduce', as do certain types of crystal.

A much better definition is to say that all living things reproduce *and pass on genetic material* or inherited characteristics to their offspring and that this material has undergone some degree of mutation. In other words, they have taken part in the evolutionary process via natural selection, they haven't simply produced exact copies of themselves. But perhaps the final word on the matter should go instead to the late Carl Sagan who, shortly before his death, defined life as '. . . any system capable of reproduction, mutation and the reproduction of its mutations'.[1] What he meant by this was that life was represented by any entity that allows for variation from generation to generation using the mechanism of evolution via natural selection, an entity that can pass on its characteristics, reshuffled by the processes of reproduction so that those characteristics will not appear to be exactly the same in the next generation.

But even this is actually not a totally satisfactory definition for several reasons, not least of which is the question of whether a cloned creature (which was produced without sexual reproduction and is a pefect copy of its parent) is actually alive. Dolly the sheep looks very much alive, but would not fit the above definition.

So, if we want to move on in this exploration we have to accept a definition which links life with the ability to reproduce via a mechanism that allows for mutation. This is because the only way we know that life can evolve is via this route. Dolly the sheep may be a fully functioning sheep that can do anything any other sheep can do, but she and any descendants produced via cloning will play no role in the evolutionary development of the species of which she is a member, although her naturally-produced ancestors could of course.

So, it is clear that evolution and life are linked. Indeed, any biologist would support the idea that without evolution there can be no life. So, whether that life is on Earth or a planet orbiting Sirius, evolution will be a fundamental process steering life there.

So, how would evolution work on an alien planet?

Well we cannot be sure, but it would seem likely it would operate in the same way it does on Earth. And to understand this, we have to explore the link between evolution and genetics.

Evolution relies upon a complex series of operations involving gigantic organic molecules such as DNA (deoxyribonucleic acid) and RNA (ribonucleic acid) commonly known as 'the molecules of life' and a set of smaller building blocks, molecules called nucleotides, that go to form these massive structures as well as the proteins, enzymes and some other biochemicals needed to run cells and sustain our existence.

But do we not have to go back even further? To begin with, how do we know that life on other planets is based upon DNA or even reliant upon the element carbon?

Well, of course, at some point we have to make some assumptions. If we keep questioning at every level we hit a wall of incomprehension and can go no further. So, to avoid this we have to apply some basic principles. Scientists accept that there are certain fundamental axioms – concepts and theories that seem to lie at the heart of the universe. The theory of relativity appears to be one of these, Darwinian evolution is another. A still more fundamental concept is what is called the 'principle of universality', or the idea that the universe is homogeneous. Put into everyday terms this could be translated as 'what happens here, happens there'.

How do we know this is true? Well, one example is that we can observe distant stars from Earth and determine that the chemicals present in those stars are the same as those we find on Earth and present in our own star – the Sun (but in different proportions).

So where does this lead us in our exploration of the laws governing alien biology?

Firstly we have to clear up what we mean by alien life. The chances are there is an infinite variety of alien life forms in the universe. There may well be many ways in which life could develop and change. It would seem likely that some form of mechanism always has to allow for evolution or else the life form could not develop, but it is conceivable that this life form may not be based upon DNA. If this was the case, it is equally probably that we would not recognise such life forms and would almost certainly not be able to communicate with them. Therefore, I would like to leave this possibility and restrict this chapter to an exploration of DNA-based life.

For life to have evolved in a recognisable form, it would almost certainly be based upon the element carbon, which would then allow for a biological framework involving DNA and therefore a system involving evolution via natural selection (Darwinian evolution). This is a limitation, but as we know from living on Earth where all life forms are carbon-based, it still offers the potential for a massive diversity of life.

So, why carbon? Thanks to the principle of universality we can safely say that carbon is the only element that will lie at the centre of a biological system yielding life as we know it. The reason for this is that carbon possesses unique properties. In many ways it is very similar to any other element, but in one vital respect it is different to any other atom – it is the only known atom which can form the backbone of really large molecules, called *organic* molecules, and even larger conglomerates called *biochemicals*. It also has an almost unique ability to form long chains and rings of atoms around which other atoms can be attached. I say 'almost', because other atoms can form chains and rings but they do not show anything like the versatility of carbon. The best example of this is silicon, which shares some of the characteristics of carbon, but because the bonds formed between silicon atoms are not so strong as those between carbon atoms, it can only form stable chains up to five or six atoms in length and is unable to form multiple bonds or cyclic structures, which carbon finds easy.

Because of these facts, carbon is unique. It is the only atom able to form huge molecules – the building blocks of life.

And, because of the principle of universality, we know that this is true not only here in our local environment but is a fact of life everywhere in the observable universe. We know that there cannot be another atom like carbon. There are no elements we have inadvertently overlooked, because such an element would not fit into what is called the periodic table – a scheme in which all the different types of atom in the universe have a strict position and interconnect in a precise pattern. This periodic table, devised over a century ago by a Russian chemist named Dmitri Ivanovich Mendeleyev, allocates a position for all the elements and it is inconceivable that some odd element perhaps found only in the Horsehead Nebula could be squeezed in. Over the decades since it was first established, all the gaps in the periodic table have been filled, and scientists have added elements at the end of the table (unstable and very short-lived atoms found only in extreme situations such as the heart of a nuclear process) but they could never discover any other previously unknown element that somehow fits into the middle of the scheme. (See fig 8.1.)

So, the point of this diversion is to establish that carbon is the only atom that can form molecules large enough to act as 'the molecules of life' – the enormous structures such as DNA (deoxyribonucleic acid) and RNA (ribonucleic acid), or even the smaller building blocks, the nucleotides that go to form these massive structures, and the proteins, enzymes and other biochemicals needed to run cells and sustain our existence. And, because of the homogeneous nature of the universe, this is the case both 'here' and 'there'.

These biochemicals lay at the heart of genetics and are linked with the meat of the discussion in this chapter –

the question of evolution. But, how does genetics link with evolution?

At the start of this chapter we reached a definition for 'life' as a system which can reproduce and pass on mutated information from generation to generation or a commodity involved with evolutionary change via natural selection. Evolution works via reproduction.

However, this creates what seems on the surface to be a chicken and egg scenario. Consider the facts: the genetic code is carried by DNA, but, if the ability to undergo evolution is a requirement of 'life' and this process itself requires an elaborate set of processes involving DNA, how did 'life' originate in the first place? To put it another way: any entity that can evolve (or by our definition be 'alive') has to be complex enough to possess the genetic material with which it can evolve. But how could an organism reach this level of complexity without evolving?

Group / Period	I	II											III	IV	V	VI	VII	0
1							1 H											2 He
2	3 Li	4 Be											5 B	6 C	7 N	8 O	9 F	10 Ne
3	11 Na	12 Mg											13 Al	14 Si	15 P	16 S	17 Cl	18 Ar
4	19 K	20 Ca	21 Sc	22 Ti	23 V	24 Cr	25 Mn	26 Fe	27 Co	28 Ni	29 Cu	30 Zn	31 Ga	32 Ge	33 As	34 Se	35 Br	36 Kr
5	37 Rb	38 Sr	39 Y	40 Zr	41 Nb	42 Mo	43 Tc	44 Ru	45 Rh	46 Pd	47 Ag	48 Cd	49 In	50 Sn	51 Sb	52 Te	53 I	54 Xe
6	55 Cs	56 Ba	57* La	72 Hf	73 Ta	74 W	75 Re	76 Os	77 Ir	78 Pt	79 Au	80 Hg	81 Tl	82 Pb	83 Bi	84 Po	85 At	86 Rn
7	87 Fr	88 Ra	89** Ac															

* Lanthanide series	58 Ce	59 Pr	60 Nd	61 Pm	62 Sm	63 Eu	64 Gd	65 Tb	66 Dy	67 Ho	68 Er	69 Tm	70 Yb	71 Lu
** Actinide series	90 Th	91 Pa	92 U	93 Np	94 Pu	95 Am	96 Cm	97 Bk	98 Cf	99 Es	100 Fm	101 Md	102 No	103 Lw

The fundamental problem comes down to the question: How could simple amino acids that were probably around in the primeval soup on Earth some four billion years ago have changed into what we see as *biological material* or the simple living matter that then evolved into more advanced forms, and eventually, us?

We are not so much concerned with the second part of this question – the grand sweep from single-celled organisms to twenty-first-century humans. For the purposes of this discussion it is the change from non-living or what is called *prebiotic* material to living cells that lies at the core of the problem, the jump from unorganised RNA to a bacterium.

There are two theories that attempt to explain how this occurred. The first of these is the *RNA-world hypothesis*. This suggests that somehow a small quantity of a type of RNA was produced on the early Earth which had the ability to perform a number of roles on top of the functions it demonstrates today. The RNA that is postulated would have been able to replicate (make copies of itself) without the presence of protein (presumably it would use some of the protein within its own structure) and would also be able to catalyse every step of the protein production process.

This may seem unlikely, but recently scientists have found molecules called *ribozymes* which are RNA catalysts or enzymes made from RNA. However, these molecules are still some way from RNA that could have self replicated.

The other contesting theory to explain the jump from prebiotic to biological material is that of biologist A. Graham Cairns-Smith of the University of Glasgow, who suggests that the organic agents that lead to the formation of living things actually evolved from inorganic materials.

Now, this may seem rather startling. After all, to most of us there is a vast difference between organic and inorganic materials. All living things are organic – the food we consume, the animals and plants that fill the planet. Inorganic materials include the rocks and stones, the gases that constitute our atmosphere, things generally deemed 'inanimate'.

Cairns-Smith points out that, like the biochemical system using DNA and RNA, complex *in*organic systems are capable of replicating and passing on information, albeit in a very much simpler way. In the system that operates in the modern biosphere, DNA carries a code in the form of an almost unimaginably complex set of instructions that is the blueprint for reproduction, whilst RNA and the proteins play their respective roles in bringing this about. What Cairns-Smith proposes is that around four billion years ago a simpler system operated which initially did not need RNA, DNA, or even proteins.

In his system, the first step was to produce what he calls a *low tech* set of machinery using crystal structures present in clays. These clays, although far less complex than a DNA molecule, can create a self-replicating system in which information is passed on from one 'layer' to another, mirroring the way DNA replicates.

From this low tech start, Cairns-Smith supposes that a gradually more complex system evolved which incorporated organic molecules. These unsophisticated systems developed over time into the *high tech* machinery we have today in which DNA, RNA and proteins facilitate genetics and allow the evolution of living things via natural selection.

So, this then leads us some way towards a model for how life may have begun on Earth and would probably do equally well for any DNA-based life form on other worlds throughout the universe. But given these possible mechanisms for how life began, how would life on other worlds have developed? Could we expect biological processes to have gone along a similar route to the way they operated here? And, if so, would it lead to human-type beings or very different creatures?

To find answers we must turn to the discipline of *developmental biology*. This is really a blend of several linked fields – evolutionary biology, palaeontology and genetics – which considers the way in which creatures on Earth have evolved from simple forms dating back billions of years to the fauna and flora of today.

Developmental biologists start with two other disciplines from biology. Firstly, they need to consider *genetic retracing*, which involves analysing how genetic material has changed over long periods. Genetic characteristics are of course one of the key factors in determining the nature and diversity of life and it is possible to trace back the way genetic material has altered both within species and across different species. In this way, biologists can reach conclusions about common ancestors of modern species and this can lead to a 'family tree' dating back many hundreds of millions of years. The other approach is *evolutionary biology* which looks at the range of modern animal structures, or the 'body plans' of animals – the fundamental groupings of different animal types we see all around us. From these it is possible to work backwards using computer models to determine the original plans.

Neither of these techniques is straightforward. Evolutionary biologists use powerful computer models that utilise a vast collection of parameters – information gained from paleontological and archaeological finds to try to determine how 'function' ties in with 'design', and how organisms have adapted to their environment. Genetic retracing is a complex science because genes (like species) evolve at different rates and the evolutionary lines can branch in elaborate ways.

Life probably first appeared on Earth around 3.85 billion years ago and although we are not sure how the change from prebiotic material to 'living' organisms occurred, it is clear that once it did, life flourished and evolved on this planet. But, it was certainly no simple development.

Until about 530 million years ago, the most complex form of life on Earth was an organism no more advanced than simple algae. Even then, algae were new arrivals. For the 2.85 billion years leading up to this point, life on this planet consisted of single-celled organisms such as bacteria. About one billion years ago the first very simple multi-cellular creatures, the algae, appeared for the first time. Then, about 550 million years ago, during what is called the *Neoproterozoic era*, more advanced organisms began to appear. These simple creatures probably resembled modern-day sea pens, jellyfish, primitive worms and slug-like animals all of which have left faint fossil remains and markings.

But then suddenly, around 530 million years ago, there was a complete and in a geological sense 'sudden' change in the evolutionary development of life on Earth. Throughout the Neoproterozoic period, the Earth had been populated by animals which displayed a relatively small collection of different body plans, but suddenly everything changed. Within a short space of time the Earth was populated by a vast range of different creatures.

This transformation is called the *Cambrian explosion*, a burst of activity in the life of the fauna of this planet. Before it, the Earth was home to only relatively few simple organisms, after it, Earth was populated with organisms that, although still simple, evolved into almost every known type of shelled invertebrates (clams, snails and arthropods). In time these gave rise to modern vertebrates, then mammals, and humankind.

Most importantly for this discussion, after the Cambrian explosion all the basic body plans of all animals on Earth had been established. From that point on, all evolutionary steps, (including what some consider one of the most dramatic – the point at which some animals left the sea to live on land), merely required subtle refinements of the basic animal types established during the Cambrian explosion.

Staggeringly, this single dramatic change in the history of life on Earth produced just thirty-seven distinct body plans that account for absolutely every animal on the planet.

Furthermore, it is now known that almost all living things share a collection of genes called 'regulatory genes' which determine the essential body plan of a creature. Most animals start from a single cell, the fertilised egg or zygote. This cell then divides and multiplies and specialised parts form – the organs, glands, skin, bone, muscle tissues. But every organism has a set of common genes which control the process of protein formation that leads to the formation of these parts. As this process continues, the genes become more and more specialised.

The simplest genetic command is that which determines the body axis of an embryo – which end becomes the head and which the tail, which is the back and which the front. Because this instruction is the most basic it is a characteristic shared by all species. Further along the process, a collection of genes determine whether a head is developed outside the trunk of the body (as in most animals) while others instruct the growth of limbs. In species as different as say, bats and eels, these instructions will be very different, but for a sheep and a dog, or even a sheep and a human they will be similar. It is only when we consider what are comparatively specialised functions and characteristics that we see very clear differentiation between the genetic nature of the various species. Even the bat's wings and the forelimbs of a sheep can be thought of as controlled by a similar set of regulatory genes.

The origin of this process is ancient. The DNA sequence – a vast and highly complex set of instructions for this process – was to be found during the *Precambrian period*, before the Cambrian explosion 530 million years ago. Indeed, it had to be in place to allow this event to happen.

The DNA sequence that does this is found in a collection of regulatory genes called 'Hox genes' that are usually found in a cluster in animal chromosomes and therefore often referred to as 'Hox clusters'. Amazingly, these clusters may be thought of as 'templates' for the animal of which they are a part – the genes are literally arranged in the gene cluster in the precise way the animal part they control is positioned in the growing embryo – genes that control the development of the head are at one end, the wings or legs part way down, the rear end holds the genes that control development of the lower parts, or the rear of the animal.

So, what does all this mean for the exobiologist?

Well, firstly it shows that only a few dozen patterns or layouts (body plans) are needed for a vast array of different species and secondly, if we restrict our vision of alien life to those based upon DNA we still end up with a universe offering an incredible variety of shapes and forms. And what does this lead us to conclude about the shapes and forms of aliens on other worlds – are we to expect little green men (the LGMs beloved of pulp science fiction circa 1920) or bug-eyed monsters straight out of a 1950s B-movie?

A way of resolving this may lie with the currently controversial idea of 'convergence'. This boils down to the idea that 'many very different starting points produce a limited number of solutions to a task'.

An everyday example is an aircraft. The 'task' is to build an efficient flying vehicle for a reasonable price that will move a small group of human beings safely through the air from A to B at high speed and in relative comfort. Now, before aircraft were invented people may have thought that there was a vast range of ways of doing this. Indeed, the experiments to make the first planes were extremely varied, and today, a century after the first heavier-than-air machines were flown, there is an array of different flying vehicles. But these fall into a limited number of types (analogous to body plans in the animal kingdom), which, on the surface, look very different from one another.

In fact, differences between aircraft are all relatively superficial and come down to appearance, size and subtle refinements in style, layout of the interior and alterations to fit specialised tasks. At their root, they are all metal cylinders with doors, wheels, wings, engines and tails, they all use fossil fuels, they have a front and a back and seats on which humans sit and they all travel through the skies (the exception is a helicopter, but even this has many of the same characteristics).

In the same way in which humans have solved this task, nature deals in a limited number of different ways with the design problems it faces. But, most crucially it always does so in the most efficient way it possibly can.

Scientists refer to this process as 'perfectibility'. And it works excellently well here, so it should work equally soundly on the majority of inhabited worlds.

So, what limitations are there to the types of DNA-based life forms we could hope to find one day on other worlds?

To establish any kind of informed answer we must look at two distinct variables. Firstly, we have to consider the evolutionary factors on an alien world and secondly, the environmental conditions.

Firstly, the evolutionary factors. Key to the evolution of life on Earth were the great events of the Cambrian explosion and it is only by looking at this singular example that we can formulate an idea of what could have, and might still be happening, on other worlds.

There are two competing theories used to explain what precipitated the events on Earth 530 million years ago. The first is simply that the time was right, that nature had experimented with various evolutionary mechanisms and eventually hit upon the right way forward. In saying this, I do not want to imply that nature in any way 'planned' this or 'knew' what to do. Nor is there anything to say that it was in some way 'guided' by an external agent, be it God or an alien in a shiny spacecraft deliberately setting in motion a process that would lead to the production of a dominant species like *Homo sapiens*. Natural selection does not operate by any sort of plan, it is driven by success and buffeted by random events, it needs neither a God nor alien intelligence. Rather, in one sense, this explanation for the Cambrian explosion is linked to convergence – nature had simply found a path from point A to point B by trial and error.

If this is the case then we can feel confident that a very similar process will have occurred on any number of alien worlds. It would be a fundamental and very simple process, therefore universal, a consequence of life reaching a certain level of complexity, a point from where it is spurred on to the next stage.

The rival theory offers a less rosy picture for the chances of there being advanced life in abundance because it suggests that the Cambrian explosion was precipitated by some unknown freak ecological event such as a giant meteorite or asteroid collision, certainly an event at least as significant as that now believed to have eliminated the dinosaurs.

Another alternative is the possibility that something caused a massive change in atmospheric conditions on the planet. An increase in the percentage of oxygen in the atmosphere would have almost certainly triggered a dramatic surge in biological activity on the surface and could explain why a vast array of fresh life forms appeared during such a brief period.

At present nobody can say which of these theories is correct, but the answer will have a great bearing upon the type of universe in which we live. One theory claims to offer the key to a highly populated universe, the other a bleaker (but not totally lifeless) prospect. It might be argued that it happened here; thus, with what are certainly a large number of other planets to choose from, it could happen elsewhere.

Beyond the initial spark of evolution from the Cambrian explosion there is a long hard road to what we call an advanced life form, one capable of developing a civilisation. But, if for the purposes of our discussion we assume the Cambrian explosion was inevitable, can we say anything about evolutionary routes on other planets?

Once again, we can only make comparisons with the one example we have – the evolution of life on Earth. To arrive at an answer to the question of whether or not intelligent life could have evolved on other worlds we have to look at what 'intelligent' means as well as its relevance to the ability to form a civilisation.

On Earth, the only animals with any form of conscious social interaction or intellect (as distinct from pure intelligence) are *Homo sapiens*. We are the only animals on the planet to keep records, to have developed a recordable language (a form of writing), to have built a civilisation based upon trade, and, crucially, to plan, to have a concept of our place in the world and flow of generations of our species.

So perhaps the first question to ask is: what is it about us that makes us different to the other species on the planet? If we can arrive at an answer to that, we might be able to extend the principle to extraterrestrials.

The difference between us and other species seems to come down, at least in part, to brain size. We have very large brains for our bodies. If the human brain was unfolded and spread out, it would cover four sheets of A4 paper. By comparison, a rat's brain would barely cover a postage stamp. However, it is not just a matter of size, but the way the brain is used. Dolphins have very large brains, but it is believed that most of their brain capacity is involved with managing their complex sonar system.

The reason brain size is so important for humans is its use in developing the incredibly complex skill of language. And language is a basic (but not the only) requirement for civilisation and social development.

In the case of human history, there was a 'sudden' four-fold increase in brain size between 1.5 and 2.5 million years ago. It is thought that before this point, early human ancestors had a brain capacity comparable to that of a chimp (about one-quarter of ours). What caused this rapid development remains a mystery, but it marks another key turning point in the development of the human race, another crucial jump along the evolutionary road. The most likely explanation is that our ancestors were faced with a severe 'challenge' to their survival.

The best candidate for such a challenge is the advent of the most recent Ice Age, the *Quaternary Ice Age*, which is believed to have acted as a 'filter' for many species including the ancestors of *Homo sapiens*. In other words, early *Homo erectus* (the immediate progenitors of the first *Homo sapiens*) learned a great deal from their experiences during this time. Biologists have reached the conclusion that the more intelligent land-based animals are omnivorous. This, biologists believe, is because omnivores can adapt their tastes to find diverse sources of food, and the effort to search out new resources is also a learning process which helps the animal develop skills not common in carnivorous or vegetarian animals. Similarly, the increase in human brain capacity precipitated by the Ice age came about because of the demands this placed on early humans. Those who survived this change in the environment did so by learning to find and use new resources, which led them to gradually develop social skills, to create communities, to develop language and to eventually take the first steps towards civilisation.

And with language comes what we call 'intelligence'. If we define intelligence as the ability to communicate and process ideas, then a huge leap in human evolution came about with the development of syntax and from that the ability to string together meaningless sounds (phonemes) to make 'meaningful' words. This ability enables us to create sentences and to communicate abstract ideas, to plan, to create social rules, taboos and hierarchies. Language really is the cornerstone of civilisation.

But, would there necessarily have been events comparable to the Ice ages on other worlds?

It would seem very likely. Although there are a number of plausible theories to chose from, nobody knows for sure why the series of Ice ages occurred on Earth and whether these are linked to very common natural processes in the life of a planet. But, it would seem reasonable to suppose they are common to a good percentage of worlds. And of course, Ice ages may not be the only form of challenge an embryonic dominate species might be offered. Other worlds may suffer environmental changes precipitated by comet or asteroid collisions, volcanic activity or short-lived irregularities in the behaviour of the planet's sun.

But what other evolutionary considerations should be taken into account? Brain capacity and brain application are only part of the developmental formula, albeit crucial ones. Another extremely important factor is physical versatility. And this leads to the question: could only humans have created a civilisation on Earth? Why, for example, have dolphins not achieved the same status?

Many people think of dolphins as highly-intelligent creatures, and they almost certainly are (by some definitions), but they exhibit a form of intelligence that appears to be very different to ours, one which has not lead them to the creation of what we understand as a 'civilisation' or a 'society'. But, why is this?

The simple truth seems to be that dolphins did not have a chance of competing with humans because they live in an environment that makes it very difficult for an intelligent animal to create any form of infrastructure. And this is due to several complex factors.

Dolphins do not have digits with which they can manipulate materials and they certainly have not developed opposable thumbs which have been one of the most important distinctions between human and non-human primate development on Earth. Dolphins are a very successful species – their physiology has evolved in a way that allows the animal to be perfectly adapted to its environment, but they were unable to even start on the road to civilisation.

Dolphin 'language', although sophisticated compared to almost all other animals on the planet, has not developed in a way that can lead to social development beyond a rudimentary level. With the bodies they possess, they could not have constructed the aquatic equivalent of buildings; they cannot easily record any knowledge they acquire in the way humans do using writing; they could not easily cultivate their territory or manage other animals, which means they are constantly at the whim of fluctuations in food supply. Finally, they could not have developed weapons so they could not have engaged in what is an extremely important developmental factor for any civilisation – war. So, extending this example it might be fair to say that any intelligent aquatic animal has only a slim chance of developing a civilisation as we understand the concept.

So, any planet that brings forth life must have enough land to allow animals to develop and for the correct ratio of plants and animals to arise in order to create a balanced ecosystem. Furthermore, any world which is entirely covered in water will almost certainly not harbour life any more advanced than the equivalent to Earth-style fish and relatively simple aquatic animals and plants, although, in theory, it might be possible for a special system to emerge and flourish on a world almost entirely covered in water which contains animals and water-based plants rather than land-based plants.

So, turning to the other strand of the arguments to determine the nature of alien life, what about environmental conditions?

Bacteria have been found in some extreme environments on Earth – in radioactive waste, thousands of feet beneath the sea bed, in hot springs and in the frozen wastes of Antarctica. Bacteria are of course extremely hardy creatures; more sophisticated animals could not have evolved within environments as harsh as those in which they appear to thrive.

This places limits upon possible environments on alien worlds harbouring any form of *highly developed* life form. Firstly, the temperature of the environment must lie somewhere in the region of 0°c to 40°c. Enzymes cannot operate at temperatures much higher than 40°c and begin to denature.* Coupled with this, the environment must not be flooded with intense radiation as this damages biochemicals and inhibits

---

* Water freezes at 0°c, (at a pressure of 1 atmosphere) and therefore biochemical processes which all take place in liquid water would cease before this limit. A caveat to this is that on a planet with a different atmospheric pressure, water will freeze at a different temperature, but, as we will see, environments with very different atmospheric pressures to that of Earth present their own problems for the evolution of life-as-we-know-it.

many of the chemical reactions required for mechanisms that control the functioning and continued growth of cells.

The environment on a particular planet cannot be too harsh or else any form of complex multi-cellular beings could not have evolved. On the other hand, the environment has to offer a challenge to living things so that natural selection can operate and evolution can occur.

If we consider first the atmosphere, what are the limitations? Would it be possible to have a successful ecosystem on another planet that supports DNA-based life but does not have an atmosphere similar to that of the Earth?

The answer is almost certainly 'no'. The reasons for this are complex. On Earth we live in a balanced ecosystem in which plants need carbon dioxide to facilitate photosynthesis which produces oxygen. All animals use oxygen, which is transported by the blood and carried to the cells of the body where it is involved in almost all the biochemical mechanisms that maintain our bodies. No alien creature could evolve or remain alive on a planet without interacting with other organisms. All organisms must be part of an ecosystem and any ecosystem must include gaseous cycles similar to the oxygen-carbon dioxide cycle on Earth. Such alien systems would have to integrate organisms similar to our plants and animals. An alien world may have an ecosystem based upon animals and some other kingdom – perhaps some form of living mineral or living rock – but the same situation applies.

This does allow scope for an atmosphere with different *proportions* of the gases we have in our atmosphere, but of course precludes too high a concentration of any gases DNA-based life would find toxic. An illustration of this would be the fact that only some very rare bacteria can survive in an atmosphere in which there is too little oxygen or too much of a 'toxic' gas such as methane.

So, what of other environmental considerations? What of atmospheric pressure and gravitational fields? How would these affect the diversity of life on an alien world?

On a planet where the atmospheric pressure is higher it is possible that intelligent creatures could have evolved that look very different to humans. The layout of the respiratory systems of such creatures would probably be very different because the pressure of the gases they breathe would not be the same as it is here, which means that the processes allowing gases to diffuse into their version of a circulatory system would operate at different potentials. But, this does not exclude the possibility of such creatures reaching a high level of development.

More difficult to resolve is the affect of high or low gravity. The strength of the gravitational field on an alien world will greatly affect the body types and the behaviour of creatures living there. All land-based mammals on Earth fall within a relatively narrow range of size – there are no mammals two hundred feet long or insect-sized. But if the force of gravity was say, fifty times greater than it is here, the creatures that developed there would be very much smaller and would be far less mobile. In extreme conditions we could imagine intelligent creatures that were almost flat.

Conversely, planets with low gravity would bring forth creatures that were much larger but lighter and they would probably move by natural methods of flight as we move around the surface of the Earth.

However, a great difference in physical size to that we witness on Earth creates its own problems. Think back to the aircraft analogy for a moment. At either end of the scale there is a definite limit to the size of aircraft that could be of practical use to humans. In the same way, very large creatures present design difficulties for nature.

One of the major problems for very large animals (and there are many such difficulties) is the fact that they would need huge hearts to supply the volume of blood needed to keep their bodies functioning, and big hearts need big lungs. As we know from the design of animals on Earth, this is not a strict limitation, but for an animal to evolve into the dominant species and to establish a civilisation, they also need a large brain that is not simply devoted to running a massive body. Such a brain would need a large head and still more blood to supply the cells with oxygen, which needs a massive heart and lungs, and so we enter a vicious circle.

Some claim that the 'success' of the dinosaur refutes this argument. It does not. By this argument, 'success' derives from the fact that the dinosaurs were around for many millions of years. Yet success is not based purely upon longevity; it must take into account the role an animal plays in the ecosystem. Humans are the only animals to have created a civilisation, the only species to control their environment in any large-scale way.

So, even if we only consider DNA-based life it is clear that there could be a range of different shapes and sizes for extraterrestrials, but these have to fit into certain limits and it may be that on planets with approximately the same gravity as the Earth, the species that formed a civilisation would be at least vaguely similar to humans. But what of the details, what exobiologists call *parochial characteristics*, or 'cosmetic' differences? What about the number of limbs, sensory apparatus or colouring? Is it likely that we will one day encounter a two-headed, five-legged green thing that we are meant to befriend?

Whether or not an extra pair of limbs or a third eye would be favoured within an ecosystem on another world is open to debate. There may be advantages in having these things. But as we saw earlier, within any environment, nature will always go for the most efficient option. If the advantages of a third eye or an extra pair of ears outweighs the demands produced by the extra weight, the extra blood requirements, the development time (both in terms of evolution and within the womb), then it could happen. If not, then evolution is unlikely to allow such creatures to dominate, and they would easily be made obsolete by better 'models'.

But, how far can we go with this argument?

There are those who do take the anthropomorphic argument to its limit. They suggest that the most likely design for a successful life form which has evolved to the point of developing a civilisation will be similar to ours – that they will look like us (or us like them). But why?

Consider the number of limbs a creature has. Do we need more than two legs? It is possible that a creature developing on a world with high gravity would need three or more legs to allow it to move more efficiently under the strain? But then it could be argued that a biped with two much better legs, could have evolved on the same world, allowing it to move around more readily than its multiped rival.

Does any creature need two heads? We have two of almost everything else, why only one head?

Quite simply, two brains would require too much blood for the same-sized heart and we are back in the same cul-de-sac as we were with the size of lungs versus size of animal. But, convergence would not allow for such a consequence anyway, it would enforce the most efficient solution – a biped with one head is better than a large ungainly biped with two.

So, a three-legged, two-headed beast may never get through the evolutionary net. Indeed, it may be argued that this latter body type is unlikely because amongst the great diversity of life on Earth there has never been a two-headed anything. However, strictly speaking, this is not an empirically sound argument because we are trying to deduce outcomes for an alien world where (within the limits required for DNA-based life) conditions could be quite different.

So, to conclude, what can we determine from these arguments? Firstly, most scientists believe that life in the universe is plentiful and many would put money on the idea that our civilisation is just one of many. Less convincing is the argument that there could be intelligent life based upon anything other than DNA-led biochemistry. If there are creatures that have flourished and become highly evolved via a non-DNA-led route, we may never encounter them and would almost certainly never be able to communicate with them.

Turning to the narrower arena of life based upon DNA,

we still have a truly mind-boggling range of possibilities
– just look at the marvellous blend of life on Earth in all
its varied glory. If we are to consider DNA-based life, it
will form and evolve on a range of planet types but there
are certain restrains, certain environmental limits. These,
along with caveats to the way evolution could progress
on alien worlds, narrows the field somewhat and can lead
us to believe that the most likely shape for an intelligent
DNA-based alien approximates to the humanoid form. But,
details could produce very different creatures. They could
perhaps use different chemicals to carry oxygen to their
cells and their sun could emit a slightly different range
of radiation. Combined, this would mean that such aliens
would be a different colour to any human we have seen
on Earth because it is the colour of the haemoglobin in our
blood and the amount of melanin in our skin that determines
our colour.

It is even conceivable that we may one day encounter little
green men.

9

MENDEL'S MONSTERS

'Right thinking people should check the procreation of
base and servile types . . . all that is ugly and bestial in
the souls and bodies of men.'

H.G Wells, *Anticipations.*

Human mutants and man-made monsters are one of the
mainstays of myth from ancient legend to the movie *Gattaca*.
They are the stuff of nightmares. Ever since Mary Shelley
created the tale of Frankenstein's monster, coinciding as it
did with the birth of modern science, people have wondered
if such things could be possible – could humans make other
humans? Can humans manipulate the very stuff of life to
'manufacture' other living things? Can we alter our bodies at
a fundamental level or imbue life into inanimate matter?

In the days when these questions were first raised, biology
was in its infancy and the science of genetics was totally
unknown. In the same way the alchemists dreamed of
transmuting base metals into gold but did not have a nuclear
reactor with which to accomplish it, early thinkers in the
realm of biological mutation had none of the technology
and little of the knowledge needed by modern-day genetic
engineers. But today, we have the technology and our
understanding of the fundamental genetic processes of life
is becoming clearer each day. The nuclear physicist is no
longer an alchemist working in his private laboratory, today

they have the key to the basic forces of Nature and the potential for great good and great evil. In the same way, genetic engineers have their fingers on the biological button offering a world of wonder and benefit, or the way to the worst techno-nightmares.

As we will see, the question of morality is an issue of major concern in the world of genetics and a contemporary dilemma for a growing number of ordinary people. We may now have the technology to manipulate our genes, to produce both angels and monsters; but should we?

The tremendous leaps we are now witnessing in the science of genetics represents one of the greatest revolutions in human understanding since ancient times, its pace almost supernaturally fast. According to one observer: 'Genetics will touch our lives in the next century as powerfully as the development of silicon chip technology did during the 1980s. Just as virtually every home now contains machines with the chip, so nearly all of us will soon have some reason to welcome or curse the advance of genetics.'[1] So important is the development of ideas in the field of genetics and their application to everyday life that 'genetic engineering' is sometimes called the *fourth medical revolution*.

The first of these revolutionary changes was the reali-sation, some two hundred years ago, that hygiene was essential for good health. The second, during the middle of the nineteenth century, was the discovery of anaesthesia, which allowed for far safer surgery, and the third was the discovery of ways to combat bacteria and viruses – the use of antibiotics and the invention of the vaccine. The fourth is the recently-developed process via which doctors can pinpoint genes and replace 'bad' genes with 'good' ones.

In much the same way that the science of nuclear physics has come to be viewed as a mixed blessing for humanity, the field of genetics is a classic, double-edged sword. The nuclear physicist has given us an alternative power source to counter the gradual depletion of our natural resources, which may one day provide the means for interplanetary travel. But the knowledge we have gained from nuclear research has produced two atomic explosions, one catastrophic accident and the potential to destroy human civilisation many times over.

In the same way, genetics provides huge opportunities as well as a catalogue of anxieties for the future. On the one hand, within a few decades scientists hope to have intimate knowledge of the estimated 5000 genetic diseases suffered by humans, be able to replace faulty genes, manufacture transplant organs and favourably manipulate whole swathes of the Earth's gene pool to our collective benefit. On the other, there is the danger that cloning could be terribly misused and lead to the creation of man-made mutants, human clones, social eugenics and the horrors these things could provide. Genetic engineering is truly a Pandora's box. But, as we shall see, it cannot possibly be left closed. In fact, it is already more than half-open.

At the root of genetics is the simple fact that all life forms pass on characteristics to the next generation via a genetic blueprint stamped into every cell in every living creature. The blueprint is different for each individual. This is what distinguishes a squid from a racehorse or Tom Cruise from Bill Clinton. The blueprint is called the 'genetic code' and it is made up of a sequence of tiny units called *genes* (there are 100,000 of them in each human cell) which are themselves made from bits of a very large biochemical named, DNA.

The study of genetics goes back a long way. Our modern understanding of the basic concepts behind it can be dated to an Austrian monk named Gregor Mendel who, during the 1850s, realised that characteristics were inherited from generation to generation by means of what he called *discrete factors*. These are what we today call genes.

Mendel realised that each individual inherited two complete sets of genes called 'alleles', one from each parent, and that these alleles change during reproduction but are passed on unaltered from parent to offspring. What makes us different is that, because each parent also has two alleles, each of their children has a fifty percent chance of getting one or other allele from each parent or a twenty-five percent chance of receiving any particular combination of genes. This 'shuffling' of genes produces variations in characteristics ranging from our colouring or build to our susceptibility to certain diseases; they even predispose our sexuality and psychological profile.

Although Mendel conceived the idea of inheritance of genetic material, he had no idea how the process worked on a chemical level. It was not until 1953, almost seventy years after his death, that the mystery was solved when James Watson and Francis Crick, working in Cambridge, discovered that genes consisted of a complex molecule, DNA – made of two strands – the now famous double helix.

DNA is found in every cell of every living thing. And, although it is a vast molecule, amazingly, it is made from just four small chemical units, or 'bases', called A (adenine), T (thymine), G (guanine) and C (cytosine). There are hundreds of millions of As, Ts, Cs and Gs in each molecule of DNA scattered throughout its structure. They combine three at a time to form specific three-letter codes (what we can think of as 'words') which allow individual amino acids to be positioned in an exact sequence to form proteins. Proteins make up the structure of all living things.

The best way to visualise how this works is to imagine a cell as being a set of huge encyclopaedias. Each volume of the collection of encyclopaedias is equivalent to a 'chromosome' within the cell. Each human cell has twenty-three pairs of chromosomes, made up of an incredibly long, tightly-coiled length of DNA. So the human 'encyclopaedia set' would consist of forty-six volumes. Each volume in this library would be billions of words long – compared to which, *The Lord of the Rings* would seem like a slender tome.

Each volume of an encyclopaedia deals with a whole range of subjects, and in the same way, each chromosome controls every physical characteristic of the organism. So, in this analogy, hair colour might be equivalent to say, 'French

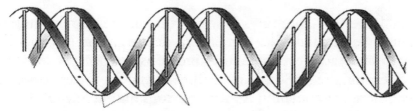

Two strands intertwined   Base pairing holds the strands together.

Colonial History'; height, 'Chinese Emperors of the fifth century'; nail shape, 'The Life of William Shakespeare'.

In our analogy, these individual entries in the encyclopaedia are equivalent to individual genes. And of course, real encyclopaedia entries are made up of paragraphs, words and letters. So, extending our model, the paragraphs are equivalent to the large sections of DNA which make up specific parts of the genes. Words are the counterpart of the three-letter words which code for the individual amino acids and the letters are the base pairs, A, T, C and G.

As well as providing the material from which genes are made, DNA also acts as the vehicle for growth by replicating itself within the cell. It acts as a template to produce new copies of itself. It is as if the encyclopaedias in our collection could be endlessly photocopied and distributed; any number of copies of each can be made by generating copy after copy based upon the original. But, as with photocopies, tiny mistakes occur during the copying. These 'mistakes' are called *mutations* and they can either be beneficial or detrimental to our offspring. But, crucially these mutations occur all the time. We all possess mutated genes – in fact at a basic level, if our parent's genes were not mutated during reproduction, we would all be biologically identical.

By the late 1960s, a decade and a half after Crick and Watson's ground-breaking work on the structure of DNA, scientists had a pretty clear idea of how the words in the encyclopaedia collection could be formed. They realised that out of the four bases, A, T, C and G, only three were needed at any one time to correctly position an amino acid to form a protein. This meant that with a supply of four letters, there would be sixty-four ways in which three-letter combinations could be created. But the rate of development in genetics has accelerated exponentially since this discovery.

During the 1980s, a new 'Big Science' project, costing almost as much as the Apollo missions and involving many more scientists around the world, was established to attempt to map every gene in the body. This is called the Genome Project and it is now reaching its concluding phase.

Along the route taking us from its foundations in the early 1980s, the Genome Project has had its dissenters and opponents but it has also unearthed a vast array of information about genetics, and in particular the genetic make-up of humans. Now hardly a day passes without the newspapers of the world heralding a new breakthrough in the study of one disease or another thanks to the discoveries of the global genetics community. In fact, we are now in the peculiar position of being able to diagnose far more diseases than we can possibly cure, which leads to problems of its own – do people really want to know they have a disease if nothing can be done about it?

This is but one of the many moral issues that has come out of the incredible and almost too-rapid advances being made in the science of genetics. But if we are to enjoy the undoubtedly huge benefits that could come from genetic manipulation then we also have to learn to deal with the potential dangers and problems it generates.

The good and the bad of genetics seem to get equal attention from the media, but just as the optimists shout from the rooftops their hopes and claims for the future and their successes of the moment, we hear of the frightening scare stories that come with it. But what are the two sides of this coin? What are the fantastic hopes and the terrifying nightmares?

Let's first look at the great opportunities the study of our genetic make-up can bring.

Top of the list must be the breathtaking advances already being made in the field of *gene therapy*. As the name implies, gene therapy is a medical treatment reliant on the potential to alter the genetic make-up of our bodies. As I discussed earlier in this chapter, the human body consists of over 100,000 genes positioned in various places in the twenty-three pairs of chromosomes present in each cell.

Many diseases known to humanity have nothing to do with our genetic characteristics. The most obvious examples are the many thousands of contagious diseases. Usually their only genetic component is our varying natural ability to resist infection and the efficiency of our defences to fight it. But there are some 5000 diseases already known that are directly affected by the presence of certain genes in our genome.

There are two types of genetic disease – those precipitated by what is called a 'dominant gene' or collection of dominant genes and those caused by a 'recessive gene' or collection of these working together.

A dominant gene is one which acts individually. It could come from either parent but it will generate a characteristic on its own without the complimentary gene from the other parent (remember we obtain a set of genes from each parent). These genes can be quite innocent. For example the gene for brown eyes will always 'dominate' that for any other colour. So if an individual receives a gene for brown eyes from one parent and a gene for blue eyes from the other they will certainly have brown eyes.

If an individual acquires a dominant gene for a disease, they will have a far greater chance of developing that disease later in life than if they did not have this gene or if the gene was of the recessive variety – the gene can simply 'switch on' at some point and precipitate a series of biochemical changes that will lead to a disease. An example of this type of serious illness is Huntington's disease (HD). This is a horrible degenerative illness that affects about one in 5000 people. It is always fatal and triggered by a solitary dominant gene. And in 1983, this gene was the first that precipitates an hereditary disorder to be located in the human genome. We still have no cure for HD, but at least individuals can now be screened to determine whether they have the gene and can therefore know if they may pass it on to their offspring.

Recessive genes work in pairs. In other words, an individual may inherit a gene that could precipitate a characteristic, but this characteristic 'good' or 'bad' will only appear if the complimentary gene is also 'switched on'. In many cases, people inherit a recessive gene that is mutated in some way so that it does not function properly. This will mean that it does not do its usual preventative job – say producing a special chemical that stops some other biochemical process occurring which then triggers illness. Alternatively, people can inherit a gene that does work properly but actually sets a disease in motion by allowing other complex biochemical pathways to open up. As we have seen, in cases where such genes are dominant then the individual has a high risk of developing the disease, but if the gene is recessive then its complimentary gene has to be 'knocked out' by some unknown factor (such things as carcinogenic compounds in the environment, exposure to radiation, hormonal disturbances, smoking, the list is a long one).

Until recently, many of these genetic diseases have only been treatable by surgery or intensive drug programmes, if at all; such illnesses as HD remain completely incurable and the greatest benefit to be derived from our genetic knowledge of them is to help prevent them being passed on. But it is hoped that in the not-too-distant future, doctors will be able to treat an increasing collection of diseases based upon an understanding of where genes are and how they interrelate. With gene therapy it is now just possible to implant healthy genes into the body of a patient with an inherited disease in the hope that the body will start to copy the healthy version and stem the deficiency or to counter the damaging affects of the gene that has malfunctioned. So far, only a very limited number of diseases have responded to this technique, but methods are improving all the time and geneticists are spreading their net further.

The first step in this process has been the effort to discover which genes do what. With 100,000 genes to chose from and considering the fact that almost all diseases are vastly complex and involve many genes, the task is incredibly difficult. But gradually, as we learn more about the genome and the Genome Project reveals many of the functions and the way genes interact, we are learning more about how the entire system operates.

A recent success in gene therapy has been the treatment of a disease called ADA (adenosine deaminase deficiency) which affects the functioning of the immune system. Another has been the use of gene therapy to combat a debilitating illness called SCID (severe combined immunodeficiency). Today geneticists are active in attempting to use gene therapy to fight a range of potentially fatal disease including an ever-growing array of cancers, cystic fibrosis, haemophilia and AIDS.

One of the great stumbling blocks so far has been the difficulty of delivering 'good' genes into the appropriate part of the patient's body and encouraging the body to take the new genes and replicate them naturally and correctly. A great deal of work is being done on this aspect of the treatment and it is very gradually improving. Some workers are even experimenting with the idea of producing a new, forty-seventh chromosome which would carry any genes that were required. The chromosome would be made outside the body and tailored to spec and then implanted where it would be replicated just as geneticists have done with single genes.

This idea is still a long way from practical use and remains very much a theoretical concept. It offers huge advantages over the simpler process of single gene implantation but is also immensely more difficult to achieve. As we will see, such advanced ideas offer huge potential for medicine, but it is also within such extreme ideas that alarmists can find potential for worrying perversions of sophisticated science. If we can tailor whole chromosomes for medical jobs could we not produce genetic monsters?

On only a slightly more prosaic level, there is the question of personal involvement in genetic engineering, because this science, developing as it is at such an extraordinary pace and taking us all into unknown territory, offers vast potential for the ordinary individual as well as for terrible misuse.

If we know the detailed structure of the genome, then it will soon be possible to map the entire genetic make-up of a foetus in the womb. This will put us in a position where parents can judge if they view the unborn child as one they would want. Now of course, this technology offers all sorts of opportunities, both beneficial and alarming. We all want a healthier world populated by fit people, but if individuals have the power to decide whether a foetus is 'perfect' enough this would be considered by most people to be a misuse of such knowledge.

Today, doctors can genetically screen for many diseases before a couple decide to start a family. There are some seriously debilitating diseases that run in families and by detecting an individual's susceptibility to such diseases, potential parents can weigh up the dangers and make their personal decision. This is considered a very positive outcome of genetic research, but exactly the same information, exactly the same discoveries and precisely the same techniques also offer scope to tailor foetuses to personal requirements.

Most people would not want to interfere in the development of their unborn child or terminate a pregnancy if a relatively minor problem was spotted, but others would. And how far does this thinking take us? There are many parents who only want a son; if technology could tell them early on that the foetus was female they might take the decision to abort. Equally, they may discover that the child will be born deaf, or have a high risk of developing a certain cancer by the age of thirty – what decision do they then make?

Current public opinion seems to be firmly against improving the attributes of a foetus. In a 1993 *Daily Telegraph*/Gallup poll in Britain, seventy-eight percent of respondents were against the notion of parents 'designing' their children. But in the US one survey found that forty-two percent of people approved of the idea of gene therapy to boost a child's intelligence.[2]

Another aspect of this is the danger that genetic information falls into the wrong hands. Should insurance companies have unlimited access to an individual's genome? Should someone applying for life insurance declare that they have a gene which gives them an enhanced susceptibility to a serious illness?

In the future these questions will be everyday problems we will all have to face one way or another. We will all be aware of our genetic profile; indeed within a decade we will probably all carry a 'genetic passport' that profiles our personal genome. We will all be drawn into the debate about privacy at the most personal level – the very internal structure of our bodies. We can only hope that as society develops these new technologies we will also produce adequate ways of dealing with them on a social and ethical level.

But society also has to find ways through a subtly different moral maze. Could our enormously enhanced knowledge of genetics lead us one day to eugenics? The considerations of the individual and the decisions they may have to make about their own unborn children presents a form of *individual eugenics*, but what of *social eugenics*?

As a civilisation, we have toyed with this dangerous idea many times – the quote at the beginning of this chapter comes from a book by H.G. Wells advocating social eugenics, and the obvious example of the application of eugenics is the Nazis' programme of *selective breeding* during the 1930s and early '40s – an attempt to produce a 'super-race'. This simplistic programme had nothing to do with high-tech genetic engineering but was purely based upon the false assumption that by choosing 'perfect' parents, 'desirable' features could be engineered to pass on to the next generation. We know now that genetics does not work like that, and that there is no way to control the inheritance of particular features over others without manipulation at a genetic level. But with the latest technology at our fingertips and the progress that is sure to be made during the next decade, we can now do just that – eradicate what some would consider to be 'negative' attributes and to promote 'positive' ones by altering the genome of a foetus or by cloning.

At first glance there seems to be little wrong with the fundamental principle of eugenics. As I said earlier, we all want a healthier world, and few would deny that a planet populated by more intelligent and more socially-responsible people would be an improvement. But there are many problems with the concept.

Firstly, who makes the decisions? Who has the right to say which foetus should live and which should die? Secondly, characteristics or attributes that would be perceived as 'undesirable' by eugenicists sometimes produce remarkable results. Take two obvious examples – Stephen Hawking and Beethoven. Hawking developed the degenerative neurological disease ALS at the age of twenty-three, yet he has gone on to become one of the most influential physicists in the world and one of the all-time best-selling authors. Beethoven became profoundly deaf as an adult yet he composed some of the most sublime music ever heard. If specially appointed individuals with the power to dictate who lives and who dies were to base their ideas purely upon empirical evidence garnered from a genetic profile, then both Hawking and Beethoven would have been terminated before they were born.

Finally, there is the problem of control. If eugenics was to ever become policy, the culling of genetically imperfect foetuses could be allowed to go to ridiculous extremes. Would the drive for perfection prevent say the birth of someone who was susceptible to obesity later in life? Or someone who may be predisposed to body odour?*

Perhaps even more exciting than gene therapy is the potential offered by the latest genetic research to hit the headlines – cloning.

Cloning has been a science fiction favourite for many years but has only recently begun to emerge as a respectable and potentially epoch-changing science. The possibility of cloning has been considered almost as long as the human race has had knowledge of how genetics works at a basic level and has now become a subject that has penetrated into the public consciousness. Indeed, cloning has been the subject of several novels. Probably the most famous is *The Boys From Brazil* in which the real-life character, Josef Mengele, the Nazi physician and experimenter, clones Hitler's genes in an attempt to produce a master race. A more chilling but less well known example of cloning in science fiction appeared in the novel *Solution Three*, written by Naomi Mitchison, the sister of the great British biologist and philosopher of science, J.B.S. Haldane. This is set in a post-nuclear apocalypse world in which the human race is all but destroyed and cloning is used to repopulate the planet – with disastrous consequences.

In more recent times there was an attempt to hoodwink the public and the scientific community into believing that human cloning had been accomplished. In 1978, a freelance journalist called David Rorvik wrote what he claimed to be a non-fiction account of how he had helped an eccentric millionaire clone himself. It was of course a rather crude hoax, and was exposed, but only after Rorvik had earned an estimated $400,000 in royalties and advances from the book.

---

* Interestingly, geneticists now have the ability to detect this last characteristic. Ian Phillips from the University of London has recently discovered a mutation in a gene which produces a defective enzyme that is unable to break down a chemical called trimethylamine, which produces the characteristic 'rotting fish' smell associated with BO.

What is most significant about this last example of cloning in literature was that it sparked off a violent reaction from the scientific community – several geneticists went on record as saying that the science of cloning was 'not even on the horizon, let alone workable'.[3] Partly because of this, for many years cloning remained in the scientific wilderness. Since Rorvik, there have been some on the fringes of the scientific community who have further marginalised themselves by making serious claims that cloning is possible and declaring that they have succeeded. For one reason or another, these have all been ignored and even openly dismissed by the scientific community.

Then, in July 1996 the world was shaken by the news that a little-known British scientist, Ian Wilmut, working in what had for long been considered a scientific backwater, the study of embryology, had become the first person to successfully clone a mammal from adult cells. The sheep, Dolly, had been 'created' in the lab.

This breakthrough was immediately splashed across the newspapers of the world and soon became the subject of books and television documentaries. But what exactly is cloning and how could such work as Wilmut's have the potential to change the course of civilisation and push society further towards some of the greatest ethical dilemmas we have ever had to face? How does this knowledge lead us to the potential to create monsters as imagined by Mary Shelley, and central to the plot of a thousand and one science fiction stories?

Cloning is the process in which the genetic material of an egg is completely removed and replaced with the entire genome (a complete set of genes) from a donor, the individual to be cloned.

Simple types of cloning have been possible for some time; indeed, before producing Dolly, Wilmut and his team had successfully cloned two sheep, named Megan and Morag. But these had been produced by splitting a single embryo creating two identical copies of the same sheep. These techniques differ from the cloning experiment that produced Dolly in two distinct ways. Firstly, until Dolly, only relatively simple organisms have been cloned by implanting genetic material into a host egg (rather than splitting an already fertilised egg). The list of cloned creatures included bacteria, plants and, in some rare cases, animals such as frogs. The second and even more important factor distinguishing Wilmut's achievement from all other previous experiments is that he used genetic material taken from an *adult* animal, a mature sheep, and implanted this into a recipient egg.

Now obviously, this has huge implications, not just for science but for all our lives in the future. For the very first time, a scientist had brought to reality the 'science fiction' idea of cloning – taking genetic material from an adult animal, removing the material already present in a recipient egg and replacing it with this 'foreign' material. What this means, if we extrapolate the science only a tiny degree, is that an adult human could have genetic material removed. This could be placed in a host egg and a new human grown in the lab. This human would not be merely a twin or close relative of the original human, it would be an identical, exact copy of the original, possessing exactly the same genome.

The process enabling this to happen may be broken down into seven clear steps:

1. Remove some donor cells. Place these in a glass dish and label it *Clone*.
2. This is what may be considered the most crucial step – the eggs need to be put in to a state of 'hibernation'. To do this they are starved of nutrients which means they stop multiplying and enter a state in which they can be 'reprogrammed'. What this really means is that they are 'tricked' into thinking they have returned to an embryonic state and become ready to multiply once the new DNA has been added to them and the old DNA

removed. No one really knows how the starving of cells sends them into this state.

3. Give a special cocktail of drugs to a large group of women to push them into a state of 'super-ovulation' in which they produce large numbers of eggs in a short space of time.

4. Harvest the eggs and remove their nuclei. The nucleus is the nerve centre or 'brain' of the cell and contains the twenty-three pairs of chromosomes which constitute the genome of the human. This stage involves dextrous practical skill because we must not lose or damage the rest of the cell's material within the outer cell membrane – the cytoplasm.

5. Place a nucleus from the removed cells of the donor to be cloned into the recipient cell in place of the removed nucleus. Fire a pulse of electricity into the cell. This facilitates the acceptance of the new material in the recipient cell. Again, no one knows why a pulse of electricity will do this, but it does.

6. Place this fused egg into the womb of another woman who acts as the surrogate mother for the clone.

7. Wait nine months. The expected success rate for mammals has been placed by Wilmut's team at about one in 300. This figure is based upon his own experiments using sheep. No one knows what the success rate would be in human cloning.

As soon as news of Wilmut's cloning of Dolly was announced, fears were voiced about the possible application of this work to the cloning of humans. The United Nations have agreed to ban any form of research that involves the use of what are called human *germ* cells – ova and sperm taken from human beings. This limits geneticists to manipulation of cells known collectively as *somatic* cells, cells other than those involved in reproduction. But, according to some this ban is flawed in a number of significant ways.

Firstly, those of a cynical disposition suggest that such

a ban, precipitated by a moral judgement on the part of the West, might only hold for a time and that as soon as a nation realises the commercial potential of experiments involving human cloning, the ban will be eased. They point to other attempts at prohibition based upon ethical criteria and the way these have eroded (for example sanctions against Iraq, the banning of land mines and others). But more importantly, some observers have pointed out that it might be ethical and wise for the West to ban human cloning experiments using germ cells, but what is to stop similar 'rogue' states (those say who are currently experimenting with germ and nerve gas warfare systems or selling arms to unscrupulous dictators) from gaining access to this technology and producing a real-life *Boys From Brazil* scenario?

The international community is gradually becoming aware of the dangers involved with cloning as well as its enormous potential. When Ian Wilmut was called to account by the House of Commons Science and Technology committee, he declared: 'We would find this sort of work with human embryos offensive. We can see no clinical reason why you would wish to make a copy of a person.'[4] But, as the scientist Professor French Anderson, director of the Gene Therapy Laboratories in the US, has recently pointed out: 'There is a real danger that our society could slip into a new era of eugenics. It is one thing to give a normal existence to a sick individual; it is another to attempt to "improve" on normal – whatever "normal" means. And the situation will be even more dangerous when we begin to alter germ cells. Then misguided or malevolent attempts to alter the genetic composition of humans could cause problems for generations.'[5]

In a recently published article entitled *Cloning? Get Used To It*, the geneticist and science writer Colin Tudge goes further, saying: 'We should face reality. There are no biological laws, apart from the underlying laws of physics, and technology might achieve anything that does not break these bedrock laws. We should also recognise that the potent new biotechnologies are already outside humanity's present control. Individual countries may have their laws, mores and customs, and influence technology up to a point through the flow of research funds. But the US in particular is driven by market forces, and while most Americans are known to deplore the idea of human cloning, that same majority supports a Constitution which defends the rights of minorities effectively to do as they please. If one percent of Americans want cloning, and it's known they do, then most of the other ninety-nine percent will not gainsay them.'[6]

Meanwhile, in Britain the debate over the uses of this new work is hotting up. The Human Fertilisation and Embryology Authority bans the use of experiments on human foetuses over fourteen days old, which means that any clone that is produced has to be destroyed after this time. Ruth Deech, chairman of the HFEA has said that: 'We would never grant a licence for any treatment that would result in the production of an actual cloned baby.'

But those opposed to the whole idea of cloning are deeply suspicious of the scientific community. Peter Garrett, research director of the anti-abortion charity Life, claims that: 'We know what a nightmare world is just around the corner if we once accept any manipulation of human life in this way. They want to lull us into allowing the cloners to get to work by proposing a fourteen-day limit on the clones' lives initially. Then we get all the usual utilitarian talk about potential benefits of research using laboratory clones. Having got us used to the idea, they will quickly relax the age limit and away we will go, full sail ahead, in a year or two's time.'[7]

Perhaps because the first cloned mammal was produced there, the country most interested in keeping up research into this new science is Britain. Recently, the British government rejected an agreement signed by nineteen other European countries including Italy, France and Spain to place strict limits on research. And, although the US Senate similarly rejected an anti-cloning research bill, the present administration in the US and in particular President Clinton, is deeply opposed to clone experimentation.

No one really knows how different human cloning would be to cloning a sheep. Of course, humans and sheep are both mammals, so there should be few fundamental differences in the methods, and if sheep cells are activated by electrical surges and hibernated by starving them, then this will also happen with human cells. Cloning is a highly technical procedure and requires skilled scientists and refined technological back-up, but it is not in the same league as the utilisation of nuclear technologies or even development of effective germ or chemical weapons along with the delivery systems and defence mechanisms they need.

To start a clandestine human cloning facility, those involved would need a team of experts (available at a price), a sophisticated biochemical laboratory (again readily available with sufficient funding), a supply of human tissue and recipients, donors and surrogate mothers, and a great deal of luck on their side. The facts are clear: for a sufficiently motivated and sophisticated state with modest funding, cloning is a technological possibility. But what would they do with such a facility?

The potential is almost limitless. The most obvious use would be to clone the country's leader. It is easy to imagine an egomaniac like Saddam Hussein or past leaders of the Idi Amin or Galtieri school being interested in such a thing. Another obvious use is the production of genetically-altered individuals for specific purposes. By combining cloning with techniques drawn from gene therapy it should be possible to generate clones possessing certain characteristics altered along the way. Using this method, it would in theory be possible to produced 'superhumans' – beings 'manufactured' to fit requirements.

However, before we get too carried away with these ideas, there are some serious limitations to the entire process of genetic engineering. It is certainly possible to clone mammals; at the same time, the techniques required to implant desired genes and to manipulate the existing genome are becoming more and more sophisticated. These genetic skills can be used to alter characteristics covering a wide variety of human attributes – from eye colour to height; they may also play a part in adjusting how an individual responds to non-physical stimuli, because it is now believed that our genetic make-up is in part responsible for our psychological nature.

Now, the important caveat here lies in the words 'in part', because we are not just simply a collection of genes, and this becomes particularly significant when we look at the psychological aspects of a human being.

A few years ago, there was a great fuss created by the announcement that a 'gene for homosexuality' had been found. At other points during the past few years geneticists have located what newspapers have dubbed 'the alcoholic gene', the 'violent gene' and others. But, what geneticists mean when they announce such findings is that they have found a gene which predisposes us to certain attributes – both the good and the bad. Of equal importance to the genetic structure of our bodies is the environment in which we mature. This is especially important when we consider such characteristics as our sexuality, our tastes and our ability to control moods.

It may be that within a very short time the potential to produce tailor-made clones will be available, but the mere manipulation of genetic material is not the whole story. Even if we consider the benign use of cloning, officially sanctioned and within a controlled environment, the outcome of such experiments would not be entirely predictable. We may be able to make an exact physical copy of someone, but would they really grow into the same person? The answer is: 'of course not'.

If we take billionaire A who wishes to have themselves cloned. He or she could donate genetic material, the experiment would be conducted and the clone born. But, even if

they were brought up under incredibly contrived circumstances, that child would experience totally different things
to the original donor; after all, the original donor was not
a clone.

A further, more subtle point to consider is that the
development of an embryo in the womb may not be solely
down to the nature of the genes in its cells. No one is sure
how the cytoplasm (the material outside the nucleus of the
cell) affects the development of the fertilised egg; or indeed
how the biochemistry of the mother and her experiences
during pregnancy impacts upon the progress of the foetus.

However, let's take the cloning scenario several stages
further, into what would now be considered the supernatural, a realm we might call *Superscience*. Consider some
of the more extreme possibilities genetic research offers.

Some neurophysiologists are currently toying with the
idea of creating a 'secondary brain' for newborn babies.
The idea involves implanting at birth a microchip into a
baby's head. This chip can record every experience the
brain has as it happens and stores the same information
as the natural brain. In other words, the chip is a 'back-
up brain'. When the human dies, the chip is removed
and plugged into a new body, enabling its owner to live
again with all the information derived from their 'first
life'.

If we couple this idea with the technology of cloning, it
is conceivable that a human could live many lives, and be
'the same' person physically and mentally – the chip would
simply go into a new body built from the old one and they
would be 'complete' again.

Of course, religious people may have a thing or two to
say about this. They would argue that the person was not
'complete'; they may have the same memories and the same
body as the original, but what of their soul?

Many scientists dismiss the entire notion of the soul as
pure fiction. They argue that what we mistakenly believe
to be a soul is just an aspect of our personality – and this

in turn is a mere product of the *gestalt* that results from the complexity of the human brain. In other words, we have such complex brains that when we are alive we have self-awareness and a personality and this is 'us' or our 'soul'. Kill the brain and the soul or personality (whatever you want to call it) ceases to exist. But if the complexity of the brain can be preserved, along with the actual information derived from experience, and this can be stored, it could be argued that the 'personality' can also be restored and preserved within a new body.

Naturally, cloning, without the added invention of storing our minds as well as our bodies, presents many problems for religious people. For instance, if humans can make another human without the need for natural reproduction – can this being really be considered human?

Such ideas lead us into a moral and ethical minefield. It raises a plethora of questions, all of which are extremely difficult to answer. For example, where does the soul derive? Is the soul created at the moment of conception as some religions profess? If this is the case, what is to be made of creatures born but not conceived? Does the activation of the cell by means of an electrical pulse, one of the key stages mentioned above, constitute 'conception'? And if it does, is a soul produced at that moment, just as some believe happens during natural conception?

These matters will occupy a growing number of people in the future. There is little doubt that somehow a human clone will be produced within the next decade; the only mystery is via which process? Will such a being come from a 'hostile' regime, or from a clandestine experiment in the West? Or will Western governments slowly relax the rules and allow this to happen – perhaps in an effort to pre-empt a pariah state getting there first?

As clones begin to appear, more and more people will start to wonder about the meaning of the soul, what is special about natural conception, what the interaction of mind, body and soul could be. Today this is really almost entirely the intellectual territory of philosophers. But tomorrow, it will by necessity become an issue argued over by everyone, as much a part of our lives as a discussion about the ecology of the planet, or the morality of abortion.

10

EARTH MAGIC, LEY LINES AND CIRCLES IN THE CORN

'Our civilisation . . . has not yet fully recovered from the shock of its birth – the transition from the tribal or "closed society", with its submission to magical forces, to the "open society" which sets free the critical powers of man.'

Karl Popper, *The Open Society and Its Enemies.*

Since the time before civilisation began, humans have believed in what has come to be known as *Earth magic*, the notion that we can in some way communicate with the natural forces at work in the world. It is now very fashionable to believe that we humans are part of a greater *web*, a network of animate and indeed inanimate matter. This holistic viewpoint embraces the idea of a gestalt within Nature, a greater force emerging from a benevolent fusing of individual parts.

To the rational observer, at the foundation of this broad concept must be the fact that in some mysterious way, some part of a human being can communicate or link up with the natural forces at work in the world in which we live. This is, of course, a central tenet of many of the paranormal phenomena discussed in this book. Many believers in telepathy think the ability to read others' thoughts works by the some form of web, a hidden link between the minds of all humans.

Those who believe we are being visited by alien beings point to the idea of a *cosmic web* which in some way interlinks beings across the universe. The alchemists, and followers of the ancient Hermetic tradition, thought (and some still believe) that the secrets of the universe may be manifest in the everyday, that there is again a pattern or net connecting the forces of nature with the beings living on this planet.

For the scientist, many of these ideas sound nebulous and vague, without any tangible root. This is not helped by the fact that like so much of the paranormal, single strong ideas are turned into a lukewarm mishmash of muddled think-ing because of hidden agendas and a willingness to accept hocus-pocus. However, some enthusiasts of the paranormal accuse scientists of harbouring what they believe to be similar ideologies. Take as an example a famous thought experiment known as Bell's experiment in which two particles from a common source are fired at a device which then sends them in opposite directions at the speed of light.

One of these particles is then 'altered'. What this really means is that the particle can be changed in a very limited number of ways. For example, its *spin* can be changed. But, the odd result is that the second particle, travelling in the opposite direction at the speed of light, is also altered at precisely the same instant by the change imposed on the first particle. This appears to go against the laws of physics, in particular Einstein's theory of relativity which puts a speed limit – the speed of light – on everything in the universe.

The current interpretation of this experiment is to say that if the two particles have been linked at any time during the history of the universe they will always be able to communicate with one another. The physicists who discuss and analyse this interpretation do so using mathematical tools, and they are usually clear-thinking individuals who have little time for the vagaries of the occult and metaphysics. But researchers into supernatural phenomena point to such concepts as mirroring their own non-mathematical theories and explanations.

They suggest that there are mysterious unknown forces at work in Nature. However, as I have pointed out in other parts of this book, it would appear unlikely that any major force could exist that we have no idea about, unless it was a very weak force that did not interact with the other known forces. The reason for this is simple: if it is a strong force, we would have noticed it already. But if, by some strange chance, we had not noticed it and it was suddenly discovered, such a finding would destroy science; an inconceivable thought because science *works*. You would not be reading this book if it was not for the fact that science (technology) had produced it.

The remaining possibility, according to misinformed occultists, is that some strange force we have not yet discovered does operate but only in another part of the universe. I have argued against this already in *Chapter 8: Our Brethren Among The Stars?* The law of universality rules out this possibility. Besides, if this strange force only operated somewhere else in the universe it would be of little use in explaining many of the paranormal experiences that are supposed to occur here on Earth.

Earth magic takes many forms. As I have said, it may be interpreted as the key to almost all paranormal phenomena, certainly telepathy, clairvoyance, remote viewing, astral travelling, perhaps even ball lightning, ghosts and poltergeists. But, it also finds a home in explanations for a rostrum of other occult and metaphysical ideas including the reason for standing stones, ley lines, divining, pyramid-building and crop circles.

Ley lines are one of the most frequently written about and discussed manifestations of Earth magic. The lore surrounding the phenomena is ancient but, like many ideas of the occultists, it had been forgotten or lost for perhaps thousands of years until it re-emerged early in the twentieth century and gained a following amongst New Age enthusiasts.

The name *ley* was first coined by an amateur researcher into ancient paths and road systems, an Englishman named

Alfred Watkins, who wrote a book on the subject called *The Old Straight Track*. Watkins's concept of the ley was that all road systems and pathways zigzagging the countryside followed ancient patterns. In other words, all roads, old or modern, followed the same route and were built along the same pathways. He gave no reason for this curious alignment and certainly saw no mystical or occult connection between the ancient paths humans created and those designed and constructed by present-day engineers.

From Watkins's idea came the metaphysical concept of ley lines being *lines of force*, a principle that was then applied to explain a whole range of occult ideas. For example, investigators of paranormal phenomena use the idea of lines of force or *channels of energy* to explain dowsing. This is a technique via which certain people appear able to locate underground water using dowsing rods which were traditionally made from forked hazel twigs, but are now produced from almost any material, most commonly wire cut into an 'L' or a 'Y' shape. The idea is that the mind of the dowser is in some way hooked up with the flow of natural energy along ley lines.

Enthusiasts point to the fact that animals are sensitive to patterns within the natural forces at work on Earth. They cite the theory that migrating birds use lines of magnetic flux to help them navigate and refer to reported cases in which animals appear to be sensitive to approaching storms or impending earthquakes and tremors. They suggest that humans still retain a primitive instinct for the lines of force around the Earth and use this to dowse. But as we saw in *Chapter 6: We Are Made of Stars*, the hypothetical force that astrologers claim facilitates the interpretation of future events, the charting of personalities and elucidating the compatibility of humans has never been detected, cannot be squared with the known forces of Nature, and really has no tangible link with the ways in which birds navigate or salmon are able to return to their birthplace to breed – phenomena which may be explained by empirical science.

The evidence both for and against dowsing is plentiful.

There are numerous documented stories of individuals being able to locate water using dowsing rods, but just as many have produced embarrassing results. During the 1970s, a well-known French dowser claimed that in a single afternoon he had succeeded in finding the precise point to sink a well for a house he had bought in England. Yet, as we saw with research into telepathy and telekinesis, scientists have never been able to pin down this talent. In 1913, a group of scientists who set out to determine the mechanism via which dowsing could work were disappointed to find that a group of well-known dowsers failed to notice they were standing above an underground reservoir which produced 50,000 gallons of water per hour. Many years later, in 1970, a study financed by the Ministry of Defence in Britain produced less than exciting results. The report claimed that: '. . . the map dowsers could not even match the accuracy of volunteers taking guesses at the locations.'[1]

So what is the scientist to make of claims linking dowsing and its apparent connection with so-called ley lines? If there are some people who are able to locate water (and in some cases deposits of other substances such as minerals and ores), then this talent may derive from a heightened sensitivity towards some known forces and energies. Perhaps there are some rare individuals who are able to detect parts of the electromagnetic spectrum that for the most of us lie beyond our senses. It is even conceivable that if there are lines of force forming a grid around the world then the energy that travels between the linked points is a form of electromagnetic radiation and that this is in some way detected by an unknown part of the human brain which has remained active in some people, but dormant since prehistoric times in the rest of us.

However, some enthusiasts of the paranormal have taken things much further than connecting ley lines with what may be natural hidden talents such as dowsing. They suggest that ley lines were used by ancient peoples in the construction of roads and in the determination of sites for ritualistic monuments, that the ancients chose these paths and places because they believed they could somehow tap the energy travelling along the ley lines for religious, spiritual or emotional empowerment.

This is far removed from Alfred Watkins's original, comparatively simplistic ideas, but the researchers of Earth magic claim that there are striking connections between the standing stones at Avebury (interpreted by some as the nerve centre or nexus of the world's ley line system), Stonehenge, and standing stones in France and other parts of mainland Europe. Others take this still further and attempt to connect these systems with the lines found at the Plain of Nazca in Peru, known to have been constructed by the Incas between 600 and 1200 BC. Still more unsupportable connections have been made between the pyramids at Giza, the ancient temples at Machupicchu, the stones on Easter Island and even the position of the legendary lost continents of Atlantis and Mu.

The latest application for the idea of ley lines is to connect them with UFOs. Some claim that the grid system acts as a guide for alien visitors, that UFOs access the power that flows along the lines to propel their craft within the Earth's atmosphere. Others believe the ancients built the standing stones and their roads along these natural routes to emulate or to honour our alien neighbours.

In the early 1960s, a former RAF pilot named Tony Wedd became the first to popularise this hypothetical link between ley lines and UFOs. He believed the pilots of alien craft used the ley lines to help them navigate and claimed to find a vortex of energy where many lines met near his house in the West of England. He then went on to declare that he had been contacted by an alien called Attalita who passed on instructions for building alien machines. None of these have yet appeared in the malls of Earth.

Others picked up the baton inadvertently passed on by Watkins and metamorphosed by people like Tony Wedd. The 1970s saw a deluge of books on leys and their importance to both a secret ancient history and UFO lore. The best known of these were *The Flying Saucer Vision* and *The View Over Atlantis* both by UFOlogist John Michell. Both of these books had sexy titles but contained almost nothing of any value to support the claims of the author – that aliens use ley lines and that there is a link between the lost civilisation of Atlantis and the lines of some intangible natural energy crisscrossing the globe.

Of course there are strange connections between the positions of stones in parts of England and all sorts of odd shapes and configurations can be mapped out to link the pyramids with Stonehenge or the supposed location of Atlantis, but such connections can also be made by studying what are otherwise totally unconnected points of reference. This does not mean there is any distinct mystical value to be placed upon them.

Nevertheless, claims and counter-claims continue to confuse the issue of ley lines and their links with the paranormal. To support the sceptics is the fact that even poor, much-maligned Alfred Watkins's rather innocent and modest claims have been shown to be fallible. He wrote a second book called *Archaic Tracks Round Cambridge* in which he described sixty-two lines around the city created by lining up dozens of ancient and modern sites and monuments. But in 1979, a group of geologists from the Institute of Geomantic Research in Britain found that only nine of the sixty-two really did line up.[2]

On the other hand what many believe to be good evidence to support the importance of ley lines has come from a variety of studies made during the years since Watkins's death in 1935. Before extending his ideas to the esoteric edge and linking leys with almost anything under the umbrella of the paranormal, the author John Michell found that there are many stone rows dotted around the world, but concentrated especially in the West and the North of England and parts of Northern France. Although initially less dramatic than stone circles, some of these stone rows appear to line up for many miles across the country. The most important of these is The

Devil's Arrows in Yorkshire. This is a line of three stones that fall into an almost perfect line for almost eighteen kilometres (twelve miles). The line linking them also passes through four Neolithic earthworks including one of the most prominent in Northern England called Nunwick.

The enthusiasts claim that this is proof that ancient peoples were able to utilise an innate ability or sensitivity for a mysterious form of energy flowing along ley lines. Indeed, computer simulations of the Devil's Arrows created by mathematicians, Michael Behrend and Robert Forrest, showed that the chances of the alignment coming about by chance was negligible.

But there is another way of explaining this linking of ancient landmarks which does not rely upon the occult. It could be that ancient peoples did indeed want to place these stones and earthworks in a line for some lost religious purpose, but that need not have arisen from any form of supersensitivity towards unknown energies. Could they have aligned their stones in conjunction with a star, or the Sun at a point in its arc that was of some particular significance to them, a significance now probably lost forever? It is very common for researchers of the paranormal to jump quickly to conclusions drawn from the occult, to overlook the cleverness of ancient peoples. Such an attitude displays a condescension not unlike that demonstrated by some extreme sceptics who scoff at every aspect of the supernatural. It is quite possible that ancient people were able to line up monuments and objects of significance across a distance of eighteen kilometres without the use of mystical forces, and the reasons for the effort may not be rooted in anything more mystical than their particular religious ideology.

Whilst the enthusiasts of the paranormal have become increasingly obsessed with the apparent mystical meaning of ley lines, the public imagination has been captivated by another strange phenomena which, according to some interpretations, also comes under the umbrella of Earth magic – the appearance in fields of crop circles.

Media excitement with crop circles began in August 1980 when a Wiltshire farmer named John Scull claimed that a circle of flattened corn sixty feet in diameter had appeared overnight in one of his fields. The local newspaper, the *Wiltshire Times*, ran a report and within days the national media had leapt on the story, and photographs of the mysterious circle in Farmer Scull's field were plastered over the front pages.

During subsequent summers, more and more of the strange circles appeared in fields. Most of these were concentrated in the Western counties of England, especially Wiltshire and Hampshire. Media interest grew and theories to attempt to explain the phenomenon abounded. But for some time, the basic facts concerning what was happening in the fields of Western England remained sketchy and often contradictory.

In those early days of crop-circle reports, no one had actually seen one being formed and the earliest any investigators could reach the site was the morning after the event. There were plenty of claims from local residents, stories of strange lights seen in the vicinity of the circles at night, odd sounds emanating from the fields. Investigators arriving on the scene sometimes spoke of mysterious electronic effects inside the circles, of their apparatus being disturbed by high levels of static electricity. Others declared that dowsing equipment had gone haywire inside crop circles and that photographic equipment had malfunctioned. The stories grew more and more elaborate as time passed. Some would also point out that the tales became more colourful as the interest of journalists escalated.

In the midst of this mounting fascination, several well-timed books appeared. The most successful of these was *Circular Evidence*, a book that became an international bestseller. Published in 1989, it was written by two UFO enthusiasts, Pat Delgado and Colin Andrews. Delgado was a space engineer who had worked on the British missile project in Australia and then for a time at NASA in the US;

Andrews was a highly-qualified electrical engineer. Both wrote frequently for such journals as *Flying Saucer Review* and became interested in the paranormal aspects of crop circles as well as the apparent physical anomalies they offered. Their book was widely condemned by scientists but found a large and enthusiastic audience amongst believers in the occult and the UFO investigation fraternity, although, to be fair, quite a few followers of UFO lore doubted many of the authors' claims.

Even by the mid-1980s, when Delgado and Andrews were researching *Circular Evidence*, the facts about crop circles were still scant but allowed for a range of often colourful theories. It was known that the corn was not broken at the base, but simply bent. It was also observed that the crops were forced into a swirl rather than a circular pattern, as though a vortex at the centre of the circle was flattening the stems like a spinning top or the conventional image of a tornado. Some claimed the effect was caused by rutting hedgehogs, others that a strange weather effect was behind them.

Dubbing themselves *cereologists*, Delgado and Andrews pointed to the fact that during the time from the first appearance of the circles in 1980, to the writing of their book, the markings had become increasingly elaborate. They contested that this was evidence the crop circles were being produced by an alien intelligence as part of an effort to communicate with humanity. This idea was then expanded upon by other authors and this theory developed, gradually drawing in other aspects of occult lore.

But others disagreed, and suddenly there seemed to be as many theories as there were subdivisions of UFO legend; each group managing to adopt crop circles for themselves. There were those who believed that the circles were created by what they called *pan-dimensional beings* – what we are to believe are beings from other 'dimensions'. And this intriguing theory is still alive and well today long after most sane individuals have grown convinced of rational (but nevertheless fascinating) explanations for the phenomenon of crop circles. As recently as the summer of 1997, a photographer who specialises in aerial images of crop circles, Lucy Pringle, claimed that: 'Crop circles are the work of beings in a "parallel world".' And warned that entering a crop circle may represent a health risk to pregnant women because of 'microwave emissions'.[3]

Others subscribe to the view that there is a race of intelligent beings who live inside the Earth – this is linked to the concept of the *hollow Earth* and believers claim that flying saucers are not from other worlds but from this secret civilisation who live in an alternative world beneath our feet, a world that may be reached through portals at the Earth's poles. Puzzling though it may seem, supporters of this idea believe the inhabitants of the hollow Earth are using crop circles to communicate with us.

Not surprisingly the number of accounts of crop circles grew almost exponentially as the media picked up on the story and ran with it throughout the 1980s. More books and, finally, television programmes began to appear. Suddenly, everyone was a crop-circle spotter, a dedicated cereologist. Helicopter trips were laid on for tourists willing to pay £100 per hour to hover over West Country fields and skirt the hillsides where fresh circles appeared on a daily basis. Farmers began to open up their fields for the fee-paying public who were then charged extra for each photograph they took or video film they shot. Film and TV crews found access to farmland depended upon how much the networks were willing to pay, and landowners vied with one another to offer the best and most sensational new pattern in the corn.

Then, just as the furore reached a peak in August 1991, two people reported seeing a crop circle in the making, and Press excitement reached a new peak. Gary and Vivienne Tomlinson were walking along a track beside a field close to the village of Hambledon in Hampshire when they heard and saw what they later claimed to be a corn circle forming.

'There was a tremendous noise,' they reported. 'We looked up to see if it was caused by a helicopter but there was nothing. We felt a strong wind pushing us from the side and above. It was forcing down on our heads – yet incredibly my husband's hair was standing on end. Then the whirring air seemed to branch into two and zigzag off into the distance. We could still see it like a light mist or fog shimmering as it moved. As it disappeared we were left standing in a corn circle with the corn flattened all around us. Everything became very still again and we were left with a tingling feeling.'[4]

But then, only a month later, the hopes of the enthusiasts heightened by this eyewitness account of corn circle formation seemed dashed when two men came forward announcing that all along they had been responsible for creating the circles.

Doug Bower and Dave Chorley, two retired artists, demonstrated how they had faked dozens of crop circles during the previous ten years, even leaving their 'DD' trademark close to some of their creations.

When this news broke, there was an immediate and impassioned response from enthusiasts and sceptics alike. The enthusiasts were initially devastated but then fell back upon the idea that the artists were themselves fakes, that the CIA, MI5 and the FBI were all conspiring to dispel the idea that the circles were part of a huge plan for aliens to make contact. The sceptics made as much capital from the news as they could. Newspapers began to run 'fake-a-crop-circle' competitions, whereas only a year or two earlier they had offered £10,000 rewards to anyone who could present a clear and convincing explanation for the phenomenon.

Although Bower and Chorley received their fifteen minutes of fame from this stunt, much to the delight of the enthusiasts, it soon became clear there were some major flaws in their claims. Firstly, it was obvious that two men working with simple tools could not have produced the hundreds of crop circles that had appeared regularly each year, some of them as far from the West Country of England as Australia and the US. But then other teams of fakers went public and circles were soon discovered that carried their hallmarks – coded messages cut into the corn close by. Sometimes the hoaxers even added their names: The Bill Bailey Gang, Merlin & Co., and others.

But there were more serious problems with the claims of the fakers; it was slowly dawning that there were 'natural' crop circles that no one had faked. Some of the circles were so perfect it was almost impossible for the doubters to explain how they could have been the handiwork of practical jokers. Other circles were found in remote places stumbled upon by chance – hardly the location a self-publicising joker would choose. Coupled with this was the testimony of the Tomlinsons who had not been involved in the debate until the night they had stumbled upon a crop circle being formed and had no hidden agenda or even any particular interest in crop circles.

However, the most convincing argument that the fakes were only part of the story came from the fact that crop circles had been reported hundreds of years before any of the players in this modern game were born.

The first documented case occurred in Assen, Holland in 1590, but the most famous incident took place in a field in Hertfordshire in 1678. The farmer who owned the land reported finding the circle in one of his corn fields and wrote a pamphlet about it (these were the days before newspapers). He suggested that the markings were produced by what he called a 'mowing devil'. The pamphlet was illustrated with a cover depicting a devilish figure cutting a swath through the field with a scythe. Intrigued by this case and other reports, a seventeenth-century scientist named Robert Plot investigated the phenomenon and came to the conclusion that the circles were produced by air blasts fired at the ground.

It is a depressing fact that in the seventeenth century, an age of great superstition and widespread belief that the occult controlled everyday life, Dr Plot could study the phenomenon with empirical detachment; yet in our own time, so many people have leapt at the supernatural to try to find answers.

Thankfully, amidst the hysteria generated by the enthusiasts of all things paranormal and the cynicism of the sceptics and the Press, farmers cashing-in and proud fakers, there were still a few people in the early 1990s who were willing to look at the phenomenon objectively. And, one of them, Dr Terence Meaden, head of the Tornado and Storm Research Organisation and editor of the *Journal of Meteorology* may well have come up with an explanation for how genuine crop circles (as opposed to the faked circles of Bower and Chorley) could have been created.

Meaden proposes that the circles are formed as a result of what he calls a *plasma vortex*. If a hill obstructs a gust of wind, the wind can eventually meet stationary air on the lee side of the hill. This creates a vortex, or spiralling column of air, which then sucks in more air and atmospheric electricity. This hovers close to the ground until it encounters a corn field, where it flattens the stems into the now-familiar spiral pattern. The static electricity generated in the vortex (produced from high concentrations of ionised air) could be the reason for the high-pitched whirring noise (a sound like a helicopter) reported by witnesses who have been close by a corn circle as it formed. It may even account for the reports of odd electrostatic effects within the circle sometime after it is created. Some residual charge may disturb machinery and photographic equipment.

In an effort to quantify the forces at work in crop circle formation, others have taken Meaden's work further. Professor John Snow working at Purdue in the US and Professors Yoshi-Hiko Ohtsuki and Tokio Kikuchi from the University of Tokyo have all visited prominent sites in England and have studied the vortex effect in the lab. They produced computer simulations and created virtual crop circles with exactly the characteristics observed in fields in Wiltshire and Hampshire.

The Japanese team took their research another stage further and produced a real vortex on a small scale and used it to create circles in metal sheets. They then persuaded the Tokyo underground railway to allow them to conduct a larger-scale experiment in a subway tunnel along which they passed ionised air. In the confined conditions of a subway tunnel the effect of air and high concentrations of electrical energy from the tracks did indeed produce a set of small circles in the dust close to the live lines.

So, what should be concluded from the evidence gathered about crop circles in recent years and how does it relate to what occultists call Earth magic? Indeed, what is Earth magic?

Crop circles are clearly a complex phenomenon and no single explanation covers all of those found. In recent years, more and more complex patterns have been appearing in fields around the world. The last years of the millennium have produced a bumper collection of amazing designs including the Star of David, snowflakes, Florentine needlework patterns, Maltese crosses, even torus knots and symbols from the kabbala. Unless you are willing to believe that these are produced by bored aliens or it is some part of a larger secret scheme to initiate humans into the great galactic brotherhood, these are obviously very clever and quite beautiful fakes. But simple crop circles still appear spontaneously in farmers' fields. Naturally, these are increasingly ignored as the more glamorous models take centre stage, but they are there nevertheless and are almost certainly produced by natural means.

Research into the meteorological anomalies that could account for these natural crop circles is continuing, but researchers face pressure from the cynics who would like to discredit anything to do with crop circles. This is a shame and actually hands a Pyrrhic victory to the crank element who, together with the Press, generated the hysteria and overblown hype surrounding crop circles in the first place.

*   *   *

How do crop circles fit into the larger picture of Earth magic? Well, as we saw at the start of this chapter, what the enthusiasts of the paranormal call earth magic may well be a collection of known forces acting in strange ways and interacting with human beings in a perfectly natural rather than supernatural way.

We are constantly buffeted by forces and energies, some of which scientists understand clearly while others remain only partly clarified. Crop circles are a perfect example of how odd physical effects can be produced by these forces. If we discount the fakers and showmen (just as we should when analysing all aspects of the paranormal), crop circles represent a phenomenon which, on the surface, defies explanation. But as is always the case, this is merely due to a dearth of information. Dig deeper and an explanation unfolds. In the case of crop circles they are the result of a natural but rare process that creates an effect only seen occasionally until recent times.

People living in the eighteenth century, say two hundred and fifty years ago, placed supernatural meaning upon the mysterious illnesses and deaths suffered by their loved ones. Only when humanity learned of the existence of bacteria and viruses were we able to substitute the concept of evil spirits with the reality of microorganisms. Suddenly, the demons and devils that killed us were known to be nothing more than other physical creatures with whom we share the planet.

There is an Earth magic, a natural magic that can cast its spell and perform its wonders. It's called biology. At other times it takes on the guise of physics, chemistry, geology. It is the natural wonder of existence and it is miraculous enough.

11

REMOTE VIEWING AND THE PSI DETECTIVES

'Fighting is the most primitive way of making war on
your enemies. The supreme excellence is to subdue the
armies without having to fight them.'

Sun Tzu, Fourth Century BC.

I was once involved in a remote viewing experiment. In 1997
I was the science consultant for a series for the Discovery
Channel called *The Science of the Impossible* and one of the
programmes was devoted to 'Mind and Matter'. Short of an
'actor', they decided I would do for a sequence in which an
experienced remote viewer would try to determine where in
the world I was and what I was doing.

The arrangements were necessarily convoluted. The idea
was that I would be taken to a secret location. I would only
be told where I was going on the morning of the shoot.
Meanwhile, in Virginia in the USA, remote viewer Joe
McMoneagle, a Vietnam veteran who had discovered his
talent after being wounded, was to be filmed live trying to
get into my mind and to describe what I was seeing across
the other side of the world, in England. The only thing he
was told was that (much to my disappointment) I would not
be leaving the country.

Why I could not have been whisked to the Bahamas I

don't know. Instead I was treated to Stansted airport in
sunny Essex. This is an impressive glass and granite homage
to the 1980s boom, a beautifully-designed building which
is also one of the largest open structures in Europe. We
arrived on time and walked around the airport, had a coffee
and waited for a private guided tour which was to take us
onto the runways and around a few aircraft. Meanwhile, the
second crew started filming Joe trying to 'see' where I was.

But then we hit a problem. The tour guide, the PR
executive for the airport, was late and so far I had not seen
a single plane – not even as we had parked and entered the
building. As far as actually seeing anything was concerned
I could have been anywhere. Then, via a mobile phone,
we heard that Joe had started to draw, and as he produced
the pictures they were faxed to a mobile fax machine the
producer had in one of the film crew vehicles. By the time
our guide arrived and escorted us out onto the runway and
I saw my first plane, the test was over and Joe had said that
he had finished with the location.

So how did Joe McMoneagle's illustrations match up with
reality?

Well, things were confused by the mix-up at Stansted
airport, but even so, I can't honestly say the experiment was
terribly convincing. Joe made a few striking connections. The
most surprising was that just at the moment I had turned
to the producer to draw attention to the amazing granite
floor in the building, Joe had described the place in which
I was standing as 'made of lots of stone and glass'. He then
went on to draw archways and canopies of stone; the roof
of the airport is held up with metal supports, which could
be described as 'arched'. He said we were near a main road
and a railway line, that there was a church or place of worship
nearby. But, most importantly, he did not mention aircraft,
flying or anything to do with an airport.

The interpretation of this experience was as confused as
the events. The producer claimed that it was really a success
because Joe could not have known I was at an airport because

I had not seen a plane until after he had finished viewing. He pointed out that there were two major motorways close to the airport and that there was an underground railway that we had passed as we entered the airport. Most significantly, he discovered there was a chapel on the lower ground floor of the airport.

However, for me there were problems with these interpretations. Firstly, I had been totally unaware of the underground railway we had passed, although I admit I may have been aware of it subliminally. I was quite unaware of the chapel, yet Joe was supposed to have picked that up from me. If this was true, why had he failed to pick up the aircraft I had not seen? Finally, the fact that he had correctly realised there was a major road close by is hardly an amazing feat of supernatural skill – it is rather difficult to get away from roads in 1990s Britain.

My feeling was that Joe thought I had been in a church or a cathedral. His drawings consisted of stone arches, glass and ornate decoration and he was keen to push the idea that I was in a city and that there was something to do with worship at the centre of the experience. My interpretation of the experiment was that he thought I was in St Paul's Cathedral or Westminster Abbey.

Remote viewing (or RV) is a boom industry and for some it is the most lucrative application of supposed powers linked to telepathy and the use of what some believe to be powerful mental energies. It is also an application taken seriously by some senior executives of multinational companies who employ remote viewers, by the military establishment of many nations around the world, by government agencies and police forces who frequently use people known as *psi detectives*, who have helped to solve serious crimes.

There have been some impressive examples of remote viewing and psi detection during the past three decades. A great deal of secret work was conducted on both sides of the Iron Curtain during the Cold War, but much of this is still kept under wraps. More readily available are the details of how certain individuals appear to have helped police around the world in their work.

Two of the most successful exponents of psi detection are from Holland: Peter Hurkos and Gerald Croiset. When he was thirteen, Peter Hurkos fell from a tree and suffered concussion. Soon after, he started to realise that he could locate lost objects by just thinking about them and had strange 'impressions' of distant locations and activities which, according to witnesses, could be matched with the behaviour of individuals he had never known and with whom he had no other contact. From the late 1950s he helped the police forces of several countries solve serious crimes, determined the location of murder victims and gave descriptions of perpetrators including a period working with American police hunting the Boston Strangler. Hurkos was especially effective at passing on data he gathered from the technique of *psychometry* in which a psychic appears to 'sense' information about an individual by handling some of their possessions, usually clothes or items that had a particular significance for the missing person.

Gerald Croiset's successes were, if anything, more impressive. He has never charged for his services and is not happy travelling, usually helping police with their investigations via the telephone. In this way he helped the New York Police Department to find the body of a four-year-old girl and the identity of her killer. In 1967, he received a call from a journalist named Frank Ryan who wanted him to help find a teenage girl called Patricia Mary McAdam, who had gone missing from her home in Scotland. Croiset told Ryan that the girl was dead, where she would be found and even details such as the fact that the body lay close to a car wreck and that a wheelbarrow was leaning against the car. Strangely, the area was located, the wrecked car and even the wheelbarrow were found, but no body. To this day Patricia Mary McAdam's body has never been discovered.

Another famous case yielding what appears to be impressive results for the psi detective involved the hunt for the Yorkshire Ripper. During the late 1970s, there was a series of gruesome murders concentrated primarily around cities in the north of England, especially Sheffield and Bradford. The victims were always young women, many of them prostitutes and the murderer dismembered the bodies, earning his nickname because of the way he butchered the bodies in a similar fashion to the Victorian murderer, Jack The Ripper.

The hunt for the Ripper lasted years and became the biggest murder case in modern British history. During the latter stages of the investigation several regional police forces turned to psychics for help. The famous medium, Doris Stokes, gave information to the police which turned out to be of little use; but then another female psychic, Nella Jones, volunteered her services. She told police the murderer lived in a large house in Bradford, Northern England, that the house was Number 6, but she could not pinpoint the name of the street. She claimed the man was called Peter and that he was a long-distance lorry driver and that the name of the company he worked for was embossed on the door of the cab. She claimed the company name began with the letter 'C', but she could not make out the full name.

Early in 1981, the Yorkshire Ripper was caught and jailed for life. His name was Peter Sutcliffe, he had been a long-distance lorry driver who had lived in a large house, No. 6, Garden Lane, Bradford, and he had worked for a company called Clark Holdings.

Similarly impressive results are sometimes obtained through remote viewing and used by the military as well as government agencies such as MI5, the CIA and the KGB.

The Russians appear to have been the first off the mark with research into remote viewing and the uses of mental powers for military purposes. Some claim that research began in the 1920s and continued until the Berlin Wall came down and communism crumbled. However, there is plenty of the usual hyperbole surrounding accounts of anything to do with military use of telepathic energies. A journalist in the magazine *Encounters* recently stated quite categorically that: 'First developed in the Soviet Union and then adopted by the West, psi makes some use of the ninety percent of the human brain that is normally left unused.'[1]

But even if we ignore such bland statements unsupported by any form of evidence, it is certainly true the Russians and the other major powers have been very interested in the possible practical application of psi since at least the 1940s, and despite the collapse of communism, there are almost certainly research establishments still investigating its use for military purposes. And why not? It makes perfect sense to study such things. Compared to the development of conventional weapons, the money spent on research into the paranormal would be almost insignificant, perhaps a few million dollars. Yet, if a mysterious form of telepathic power could be isolated and controlled, it would be one of the most effective weapons any nation could wish for.

Some claim that such powers have been used; but even the most enthusiastic supporter of such ideas as psi admit that, at best, the application of these powers is inefficient and produces only patchy results.

The most popular use for mental powers by the military is its use as an aid for spying and many people formerly involved with psi espionage have come forward in recent years. Some are still bound by security to keep sensitive material to themselves, but others, such as those who worked for the KGB and other Communist Bloc agencies have been more forthcoming. As well as this source, information about the fascination with parapsychology in former Warsaw Pact countries has been known since the 1960s via investigators and research groups in the West, some of whom gathered first-hand experience by clandestine means during the Cold War. According to some authorities these sources alerted the Pentagon to the potential of research into psi powers.

In 1968, two investigators of paranormal activity, American Sheila Ostrander and Canadian Lynn Shroeder, visited the

USSR and detailed their findings in a book called *Psychic Discoveries Behind the Iron Curtain*. Soon after the publication of the book, they claimed they were each visited by agents from the FBI and the Canadian Mounted Police, although this could have been a convenient story to enhance sales of their book.

By this time, the US government had detailed knowledge of the Russian interest in psi research, and in particular, claims that the Russians had people who could influence the behaviour of others and to remote-view secret installations. Even so, it took some time for this to be made public, and it was not until the 1980 issue of the *US Military Review*, that a Lieutenant Colonel John Alexander was sanctioned to declare his belief that Russian psi research had developed to the point where they could interfere with US military operations. This was followed by an official recommendation that the Pentagon set up a counter investigation. In fact, such an organisation had already been in operation for many years.

The research that the Russians had apparently developed into a practical tool was based on a technique which has become known as *Sleep-Wake Hypnosis*. This is a trick used by professional hypnotists and showmen which, some claim, enables them to induce hypnotic effects at a distance. The power to do this on a stage is one thing, but some have claimed that highly-skilled practitioners have the power to turn on and off hypnotic states at distances of thousands of miles.

These claims have yet to be studied thoroughly by investigators outside the military, so little information is available in the public domain. It could be that secret institutions have made some headway in the study of Sleep-Wake Hypnosis, but there is no documentary evidence available to support this. All we have to go by at present are the performances of professional hypnotists who insist they are not using any form of trickery, yet are able to produce what seem to be impressive results. One famous hypnotist who appears regularly on British television, Paul McKenna, has been filmed raising and lowering the heart-rate of a volunteer seated in another room. However, it is important to note that to date, this particular claim has not been verified rigorously by scientists under laboratory conditions.

Yet, to the believers in the practical uses of psi, the implication from the Russian research is that their military have had the ability to influence the actions of unaware individuals across the world for the best part of two decades. But even this extraordinary claim is not enough for some. It has been suggested recently that the Russians have mastered a technique via which they are able to create, store and transmit at will what is dubbed *negative energy* and to pervade an area as far away as the West Coast of the United States with this energy.

One of the most extraordinary accounts of what some believers think is the use of this mysterious energy comes from a 'mystic' named Michael Bromley, a self-styled 'Celtic shaman'. Bromley claims to have the ability to sense negative energy and has been employed on numerous occasions by security agencies around the world to help them plan events and to know in advance when and where there is likely to be trouble. He claims to have been successful in pinpointing key areas in Los Angeles where he thought problems might arise during the 1984 Olympic Games held in the city, and was able to tell police in advance about a security guard he believed would attempt to rape one of the athletes performing in the games. He impressed the local police (and, it was revealed later, the FBI and the CIA) when he told them before the start of the games that the district of Westwood was particularly vulnerable and awash with negative energy.

On the opening day of the games a young man drove a car deliberately at a queue of twenty people in Westwood. At his trial, the offender told the jury that he had been hit by what he called 'waves of energy'.

For Michael Bromley and others, the 1984 Olympic Games was particularly significant because it was a time of increased pre-Glasnost political tension and the Russians had refused to take part, just as the US had done four years earlier at the Moscow Olympics. Bromley was convinced that something sinister was going on during the 1984 Olympics. 'I lived outside Los Angeles,' he reported. 'Quite independently people were calling me from the city saying they felt waves of energy coming into the area. The Soviets didn't come to the games. All the phone lines from that country to America were engaged a lot of the time. I realized that phone lines were carriers of energy. Now if it was possible to send *psychic* energy down those lines ... I believe the Soviets were projecting negative energy into Los Angeles. I know it sounds far-fetched, but we do it every day. It's the same as wishing someone well, sending their love, or wishing them harm. The Russians have been carrying out scientific experiments into parapsychology for decades.'[2]

For the scientist this statement illustrates many of the misguided attempts at explanations offered by enthusiasts and what is often muddled thinking concerning any attempts to bring the occult into the arena of scientific investigation. It is worth looking at in some detail.

Firstly, the whole account is an odd blend of emotive statement and wild speculation. I would like to give Michael Bromley the benefit of the doubt and assume he is not combining these elements to deliberately manipulate the reader and that he is sincere about what he believes. However, this technique of mixing stirring, thought-provoking one-liners with suggestive remarks is used frequently by politicians and speech-makers who are trying to convince an audience. So for example, we have a description of how Mr Bromley was being called by people from Los Angeles reporting 'waves of energy'. He follows this sentence immediately with: 'The Soviets didn't come to the games.' Then we have a long discourse about how energy could be transmitted via telephone lines followed by: 'The Russians have been carrying out scientific experiments into the paranormal for decades.' This has the effect of reinforcing a link between the two statements that is not really there.

And what are we to make of the theory postulated by Michael Bromley, that the negative energy sent by the Russians could be transmitted via the telephone lines?

He presents no evidence for this hypothesis. He may think he has, because he says things like: 'I know it sounds far-fetched, but we all do it every day. It's the same as wishing someone well, sending their love, or wishing then harm.' This is not evidence, this is bland statement actually contradicted by fact. Yes, we may all send our love to people every day, but does it actually do any good? We do not live in a world where things happen because we wish they would. There are undoubtedly forces known as positive and negative *thinking*, but these have nothing to do with projecting our desires or wishes upon the world or other people. Positive and negative thinking are emotions or drives within us that dictate how confident, optimistic, or indeed pessimistic we feel, and this in turn affects our performance. If we were really able to influence events by wishing alone, would it not be an everyday occurrence to see the sick rise up from their hospital beds because loved ones wished it so?

And what about the telephone lines? Telephone lines do indeed carry energy, electrical impulses with tiny electrical potentials. But how can we accept a leap from a documented, practical scientific principle such as the use of electrical impulses to communicate around the world, to some vague notion Mr Bromley proposes such as the use of telephone wires to carry an unknown force?

For Michael Bromley, the phone lines carry energy, therefore the Russians must be sending negative energy down those lines. How does he know this? Because the lines were engaged! Does it not seem more likely that the phone lines were jammed with people wanting to talk across the world, disappointed people who had been hoping to meet their friends from Russia?

Which then leads us to another problem with this story

– where is the motivation for such an act? Why would the Russian military waste so much effort upsetting the people of Los Angeles during the Olympic Games? It might be argued that during the Cold War, agencies in the Soviet Union and in the West did some crazy things for little gain, but is this really the most likely explanation for why people felt what they called 'waves of energy'? Is it not more reasonable to suggest that these waves of energy were imagined, that someone contrived the idea that because those dastardly Commies were not attending an American Olympic games, they must be transmitting negative energy; after all: 'The Russians have been carrying out scientific experiments into the paranormal for decades.' Once the idea was circulated, others started to believe it, and in the summer heat and with the excitement of the Games fuelling the hysteria, even criminals trying to find excuses for their murderous intentions realised they could tap into the *Zeitgeist*.

But there is actually more to this story than meets the eye. People have been fascinated by the thought that the Soviets have been very interested in the occult for a long time, and this undoubtedly played a part in starting the rumours in Los Angeles and sending people to their telephones to call up Michael Bromley. As I mentioned earlier, at least one highly successful book has documented some of the experiments conducted by Russian scientists and parapsychologists working for the military, and it is worth noting that 1984 was a time of heightened political friction between the two superpowers, a time reminiscent of the Cold War hysteria of the 1950s and '60s.

There is a rich history of attempts to apply psi powers, not just as a tool for the spy, but also in efforts to exert some sort of mental control at a distance, of which Paul McKenna's media-friendly effort to utilise Sleep-Wake Hypnosis is only one example.

In 1977, a psychical investigator named Andrija Puharich told a surprised audience at one of his lectures in London that the Russians had for years been developing a device which was able to control minds at a distance. This, he claimed, was based upon the work of the great physicist Nikola Tesla, the man who had made practical the use of alternating current.

According to Puharich, around the turn of the century Tesla had developed a method of sending an extremely low frequency wave (an ELF wave) which has a frequency of 4–15 pulses per second (4–15 Hz) through the core of the Earth. The idea was to use huge transmitters positioned diametrically on the surface of the planet that would set up a *stationary wave* (a set of waves all vibrating at the same frequency to produce a single wavefront) able to penetrate the Earth's core and emerge at a predetermined spot somewhere in the world.

The use of a frequency between 4 and 15 Hz was no mere coincidence. This is the frequency range of alpha rhythms produced by the human brain. These rhythms are usually linked with relaxation but have also been identified as the frequencies most usually enhanced in the brains of fakirs during feats of extreme physical endurance.

In an attempt to explain how the stationary wave generated by Tesla's transmitters could affect the thoughts and behaviour of a target, supporters suppose that a *resonance wave* is established in the brain of the recipient of the signal. A resonance wave is created when two waves vibrate in harmony – an everyday example is the way an opera singer can shatter a glass because their voice vibrates at the same frequency as the molecules in the crystalline structure of the glass. The implication is that a controller using the Tesla device could alter the brain waves in a target subject by establishing a resonance wave and then fine-tuning the frequency.

These ideas have found plenty of support within the community of investigators of the paranormal and there have been many attempts to link these studies with the phenomenon of telepathy and psychokinesis. But, there is still no clear empirical evidence to support these claims, and the concept that rhythms in the human brain, operating at whatever frequency, lay at the root of apparent psi powers is unproven.

In some ways, this scenario is an illustration of the problems anyone faces in trying to find genuine legitimate and provable links between science and the supernatural. Tesla's machine is theoretically sound, extremely low frequency waves can be produced, and, again in theory, if sufficiently powerful generators were used it is conceivable that a stationary wave powerful enough to penetrate the Earth's core could be produced. Where science and the paranormal do not harmonise is in the linking of this man-made wave to the natural rhythms produced in the brain. The elements are all there – Tesla's machine could be built, the brain does produce alpha rhythms, there is such a thing as resonance; but these ideas do not link up except in the minds of the enthusiasts.

The Western powers have been just as keen as the Russians in attempting to exploit any possible practical use for psi powers. In a 1992 Symposium on UFO Research, US Major General Albert N. Stubblebine III chaired a seminar on remote viewing and became the first high-ranking military official to reveal the degree to which the US government had used RV for military purposes.

Stubblebine himself headed a research group called Psi Tech which was set up by two respected physicists, Hal Puthoff and Russell Targ at Stanford Research Institute in California, and jointly funded by the CIA and the US Navy. At the talk, he claimed that RV training took about one year and that selected individuals with appropriate discipline and commitment could do amazing things using the power of their minds. 'Time is no object,' he claimed. 'I can go past, I can go present, I can go future. It is independent of location so I can go anywhere on Earth . . . I can access information at any location I choose.' He then went on to describe how in 1991 his group had helped a large American corporation assess the effect of the Gulf War on the price of oil. His group came up with an answer by, he claimed, 'looking inside Saddam Hussein's head'.[3]

To the dispassionate observer, there are many problems with this account. We can assume that such a group was established, but the successes they claim to have achieved are highly dubious. The overriding reason for this is that if such a group had been able to truly 'go past, present or future at any location on Earth', there would be no need for any conventional spies, the US government would know everything there was to know about any foreign power. In fact, such a group could easily have become billionaries and would by now rule the world!

We must assume that Major General Stubblebine III is, like many of us, prone to hyperbole and exaggeration. Caught up in the enthusiasm of his delivery, he must have failed to add caveats to his claims, not least of which is the fact that even the most successful remote viewers are often vague, get things wrong as often as they get things right, and are quite unable to give precise details except on extremely rare occasions.

The second point concerns Stubblebine's story of his involvement in Gulf War espionage. This is unconvincing on two counts. Firstly, when a corporation funds a project, there is pressure on those employed (in this case, the remote viewers) to come up with something, anything that might justify a cheque. This understandably casts everything they do in a suspicious light. But, the second, and far more important issue, comes from the simple fact that anyone with any awareness of world affairs and global finances would be able to produce a coherent report detailing the effects of the Gulf War on global economics. You certainly don't need to have psi powers to do that, and one of the last people to be of help would have been Saddam Hussein.

Yet, beyond all this, in order to validate or refute this research we must look at the work of the two men who started the project, Hal Puthoff and Russell Targ. According to their own accounts, they conducted over one hundred RV experiments during the late 1970s and claim to have achieved remarkable results.[4] In at least one set of experiments, they described a remote viewer who was able to find precisely a location not simply when a 'sender' was there but before the site was even chosen.

To the scientist, this alone would imply that something suspicious was going on with their procedure – that there must be a security leak somewhere. But putting this aside, other researchers have tried unsuccessfully to duplicate Puthoff's and Targ's results. The most thorough and well-publicised of these was a set of experiments conducted by two other physicists, David Marks and Robert Kammann. They found that their subjects produced results that were no better than would be expected from chance or simple guesswork.

In a book the pair wrote in 1980, entitled *Psychology of the Psychic*[5], Marks and Kammann described their experiments, how they then contacted Puthoff and Targ to request access to their data and how, to their amazement, their request was refused.

To deny other scientists access to one's work is almost unheard of, and immediately sets alarm bells ringing in the ears of other researchers trying to verify results. Consequently, Puthoff's and Targ's refusal to release their data gave Marks and Kammann renewed enthusiasm to track down what could be happening in RV experiments.

After extensive investigation, they came to the conclusion that in all the tests they performed, the remote viewer was either totally inaccurate or when they had succeeded they had been provided with subliminal cues or unconscious hints by those involved in the experiment. By matching the transcripts of the conversation between the viewer, the 'sender' and the experimenters, Marks and Kammann showed how these clues are picked up.

Suppose a viewer is told that they will be required to identify three locations: 1, 2 and 3. The viewer is told that one location is a building, another is an open area, a third is a road, but they have no idea of the order in which they will come during the tests. However, in the transcript of the dialogue, there are a series of cues the experienced viewer can use. For example, the experimenter says before one of the tests: 'Third time lucky.' During another of the three, they say: 'OK, take it slowly, we've got a long day ahead of us.' With these hints, the viewer knows which site is 1, 2 or 3.

After holding out for five years and facing renewed requests from others in the field, Puthoff and Targ did eventually publish their findings, in 1985. And, upon detailed analysis of these documents, independent investigators found that there were many cues given in their transcripts, particularly during the most successful remote viewing tests.

Other researchers have conducted their own investigations similar to the work of Marks and Kammann and have obtained concurring results. In a paper published in *Nature* in 1986, co-authored by Dr Marks and an independent colleague, Dr C. Scott, the researchers came to the scathing conclusion that: '. . . remote viewing has not been demonstrated in the experiments conducted by Puthoff and Targ, only the repeated failure of investigators to remove sensory cues.'[6]

But is this really the whole picture? Naturally, like all areas of the paranormal, there is a high proportion of misinterpretation, misunderstanding, wishful thinking and out-and-out fraud involved with remote viewing and psi detection: but is it possible that a few individuals do not rely upon cues, do not fake their abilities and are able to pick up incomplete and often hazy images from distant locations? Is it possible that some special individuals are able to picture scenes and people in the past, present and future? What are we to make of some of the remarkable success stories of people such as Nella Jones? Do such people have a genuine talent, and if so, how does it operate?

Remote viewers claim they can 'see' distant locations, they can 'get inside the heads' of the person they see through. However, the energy needed to do such a thing would destroy the cells of the brain. A safer option may be the use of some form of 'channelling'. This is an idea that has gained popularity during the past twenty-five years and is based upon the principle that some talented people can 'tap into a mental network', some mysterious 'level of human consciousness' where all humans are linked.

Parapsychologists are fond of trying to involve quantum mechanics in their explanations of how this could work, but these links are tenuous in the extreme. As I have said elsewhere, well-meaning but untrained investigators are often too keen to drag out Bell's experiment and other seemingly odd aspects of quantum theory to explain what could be happening with telepaths, clairvoyants and indeed, remote viewers.

It is conceivable that remote viewers may be able to utilise some strange talent involving receiving information passed through a wormhole. In other words they could be receiving data via a wormhole linking two places on Earth.[7] To do this, they would have to have the extraordinary ability to not only access random information as clairvoyants seem to do (people who receive uninvited images of future events), but to actually manipulate the wormhole so they could see and sense anywhere in the world they wish to probe.

For even the most open-minded scientist, this last hypothesis appears so far-fetched as to be impossible. For this idea to work successfully, it would mean that Nella Jones and other successful psi detectives, along with the rare individuals who have produced successful remote viewing results unaided by cues and strong hints were able to manipulate the very matter of the universe and such fundamental entities as wormholes, without consciously realising it.

This is no explanation, simply a wild idea, an attempt to match up the meagre facts unearthed by parapsychologists with the latest ideas on the fringes of science. But, until we have more information about how the mind can process information, how subliminal information may seep into our subconscious and be dredged up by the human brain, and indeed until we know a lot more about how the universe functions at the most fundamental level explored by quantum mechanists, some very rare cases of remote viewing and psi detection remain totally unexplained.

12

THE GODS
THEMSELVES?

'There were vast heaps of stone . . . There . . . under my
eyes, ruined, destroyed, lay a town – its roofs open to the
sky . . . Further on, some remains of a giant aqueduct . . .
there traces of a quay . . . Further on again, long lines
of sunken walls and broad, deserted streets . . . Where
was I? Where was I? . . . Captain Nemo . . . picking up a
piece of chalk . . . advanced to a rock . . . and traced the
word . . . "Atlantis."'

Jules Verne, *Twenty Thousand Leagues Under the
Sea*, 1869.

Most of us love the idea of Atlantis, and upwards of three
thousand books and articles have been written on the subject
during the past two hundred years. There are many reasons
for this interest. Psychologists might argue that the image
of Atlantis holds a mirror to our world, that it has a similar
emotional energy to the biblical Garden of Eden. For others,
Atlantis represents an idealised version of our future as a society, a culture closer to our human roots, but technological
and global.

In some respects, Atlantis is all things to all people. For
some, it is nothing more than a myth, to others, it is a lost
continent that may one day be found. For a smaller group,

it was a place visited by aliens, perhaps even established by extraterrestrials who then passed on their knowledge to the Egyptians. In this last scenario Atlanteans are the forebears of our technological existence, the progenitors of ancient knowledge, keepers of what the alchemists and Hermeticists called the *prisca sapientia*.

But what lies at the root of these ideas? Was there ever an Atlantis, and if so, what sort of place was it? And who were the Atlanteans?

The story of Atlantis has come to us from the Greek philosopher Plato who lived during the fourth century BC. Renowned for his ten-volume masterpiece, *The Republic*, devoted to political structure and the nature of government, he also wrote a pair of dialogues (books in which two or more characters argue over a subject) which dealt with philosophy, history and science, entitled *Timaeus* and *Critias*. In these texts, Plato's teacher, Socrates, holds an imaginary conversation with three of his friends. One of these is Plato's maternal great-grandfather, Critias, who had heard a story about a place called Atlantis from his grandfather, Critias the Elder. He had been told the story by his father who had learned of the legend from the great Athenian thinker and lawgiver, Solon, who had died 130 years before Plato's birth. Solon claimed to have come by the tale when he visited Egypt where an ancient priest and guardian of the Temple of Sais had been privy to ancient records documenting all remaining knowledge of the lost continent.

According to these ancient texts, Atlantis was a vast landmass populated by peace-loving demigods who presided over a global culture that existed some 9000 years before Solon's time – about 11,500 years ago.

According to Plato: 'There was an island opposite the strait you call ... the Pillars of Hercules, an island larger than Libya and Asia combined ... On this island of Atlantis had arisen a powerful and remarkable dynasty of kings, who ... controlled, within the strait, Libya up to Egypt and Europe as far as Tyrrhenia [Italy]. This dynasty . . . attempted to enslave at a single stroke . . . all the territory within the strait.'

Originally a noble people descendent from the gods, the Atlanteans eventually became greedy and sought to dominate realms beyond their boundaries, invading neighbouring states and oppressing less-developed cultures. Finally Zeus became angry and destroyed them at a single stroke, the grand palaces and the golden wall was swept aside and sunk beneath the waves as the land of Poseidon's children was deluged by the ocean.

'At a later time,' Plato tells us, '. . . there were earthquakes and floods of extraordinary violence, and in a single dreadful day and night . . . the island of Atlantis . . . was swallowed up by the sea and vanished; this is why the sea in that area is to this day impassable to navigation, which is hindered by mud just below the surface, the remains of the sunken island.'[1]

Plato's *Timaeus* and *Critias* also detail the political structure and society of Atlantis. The Atlanteans were ruled by ten kings, descendants of five pairs of twins, the off-spring of the union of the mortal woman Cleito and the god Poseidon. The kings met at intervals of five years to make far-reaching decisions using a system of votes. Their meetings took place in the great capital city which was surrounded by a golden wall. The city had hot springs, temples, exercise areas and, oddly, a racecourse.

For many historians, the account outlined in Plato's dialogues is an example of a technique he used often, most famously in *The Republic*, portraying his philosophical ideas through morality tales and stories that highlighted ethical issues. With such details as a racecourse, the description of the Atlantean capital sounds suspiciously Greek, which would imply that the original tale as handed down to Plato has been greatly elaborated and embellished by the author to make it fit the requirements of his own culture and to convey his own ideology. The structure of the story is also an ancient one – the notion of a people acquiring too much power and becoming corrupt before being taught a lesson, or in this case, facing destruction by the all-seeing, all-knowing gods. But this of course does not mean the story is completely contrived. It might be simply that Plato used an ancient legend for his dialogues and altered the details.

Plato's pupil, Aristotle, took the view that in writing *Timaeus* and *Critias* his master had expanded upon a kernel of truth in order to create a myth to convey his philosophical teachings, calling Plato's work 'political fable'. But despite the fact that Aristotle became a colossus of teaching throughout the world for at least 1500 years after his death and his ideas were the cornerstone of philosophy and science until the Enlightenment, there remained a large contingent of people who did not see *Timaeus* and *Critias* as a mere 'fable'.

Even by the time of the philosopher Gaius Plinius Secundus, known as Pliny the Elder, who wrote the encyclopaedic *Natural History* in the year 77 AD, four centuries after Aristotle, the idea of Atlantis in the world of philosophy and history was ambiguous, and opinion about it divided. Some scholars held the view that Atlantis had been a real place, lying opposite the Pillars of Hercules, whilst others saw it as simply a myth.

Plato's is the only original surviving source of the Atlantis story and all other accounts are based entirely upon it. And, because there is so little to go by, it is almost impossible to judge the political structure or the form of society that may have been adopted by the Atlanteans. Consequently, those fascinated with the subject have concentrated on attempting to find the location of the lost continent in the hope that one day an expedition will unearth the great walled city and reveal the secrets of the demigods who some believe once ruled the world.

Throughout ancient times, and indeed until the late fifteenth century, the Atlantic was a largely uncharted ocean. Roman and Dark Age historians and geographers described the location of numerous unexplored islands and isolated lands throughout the Atlantic, almost all of which turned out to be fictitious. These included the islands of the Seven

Cities, the Fortunate Isles, St Brendan's Isle and a mysterious place named Hy Breasil which remained on mariners' charts the world over until the late nineteenth century.

Plato had described Atlantis as lying beyond the Pillars of Hercules, by which he meant the Straits of Gibraltar, the gateway from the Mediterranean to the Atlantic. It was only natural then that this information should lead cartographers and explorers to place the mysterious lost continent of Atlantis somewhere in the Atlantic Ocean. But where exactly?

During the first few decades after America was discovered by Columbus, European philosophers thought that this new landmass might be the remains of the lost continent. In the 1550s, the Spanish historian Francesco López de Gómara believed that some of the features of what was then known of America and the West Indies fitted the description Plato had offered in *Timaeus* and *Critias*, and the English statesman and philosopher Francis Bacon placed Atlantis in the New World in his masterpiece *Nova Atlantis*, published in 1618.

But gradually, as America was explored and mapped, it became clear that it had nothing to do with Atlantis. However, the idea that Atlantis was to be found some-where in the Atlantic Ocean persisted. One of the most determined adherents to this view was the American author and historian Ignatius Donnelly, who was convinced that the Azores are the only remains of Atlantis above sea level. In his book *Atlantis: The Antediluvian World*, published in 1882, Donnelly propounded the theory that Atlantis sank beneath the Atlantic waves and that a feature called the Mid-Atlantic Ridge, discovered in the 1870s (of which the Azores are the volcanic peaks), was a major geographical component of the continent.

Donnelly went to his grave believing he had solved the mystery of the location of Atlantis, but in the 1960s the study of plate tectonics showed that his theory could not be correct. Plate tectonics describes how the present configuration of the Earth's crust was produced by shifting plates (large segments

of the Earth's surface) which have created features such
as mountain ranges and ocean ridges including the Mid-
Atlantic Range. Rather than this range and the Azores being
the remains of a sunken continent, as Donnelly believed, the
Ridge was generated by the movement of the Earth's tectonic
plates in relatively recent times.

Today, Donnelly's idea is dismissed by scholars and scientists. The Greek historian Professor A. Galanopoulos has
said of the idea: 'There never was an Atlantic land bridge
since the arrival of man in the world; there is no sunken
landmass in the Antarctic: the Atlantic Ocean must have
existed in its present form for at least a million years. In
fact it is a geophysical impossibility for an Atlantis of Plato's
dimensions to have existed in the Atlantic.'[2]

Yet, to this day many believe the theory that Atlantis was
a large landmass in what is now the Atlantic Ocean and
some contend that there is particularly compelling evidence
to support the argument that it was located close to the
West Indies.

In 1968, a diver in the Bahamas known to the locals as
'Bonefish Sam', met an American zoologist and keen amateur archaeologist called Dr J. Manson Valentine, who was
visiting the island. Bonefish Sam showed him an underwater anomaly which he thought might be of archaeological
interest.

The anomaly is about a kilometre off Paradise Point in the
Bahamas and consists of what could have once been a wall
(interpreted by some as a road) made from large stones lying
under about six metres of water. The stones, now known as
the Bimini Road, are each estimated to weight between one
and ten tons and several dozen of them are aligned to run
for about half a kilometre in a straight line before ending in
a sharp bend.

Dr Valentine described the structure as '. . . an extensive pavement of rectangular and polygonal flat stones of
varying size and thickness, obviously shaped and accurately
aligned to form a convincing artefactual pattern . . . Some

were absolutely rectangular and some approaching perfect squares.'[3]

Occultists became very excited by this discovery. This was mainly due to the clairvoyant Edgar Cayce, who during the 1920s and '30s claimed to enter a trance in which messages from 'higher authorities' informed him of mystical connections. Before he died in 1945, he was quoted as saying: 'A portion of the temples [of Atlantis] may yet be discovered under the slime of ages of sea water near Bimini . . . Expect it in '68 and '69, not so far away!'

Initially this does seem a rather startling prediction, but it should be borne in mind that the underwater feature was called the Bimini Road because of its proximity to North Bimini island in the Bahamas and was a well-known tourist spot, but had been overlooked by scientists until Bonefish Sam's revelation in 1968. Cayce may also have known of the feature and used it in his prophecies. It is also possible that many people on the islands knew about Cayce (he was a very famous mystic in his day) and had deliberately chosen to inform the scientific world through Dr Manson Valentine when they did in order to fit the prediction.

But, to the increasing satisfaction of the Atlantis enthusiasts, there was soon more ammunition for their arguments. In 1975, a Dr David Zink, author of *The Stones of Atlantis*, discovered what appears to be a block of stone that looks very much like concrete and is certainly man-made because it contains a tongue-and-groove joint.

Sceptics were soon able to show that this and other artefacts, including some anomalous marble pillars (marble is not found in the area naturally), are relics of shipwrecks. These arguments were strengthened when a building found alongside the Bimini Road and originally thought to be an Atlantean temple was shown to be nothing more exotic than a sponge store that had been built in the 1930s. This has led doubters to encourage the theory that the Bimini Road was actually produced by a natural phenomenon, via an accepted geological process called *Pleistocene beach-rock erosion and cracking*. Others tread a middle road suggesting that the underwater feature is natural, but could have been used by ancient peoples.

Today, the mystery of the Bimini Road remains unsolved and it is the battleground for supporters and opponents of the many theories surrounding the reality and the location of Atlantis. In 1997, a group of British researchers from the Building Research Establishment (BRE) analysed samples from the man-made block close to the Bimini Road and concluded that it is made from a form of concrete manufactured by an old-fashioned technique and certainly older than the modern-day Portland cement process, devised in 1820. Just how long before this is uncertain, so the block could have been produced in Europe anytime between the sixteenth and early nineteenth centuries or it could be far more ancient.

Using an electron microscope, one of the BRE team, Dr David Rayment, head of the organisation's Electron Microanalytical Unit, has found a strip of gold in the concrete block which shows clear signs of having been worked by a skilled craftsman. But, although this is a fascinating development, it does not mean that the block was part of a building in Atlantis. As Dr Kelvin Pettifer of the BRE's Petrographic Unit points out: 'Much as I'd like to believe it, there is nothing in any of the samples that is enough to convince me. It could have been that the marble pillars and other man-made materials were intended for a cotton plantation mansion but ended up on the sea bed following a shipwreck.'

Clearly, more research on these materials is needed before a definite conclusion can be reached. Carbon dating would be of little use in this case because the concrete block is man-made, but one possibility would be to try to find pollen grains or other organic materials inside the core of the block which may have been deposited there when it was being produced, these could be matched with samples found in different parts of the world in an effort to determine where the block was made. And of course, the pollen grains or other natural materials could be carbon dated.

Meanwhile, a Russian team, lead by Professor Viatcheslav Koudriavtsev, director of the Moscow Institute of Metahistory, which studies how natural catastrophes affect human development, are investigating the idea that Atlantis could have been positioned off Land's End, in Cornwall, England. They are sending a group of divers to explore a little-known set of sunken ruins that lie one hundred miles off the western tip of Cornwall clustered around Little Sole Bank, an undersea hill that rises to fifty metres below the surface.

Koudriavtsev has based his theory upon a combination of Plato's descriptions in *Timaeus* and *Critias* and ancient Cornish myths that tell of a rich land on which stood the City of the Lions containing no fewer than 140 temples. In these tales, the area now under the waves was called Lyonesse, a land that has featured in many ancient fables and legends including *The Faerie Queen* by the Elizabethan poet Edmund Spenser and Alfred Lord Tennyson's version of the Arthurian legend, *Idylls of the King*, published between 1859 and 1885 in the form of twelve poems.

The Russian professor has said that the idea Atlantis existed off the coast of Cornwall is backed up by plentiful research, claiming that his conclusions are 'based upon fresh translations of the Greek texts, which have fascinated me since I was a student at Moscow University many years ago'.

Indeed geologists do believe that a series of natural disasters set in motion by the melting of the last icebergs left over from the most recent Ice age could have flooded a fertile plain that may have existed at the location marked by the Russian investigators. Dr Geoff Kellaway, a local geologist, has called the Russian theory: '. . . not unreasonable. Billions of gallons of Ice-age waters flooded fertile lands that could have supported civilisations. Mammoth teeth have been washed ashore. But the Celtic Shelf is a massive area – the Russians will be looking for a needle in a very deep haystack.'

Sadly, even if Professor Koudriavtsev's team do locate evidence that Little Sole Bank represents a part of Atlantis, it will solve one mystery but offer another, because just miles away from this point, the Celtic Shelf falls away to a depth of 4000 metres and much of the lost continent will be truly lost, having slid to the bottom of the Atlantic Ocean.

But these are just a few of the disparate ideas that surround the possible location of Atlantis based upon one interpretation of Plato's descriptions and combined with other seemingly connected ideas. There are many who refuse to accept the notion that Atlantis was anywhere near the Atlantic. According to a growing body of experts who have in recent decades held sway over the official line in linking the myth with the reality of Atlantis, the lost continent was actually thousands of miles away from the Atlantic Ocean.

Close inspection of Plato's account shows many confusing contradictions and anomalies. Firstly, it seems that he has exaggerated all the dimensions by a factor of ten. This was noted by Professor Galanopoulos, who points out that in his description of the great capital of Atlantis, the Royal City, Plato ascribes a length of 10,000 *stades* or 1135 miles to the city wall.[4] Even Plato questioned the validity of this figure in his transcription and it does indeed seem excessively large even for a culture ruled by demigods. The Great Wall of China (which is incidentally the only man-made object visible from Earth orbit), is 1500 miles long, but a city wall over eleven hundred miles in length would circumvent Greater London twenty times. If we reduce the length of the wall by a factor of ten we have a more reasonable number.

Plato also says that Atlantis existed 9000 years before his time, which places it in an era when the rest of the world was still in the Palaeolithic period or Old Stone Age, at least 6000 years before the origin of the Egyptian civilisation. And, although it is argued that the mythical flavour of the lost continent is eradicated if we again divide Plato's figure by ten, placing the high point of Atlantean culture 900 years before Solon, this does then fit neatly with the description offered by Plato of battles between the Atlanteans and the embryonic state of Athens during the time in which the kings of Atlantis were attempting to expand their empire.

This mistake could have occurred, it is argued, because the Egyptian copyist mistook the ancient Egyptian symbol for '100' (a coiled snake), for the lotus flower, the symbol for '1000'. This would be analogous to us confusing the British billion (one million million) with the American billion (one thousand million).

A further confusion arises over a simple phrase in the original tale. Plato was told that the lost continent was 'larger than Libya and Asia combined', but the Greek words for 'greater than' and 'between' are almost identical, which suggests that Plato should have described Atlantis as 'between' Libya and Asia.

If for the moment we take these ideas as facts, it places an entirely different complexion on the tale of Atlantis, at once making it eligible for links with another culture that is known to have existed at the same time, but far from the Atlantic Ocean – the Minoan civilisation of Crete.

Beginning in 1900 with Sir Arthur Evans, a succession of archaeologists have studied the region encompassing the islands of the Aegean lying south of mainland Greece and have gradually pieced together a picture of what may have happened to a great civilisation that once lived there around 1500 BC.

The most southerly of the Greek islands is Santorini. Today it is actually a collection of three islands, the largest is the beautiful isle of Thera, which is a major tourist attraction with its black sand and crystal clear waters. 3500 years ago, Santorini was a single, almost circular island which was blown apart by a massive volcanic eruption thought to be four times more powerful than the eruption of Krakatoa in 1883.

The eruption of Krakatoa has been estimated as equivalent to one million Hiroshimas, and although this may be an exaggeration, the explosion that occurred on Santorini around 1520 BC must have been truly devastating. It is believed to have created 100-foot waves that swept in all directions from the island, entirely engulfing another advanced community living a mere ninety-six kilometres north – the Minoan civilisation that was then thriving on the island of Crete.

Evans, who discovered the Palace of Knossos on Crete and with it unearthed the lost history of Minoan culture, did not link the destruction of this civilisation with the volcanic eruption on Santorini; but others did soon find a link. As early as 1909, some scholars were suggesting that the ruins of the Minoans were in fact the lost Royal City of the Atlanteans. By the 1930s, the Greek archaeologist Spyridon Marinatos took up this idea and made the link between the eruption on Santorini and the destruction of Knossos after he found more Minoan remains in the north of Crete along with pumice, a frothy form of volcanic glass left over from a volcanic eruption. Later, during the 1960s, ruins of an advanced culture were found on Thera, including the remnants of a massive circular channel on the edge of what remains of the original island which matches Plato's description of channels circumventing the great metropolis of Atlantis.

Other possible links come from a comparison of the Minoan culture and the legends of Atlantis. According to Plato, the Atlanteans worshiped the bull and it was discovered from the ruins at Knossos that the bull-cult also lay at the heart of the Minoan religion.

If we take Plato's geography as misguided (along with his time-frame) and wrong by a factor of ten, then the evidence to superimpose Crete with Atlantis is compelling. This then suggests that the tale of Atlantis that passed from Solon to Plato was actually an Egyptian legend based upon an event that may have taken place some 900–1000 years earlier, in the Aegean Sea.

However, even this rather neat explanation has its critics. Recent archaeological findings using accurate dating techniques suggest that that the volcanic ash from Santorini is at least 150 years older than the date assigned to the destruction of the Cretan palaces, implying that the volcanic eruption on Santorini did not destroy the Minoan culture after all.

Evidently, a great deal more work has to be done on the possible links between Santorini and Crete before a plausible hypothesis linking this area with Atlantis can be formulated; but for many, what appeared to be a promising connection is too flawed to be accurate and they are actively searching for new solutions.

One of the best researched alternative theories of recent years has been the work of the writer Graham Hancock, who along with others has proposed a quite different location for the lost continent.

Hancock, in his book *Fingerprints of the Gods*, and archaeologists Rose and Rand Flem-Ath in their book published the same year (1995), *When the Sky Fell In*, propose that the site of Atlantis was in fact Antarctica.

Sticking to Plato's original dates for the existence of Atlantis, both authors subscribe to the idea that catastrophic displacement of the Earth's crust caused the extinction of an advanced civilisation that existed on the edge of an extended continent of Antarctica about 11,000 years ago. Their contention is that at this time Antarctica was very much larger than it is today, that its most northerly coast reached at least 2000 miles further north. They further contest that the reason no one has yet located Atlantis is because it lies beneath the frozen wastes of modern-day Antarctica.

In *Fingerprints of the Gods*, Hancock quotes the Flem-Aths as saying: 'Antarctica is our least understood continent. Most of us assume that the immense island has been icebound for millions of years. But new discoveries prove that parts of Antarctica were free of ice thousands of years ago, recent history by the geological clock. The theory of "earth-crust displacement" explains the mysterious surge and ebb of Antarctica's vast ice sheet.'[5]

The link with Plato, they contest, comes from the fact that some of the records of Atlantis were taken by survivors to the area around the Mediterranean, a group who millennia later seeded the Egyptian civilisation providing them with the technological expertise needed to construct the pyramids, embalm their pharaohs and model the sphinx.

But does Atlantis need to have existed at all? After all, the only account we have to go by is Plato's testament, and although there may have been genuine elaborate legends hidden in lost documents in Egypt, perhaps in the library of Alexandria before its destruction, it is also possible that Plato's story is nothing more than a total fabrication.

Noting the remarkable similarities between artefacts found in different cultures that developed around the Atlantic Ocean as far apart as Africa and Europe, there are some who hold the view that there had to be a real Atlantis that existed some 11,000 years ago to account for this. But the work of such pioneers as Thor Heyerdahl and others have shown that there is no need for recourse to occult explanations for such things; that indeed, people travelled more widely at this time than many believed possible.

Yet, the story of Atlantis does lie at the heart of a great occult tradition. The Theosophists (or Theosophical Society) – a group that flourished towards the end of the nineteenth century – were particularly enamoured with the legend of Atlantis.

The Theosophy Society was established by Madame Helena Blavatsky in 1875. She wrote several books that have become classics of the alternative historical tradition, including *Isis Unveiled* and *The Secret Doctrine*. The Theosophists believed in what they called the *Akashic records*, what some describe as an 'astral library' – a source of mystical knowledge tapped into by skilled mediums who then divulge secret knowledge to the rest of us.* From the Akashic records, Blavatsky and other Theosophists, most notably Rudolph Steiner, constructed an image of a train of seven civilisations or *root races* dating from the distant past, of which we are supposed to be the fifth.† The Atlanteans, who according to this idea are our immediate ancestors, the fourth race of humans, possessed an advanced technology, used flying machines, and had developed sophisticated medical techniques.

It is interesting to note that Theosophists writing in the late nineteenth century were fascinated with the potential of technology and in some respects their descriptions of ancient lost civilisations bore a marked resemblance to Victorian Western culture – the Atlanteans used airships and X-ray machines. This is even more interesting when we consider the fact that imprinting ones own culture upon alternative ancient scenarios is exactly what Plato did in his tracts describing the lost continent. It is also a common phenomenon amongst witnesses who claim to have see alien spacecraft – they describe them in a way that is fitting for their time (see Chapter 1).

One of the most prolific writers on the subject of Atlantis and the legends surrounding it was an expert of the occult, Lewis Spence, who produced over a dozen books on the subject all based upon the fantasies of the Theosophists and Plato's original 7000 words on the subject in his two dialogues *Timaeus* and *Critias*. Many of these books have

* Edgar Cayce claimed to be able to access these records and believed they were the source for his predictions.

† According to Theosophic doctrine, the first root race were invisible, made of 'fire-mist' and lived at the North Pole. The second lived in northern Asia and were almost invisible, but managed to see each other well enough to develop sexual intercourse. The third root race were the Lemurians who lived in a place called Mu several hundred thousand years ago, the fourth were the people of Atlantis and we are the fifth. The sixth root race will supposedly return to Lemuria, and after the seventh race has run its course, humans will leave Earth altogether and emigrate to Mercury.

become classics of the alternative tradition and remain in print today via specialist publishers around the world.

And in more recent times, the myth of Atlantis has found a new impetus amongst believers in the idea that our planet has been visited and perhaps even colonised in the distant past. By amalgamating some of the ideas of the Theosophists and the convoluted hypotheses of such writers as Eric Von Daniken, a large body of people claim to believe that the human race was seeded by aliens, that Atlantis was really the home of an advanced culture destroyed perhaps by a nuclear accident or wiped out by an AIDS-type disease. Ironically, some are trying to use the Atlantis story as a model for all that they perceive to be wrong with our culture. This, again, is exactly what Plato was doing two-and-a-half millennia ago in Greece.

Believers in the idea that there have been advanced human civilisations that have existed and thrived here on Earth in ancient times point to the many and diverse legends incorporating advanced but lost civilisations in our own deep past, but they provide very flimsy evidence for such a bold claim.

The 'evidence' may be broken down into three groups – ancient texts, ancient images and ancient monuments.

The first of these come from a variety of sources and different cultures including ancient India, China, Egypt and South America. These texts often describe events which could be interpreted (again using contemporary culture as a template) as describing visitations by aliens, abductions, even colonisation, and have been used by many enthusiasts in a growing collection of books that attempt to make links between extraterrestrials and ancient peoples on Earth. An example is the accounts of Old Testament prophets such as Ezekiel, interpreted by writers such as Eric Von Daniken as coded descriptions of alien visitations, cosmic travellers who passed on secret knowledge, men who some identify with the original colonisers of Earth and possibly with the establishment of Atlantis.

A favourite of the occultists is what has been claimed to be Ezekiel's encounters with an ancient astronaut taken from the Biblical passage which begins: 'Now it came to pass in the thirtieth year, in the fourth month, in the fifth day of the month, as I was among the captives by the river of Chebar, that the heavens were opened . . . And I looked, and behold, a whirlwind came out of the north, a great cloud, and a fire unfolding itself, and a brightness was about it, and out of the midst thereof as the colour of amber, out of the midst of the fire. Also out of the midst thereof came the likeness of four living creatures. And this was their appearance; they had the likeness of a man. And every one had four faces, and every one had four wings. And their feet were straight feet; and the soles of their feet was like the sole of a calf's foot: and they sparkled like the colour of burnished brass.'[6]

At first glance, this might appear to describe something like an advanced flying machine, perhaps one built by aliens, or by the people the Theosophists imagined might have lived in Atlantis, along with occupants clad in spacesuits. But it should be recalled that the Old Testament was written by simple people who had little experience of the world, who lived in constant fear of the forces of nature and the wrath of their God. To them, something as natural as a whirlwind or a volcanic eruption could be personified, anthropomorphosised with images of strange beings. It is even conceivable that these could be descriptions of real men from a slightly more advanced culture dazzling simple peasants with chariots, bright ornamentation and well-crafted weapons.

Linked with these surviving texts are records preserved by ancient cultures as verbal accounts. A striking example comes from the West African Dogon tribe who, according to some, knew of the existence of a star called Sirius B which can only be seen with the aid of a powerful telescope and was first photographed in 1970. In his book *The Sirius Mystery*, the writer Robert Temple claims the tribespeople knew this star was a part of what modern astronomers call a binary star system (a star that orbits another), in this case the much brighter Sirius. Astonishingly, the Dogon tribe even knew the duration of the star's orbit – around fifty years. The Dogon, he claims, learned about Sirius B from the ancient Egyptians some 3000 years ago. Others extrapolated further and believe that such astronomical knowledge possessed by the ancient Egyptians was passed onto the tribe by a much older race – once again, the same highly advanced people of Atlantis. However, astronomers are convinced that the knowledge of the Dogon is nothing more than coincidence and point to the fact that a high percentage of star systems are binary and that the figure of fifty years was a lucky guess.

The second type of 'evidence' proposed by enthusiasts of these occult ideas is pictorial representation, ancient images that have survived from long-dead civilisations, particularly the Egyptians who, enthusiasts believe, were the custodians of the artefacts surviving the destruction of Atlantis.

Some of these have been widely publicised as proof that we were either visited by advanced extraterrestrials or that there was a race of technologically-advanced humans who lived on Earth many thousands of years ago. Perhaps the most sensational is a drawing discovered in the ancient Mayan Temple at Palenque in Mexico. It shows a human figure seated in what looks astonishingly like a modern space capsule. The figure is squeezed into a small space jammed with levers and what could be interpreted as control panels and coming from the rear of the contraption appears to be a flume of smoke and fire not unlike the vapours expelled from a NASA rocket.

This is not the only picture from the ancient world that depicts what could be interpreted as space technology. According to some supporters of the ancient technology theory, primitive man seems to be obsessed with space-suited figures. One drawing seen in cave dwellings found in Val Camonica, Northern Italy, depicts what may be interpreted as cosmonauts or NASA astronauts. They are dressed in large suits and what look like helmets and visors.

Another interpretation may be that the drawings were actually showing nothing more exotic than the hunting gear
worn by primitive people during a period now recognised as
a mini Ice age. Similar drawings have been found at ancient
American Indian sites in North America, in Uzbekistan and
in Tassili in the Sahara.

But for those who want to believe that an ancient people
ruled the Earth using advanced technology tens of thousands
of years ago, the most important links they have to the past
are the towering edifice of the Great Pyramid at Giza, the
circle of stones at Stonehenge and other comparable sites
around the globe.

One of the original Seven Wonders of the Ancient World
(and the only one remaining today), the Great Pyramid is
a truly amazing feat of engineering. Known to have been
constructed during the third millennium BC, it contains
upwards of one million blocks of stone each weighing about
2.5 tons. It measures 230 metres (756 feet) on each side
(equivalent to four blocks of Fifth Avenue) and was originally
147 metres (482 feet) high.

Staggering engineering achievement the Great Pyramid
may be, but orthodox archaeologists are able to describe
in detail how it was built using tens of thousands of slaves
who dragged the stones from boats which had brought them
from quarries in the Lower Nile. They have plotted the route
of roads specially designed and constructed to transport the
stones, and have shown how Egyptian engineers had the
mathematical and engineering skills to construct a building
that is not only huge but demonstrates sophisticated number
relationships between the length of its sides, its height and
the area of the base.

A monument that required comparable engineering genuius
is Stonehenge. For several decades it has been associated with
enthusiasts of the paranormal who have tried to find theories
to link its construction with alien visitors or ancient humans
who possessed technological ability approximately equal to
our own today.

Stonehenge is to be found thirteen kilometres north of Salisbury, England. It was started a few hundred years before the Great Pyramid at Giza, around 2800 BC. But, unlike the Great Pyramid, the Stonehenge site evolved over a period of almost 1800 years. Conventional archaeologists have identified four different phases of construction, with Period I beginning around 2800 BC and period IV ending about 1100 BC.

Theories concerning the use of the site and the way such an edifice could have been constructed by primitive tribespeople are varied and plentiful. Again, enthusiasts of the ancient astronaut theory suggest that Stonehenge is one of many sites situated on ley lines – hypothetical lines of 'force' or natural energy that intersect at key points (see Chapter 10).

Although many books, articles and television programmes have been produced debating the idea that Stonehenge is in some way linked with the ancient people of Atlantis, or is perhaps of cosmic significance to extraterrestrials, once more, conventional archaeology can offer a clear picture of how this incredible edifice was built. A growing collection of scholarly works have gone to great lengths to explain the methods employed by the ancient Britons and the techniques they employed using the materials readily available at that time.[7]

But, whatever the arguments over who built the pyramids and Stonehenge and why, the simple fact remains that any reliance upon an occult explanation is at best an insult to human ingenuity. To many (and not just empirically minded or sceptical scientists) the occultists' attempts to dismiss the achievements of our ancestors are at once demeaning and crude. But beyond this, the reasoning of people like Von Daniken and other supporters of the idea that the ancients of traditional history could not have done the things they did, is one of the worst examples of flabby thinking.

In *Chariots of the Gods?* Von Daniken makes claims such as: 'Is it really coincidence that the height of the Pyramid of Cheops multiplied by 1000 million corresponds approximately to the distance between the Earth and the Sun?'[8]

Well, firstly, the answer is surely 'yes'; but, let us give this particular author enough rope to do with as he will. The distance between the Earth and the Sun is 93,000,000 miles. If we multiply the height of the great pyramid by one thousand million we arrive at a figure of 98,000,000 miles. This is an approximation indeed, out by no less than six percent. So, what does it prove? Does it suggest that the ancient Atlanteans, or perhaps visitors from another planet, calculate to within a margin of error of six percent? Nothing else about the great Pyramid is out by even 1000th of this figure.

On a television programme called *The Case of the Ancient Astronauts*, made to debunk Von Daniken in 1978, the producers drew an analogy between the author's pronouncements and what a wrong-headed archaeologist of the future might think about our culture. Suppose, they said, in the year 5330 AD, an impressive-looking ancient monument was unearthed in a site known to have been where a civilisation once existed, a city thought to be called 'Washington'. Archaeologists of the time calculate that the height (in miles) of a needle-like construction in the centre of the ruined city when multiplied by forty gives the distance in light years to the second nearest star, Proxima Centauri. Would the obvious conclusion be that the ancient Americans were too stupid to have made this comparison themselves and that the Washington monument was designed and built by ancient alien visitors?

So where do all these conflicting ideas leave us on the subject of Atlantis? Did it really exist? If it did, what sort of place was it, what sort of society did the Atlanteans have? Was their technology comparable to ours, or was Atlantis simply an isolated island kingdom, home to a culture just a little more advanced than its neighbours?

The problem with any suggestion that the Atlanteans had

an advanced technology is the matter of what happened to the traces. Hancock's fingerprints of the Gods are the encoded remnants of a great culture he believes can be seen in certain ancient materials and cultural heritage, but would there not be much more remaining? What would our society leave behind it? Would people eleven or twelve millennia in the future be able to say with certainty that an advanced civilisation once lived on Earth?

I think the answer to this is an unequivocal 'yes'. We are a global society and our marks are everywhere. If our culture was to be utterly destroyed, some traces would remain if people of the future were to look hard enough. We have left our stamp in the depths of the oceans, on the highest peaks and even on the surface of the Moon and other parts of the solar system. Atlantis could not have been a truly global civilisation and therefore it could not have developed to the level we enjoy. In fact, Atlantean society could not have been any more advanced than that of say, Europe before the fifteenth century, when global exploration became commonplace.

And what of the relics, the fingerprints of their time on Earth? For the believer in an alternative history there is no concrete proof, no 10,000-year-old human skull with capped teeth, no artificial hip joint from five thousand years before Christ, no laser gun carbon dated to the time of the ancient Egyptians.

The closest we have come to such a discovery occurred in 1936. Archaeologists working in Iraq stumbled across what is now known as the *Baghdad battery*. This is a tube a few inches long which consists of all the components of a working cell minus the battery acid itself, but known to be at least 2000 years old. Researchers have made an exact replica of the device and using fruit juice to substitute for battery acid, they produced half a volt of electricity.

No one has been able to explain the origin of this curious object, and it is still believed to be genuine many decades after it was first discovered. It may be a relic from an ancient technological society, but it is strange that such a find is entirely isolated. Advances in technology are always interlinked. It is extremely unlikely that a car, for example, could be built unless the society that manufactures it has an adequate support system – techniques to produce metal sheets, petrol or some other fuel, materials for the tyres, not to mention the machine tools to build the individual components.

It might be that the Baghdad battery was constructed by an unknown genius, a Leonardo da Vinci of his time who stumbled across the technique and built it from scratch; we will probably never know.

Yet, despite the marked lack of evidence, there is nothing intrinsically wrong or contradictory about the idea that a reasonably advanced civilisation could have sprung up and flourished for a while, perhaps tens of thousands of years ago. Indeed there are no real intellectual objections to the idea that we could have been visited by aliens in the dim and distant past and that an advanced culture was seeded by colonisers or perhaps a small group stranded here. But, equally, it is a quite unnecessary hypothesis.

And what of the location of the lost continent? If it did exist, the smart money is still with the idea that the Minoan civilisation was the origin of the Atlantis myth, the story handed on to the ancient Egyptians who wrote the account before it became elaborated by successive generations leading to Plato; just as it has been elaborated further still in recent centuries, and will almost certainly continue to be in the centuries to come.

And this is how it should be. Good stories never go out of fashion.

REFERENCES

Chapter 1: Swept Off Their Feet

1. John E Mack, *Abduction: Human Encounters With Aliens*, Simon and Schuster, 1994.
2. Stephen Rae, 'John Mack', *The New York Times*, 30th March 1994.
3. As 1.
4. James Willwerth, 'The Man From Outer Space', *TIME*, 25th April 1994.
5. As 4.
6. Patrick Huyghe, 'In Her Own Words', *OMNI*, June 1995.
7. Tom Hodgkinson, 'Why It Is Easier To Believe In Aliens Than God', *Guardian*, 11th July 1995.
8. Susan Blackmore, 'Alien Abduction: The Inside Story', *New Scientist*, 19th November 1994, pp.29–31.
9. Ibid.
10. *Encounters*, May 1996.
11. Jacques Vallee, interviewed in Keith Thompson, *Angels And Aliens: UFOs and the Mythic Imagination*, Random House, 1991, p.194.

Chapter 2: The Cult of the Cult

1. Eileen Barker, *New Religious Movements*, London: HMSO, 1992, p.13.
2. Anthony Storr, *Feet of Clay*, HarperCollins, London, 1996, xiii.
3. Ibid, p.12.
4. Tony Allen-Mills, 'Caught in the Net', *Sunday Times*, 30th March 1997.

Chapter 3: Mojo Rising.

1. From the journal of Georges de Rouquct, quoted in 'Beyond the Land of the Zombies', *The Unexplained*, September 1997, p.12.
2. Celia Hall, 'Zombie Culture All In the Mind', *Daily Telegraph*, 10th October 1997, p.11.
3. Herbert Basedow, *The Australian Aboriginal*, London, 1925, p.36.
4. Wade Davis, *Passage of Darkness*, Collins, 1988, p.94.
5. As ref 4, p.196.

Chapter 4: Miracles and Wonder

1. Arthur C. Clarke, *The Lost Worlds of 2001*.
2. David Hume, *Essays*, 'Of Miracles', Section X.
3. Ibid.
4. Jenny Randles and Peter Hough, *Encyclopaedia of the Unexplained*, Michael O'Mara, 1995, p.130.
5. John and Anne Spencer, *The Encyclopedia of the World's Greatest Unsolved Mysteries*, Headline, 1995, p.152.

Chapter 5: Searching For the Secrets of Life

1. From *Corpus Hermeticum* attributed to Hermes Trismegistus, quoted in: Jack Lindsay, *The Origins of Alchemy in Graeco-Roman Egypt*, Frederick Muller, 1970.
2, 3. Quoted in Jack Lindsay, *The Origins of Alchemy in Graeco-Roman Egypt*, NY, Frederick Muller, 1970. p.126.
4. Carl Jung, *Memories, Dreams and Reflections*, London, Collins/RKP, 1963, p.147.
5. Conceived and edited by Carl G. Jung, *Man and His Symbols*, Aldus Books Ltd, London, 1964, p.210.
6. For more detail see Michael White, *Isaac Newton: The Last Sorcerer*, 4th Estate, 1997.

7. Maynard Keynes, *Newton The Man*, in *Royal Society, Newton Tercentenary Celebrations*, Cambridge; at the University Press, 1947, pp.27–34.
8. Paracelsus, *Alchemy, The Third Column of Medicine*, Edited by A. E. Waite, London, 1897, p.44.
9. Thomas Birch, *The History of the Royal Society of London*, 4 vols., London, 1756–57, Vol 4. p.347.

Chapter 6: We Are Made of Stars

1. (unnamed, staff writer), *Mail On Sunday, Night and Day* magazine, pp.19–22.
2. Michel Gauquelin, *Dreams and Illusions of Astrology*, Prometheus Books, Buffalo New York, 1979.
3. Amanda Cochrane, 'Science, Art or Superstition?', *FOCUS* magazine, November 1993, pp.16–21.
4. Linda Goodman, *Linda Goodman's Star-Signs*, Bantam Books, New York, 1968.
5. Ibid, 1971 edition, p.475.
6. As 5, p.203.
7. G. Abell and B. Singer, *Science and the Paranormal*, Scribner's, New York, 1981, p.86.

Chapter 7: Fire From the Sky

1. As quoted in John and Mary Gribbin, *Fire On Earth: In Search of the Doomsday Asteroid*, Simon and Schuster, 1996.
2. Robert Matthews, 'The End of the World Is Nigh – Official', *Sunday Telegraph Review*, 21st July 1996.
3. From Plato's dialogues, *Timaeus and Critias* and quoted in Clube and Napier, *The Cosmic Winter*, Blackwell, Oxford, 1990, pp.70–1.
4. From Gildas, *The Ruins of Britain*, quoted in Clube and Napier, p.108.

5. Windsor Chorlton, 'Ice Age', *Focus* Magazine, December 1994.
6. Adrian Berry, *The Next 500 Years: Life In the Coming Millennium*, Headline, 1995.
7. As 2.
8. As 1, p.234.

Chapter 8. Our Brethren Among The Stars?

1. Leslie E. Orgel, 'The Origin of Life On Earth', *Scientific American*, October 1994, pp.53–60.

Chapter 9: Mendel's Monsters

1. Sean Ryan and Lois Rogers, 'Who's Playing God With The Gene Genie?', *Sunday Times*, 1st January 1995, p.12.
2. Janet Fricker, 'DNA's Genetic Time Bomb', *FOCUS*, May 1994, pp.26–30.
3. Gina Kolata, *Clone: The Road to Dolly and the Path Ahead*, Allen Lane, London, 1997, p.864.
4. *The Report of the House of Commons Science and Technology Committee*, August 1996.
5. French Anderson, 'Gene Therapy', *Scientific American*, September 1995, p.98B.
6. Colin Tudge, 'Cloning? Get Used To It', *Independent On Sunday*, 25th January 1998, p.25.
7. Roger Highfield, 'Human Embryo Clones Could Help Save Lives', *Daily Telegraph*, 30th January 1998, p.9.

Chapter 10: Earth Magic, Ley lines and Circles in the Corn

1. Russell Warren, 'The Craft of Dowsing: Worthwhile or Weird?', *FOCUS*, January 1997, p.51.
2. Nigel Peddick, *Ley lines*, Weidenfeld and Nicolson, 1997, p.27.
3. Christopher Oliver Wilson, 'Bumper Crop of Circles', *Mail On Sunday*, 31st August 1997, pp.52–3.

4.   Nigel Blundell, *Mysteries*, Bookmart Ltd/Amazon Publishing, 1992, p.68.

Chapter 11: Remote Viewing and the Psi Detectives

1.   Marie Louise-Small, 'Psi Spies', *Encounters Magazine*, May 1996, pp.54–57.
2.   Jenny Randles and Peter Hough, *Encyclopaedia of the Unexplained*, Michael O'Mara Books Ltd, 1995, p.110.
3.   *Report of the 1992 International Symposium on UFO Research*, detailed in *Encounters*, May 1996, p.55.
4.   R. Targ and H. Puthoff, *Mind and Reach*, Delacorte Press, New York, 1977.
5.   D. Marks and R. Kammann, *Psychology of the Psychic*, Prometeus Books, Buffalo, New York, 1980.
6.   D. Marks and C. Scott, 'Remote Viewing Exposed', *Nature*, 319, 444.
7.   Michael White, *The Science of the X-Files*, Legend, 1996, Chapter 6.

Chapter 12: The Gods Themselves?

1.   Quoted in: Jennifer Westwood, *Lost Atlantis*, Weidenfeld and Nicolson, 1997, p.5.
2.   Galanopoulos and Bacon, *Lost Atlantis*, Nelson, 1963, p.75.
3.   Quoted in: Dr Karl Shuker, *The Unexplained*, Carlton Books, 1996, p.155.
4.   Galanopoulos and Bacon, *Atlantis: The Truth Behind The Legend*, Nelson, London, 1965.
5.   Graham Hancock, *Fingerprints of the Gods*, William Heinemann Ltd, 1995, p.492.
6.   Quoted in Eric Von Daniken, *Chariots of the Gods?: Was God an Astronaut?*, Souvenir Press, 1969, p.55.
7.   For example: John North, *Stonehenge*, HarperCollins, 1996.
8.   Eric Von Daniken, *Chariots of the Gods?: Was God an Astronaut?*, Souvenir Press, 1969, p.99.